TWO KINDS OF TIME

Two Kinds

GRAHAM PECK

Second Edition, Revised and Abridged
With a New Introduction by John K. Fairbank
Illustrated by the Author

SINKIANG

AFGHANISTAN

KASHMIR

OLD SILK ROAD

TO RUSSIA

KOKO NOR

YELLOW R.

YANGTSE

MEKONG R.

SALWEEN R.

CHINA 1940-'41

JAPANESE CONQUESTS

CHINESE COMMUNISTS

TIBET

LHASA

NEPAL

BHUTAN

GANGES R. SIKKIM

BRAHMAPUTRA R.

BRITISH INDIA

CALCUTTA

BURMA
MANDALAY

BURMA RO

RANGOON

THAILAND

# of Time

Sentry Edition 1967

Houghton Mifflin Company
Boston

SOVIET SIBERIA

VLADIVOSTOCK

MANCHU-KUO

MUKDEN

SOVIET OUTER MONGOLIA

INNER MONGOLIA

KOREA

YELLOW R.

GREAT WALL

PEKING

TIENTSIN

SEOUL

YENAN

BLOCKADE

TSINGTAO

CHOW

HUI

PAOCHI

SIAN

SHUANGSHIHPU

KWANGYUEN

LOYANG

CHENGCHOW

HSUCHOW

JAPAN

CHENGTU

ICHANG

HANKOW

NANKING

SHANGHAI

YANGTSE R.

CHUNGKING

CHANGSHA

NINGPO

HENGYANG

WENCHOW

KWEIYANG

KWEILIN

KANHSIEN

FOOCHOW

OKINAWA

NMING

LIUCHOW

WEST R.

CANTON

AMOY

TAIPEI

WUCHOW

TAIWAN (FORMOSA)

HANOI

HAIPHONG

HONG KONG (BRITISH)

MACAO (PORTUGUESE)

NAM

HAINAN

0   100   200   300   400   500
APPROXIMATE MILES

PHILIPPINES

··· Author's Note

As I WROTE *Two Kinds of Time* in the late 1940's I became increasingly aware how indebted I was to the many Chinese friends who had helped me learn so much about their country. It was too much for one book, actually, and I am also grateful to Kay Thompson and Christopher Rand, who helped me cut and organize. The original edition still ran to seven hundred and twenty-five pages.

When the prospect of republication arose, further cutting seemed advisable. I finally decided to slice the book in two and publish the first half by itself. It is a complete book, and is indeed the volume I went to China to write in 1940. Because the Pacific War began about the time I had planned to return to America, I found myself staying an extra five years and saw the growth and doom of America's involvement in China. That is the central subject of the second half of the original edition. It is really another story, and may someday be another book.

GRAHAM PECK

South Pomfret, Vermont
1967

Cover design by the author

Contents

TWO KINDS OF TIME

Introduction
by John K. Fairbank

AMONG CHINA SPECIALISTS *Two Kinds of Time* is an insider's book, an intimate account of wartime China in 1940–1945 by a traveler among the common people. From its bizarre incidents and earthy stories there emerges a clinical description of the death throes of the old Chinese society. It has disintegrated not only under Japan's aggression but also through the seepage of modern ideas and gadgets into the village, the breaking of family bonds, the decline of the old authorities, the collapse of peasant livelihood, and all the other complex changes one reads about in textbooks. Graham Peck documents them in more human terms than any other writer of the time.

The sights and conversations he records show situations out of control, people demoralized, to the point where self-preservation justifies the grossest inhumanity. He gives us a portrait from life of those evil "old customs, old habits, old ideas," that the Chinese Communist revolution set about to destroy after 1949 and that Mao Tse-tung in his last years has feared might reappear.

In *Two Kinds of Time* there are no heroes but many victims. There is much humor, but Chinese life on the whole is a "cruel joke." What the Japanese invaders do to the Chinese in warfare is no worse than what the Chinese habitually do to one another in peace time. Suffering and personal disaster take myriad forms in this overcrowded society. To get them down on paper calls for a touch of Dante, Defoe and Rabelais — all three.

Graham Peck is a big, sympathetic, gregarious man who found friends easily, not a careerist dutifully on the make nor a man with a mission but rather like Kipling's Kim, a friend of all the world, interested in everything around him. Unlike most Americans in China, he was an observer who participated. Finally, he was a practicing artist with a keen eye for everything visual, as his illustrations attest. This gives his writing an extraordinary immediacy conveying the colors, textures, sounds, and smells of travel through the dusty Chinese landscape.

He first went to China in 1935 on a *Wanderjahr* after graduation from Yale. In that period before the Japanese invasion of 1937, he traveled through many provinces, often by bicycle, picking up a knowledge of spoken Chinese such as travelers need and making sketches to go with a book. He was fascinated by the Chinese landscape and even more by the people, whose way of life was still considerably bound by tradition. War had not yet shaken their society to pieces. After returning to the United States he published *Through China's Wall* in 1940.

When Graham Peck came to China again via Hong Kong and ran the Japanese blockade below Canton, as he recounts so vividly in the opening pages of *Two Kinds of Time*, it was June of 1940. The Japanese were still doing their worst but were now stalemated. China had resisted the aggressors with a policy of "scorched earth," destroying her modern installations that could not be dismantled and carried to the interior beyond Japan's reach. Chiang Kai-shek had personified the new national pride and stubborn determination. "Trading space for time," as the strategy of grudging retreat was called, the government had moved up the Yangtze to Chungking in Szechwan. Free China's resistance had electrified the American public, and wartime publicity had naturally done little to describe to foreigners the dislocation and demoralization that were now overcoming a war-weary and impoverished country.

Against this background, Graham Peck's experience from the first was disillusioning. For six years, through the latter half of China's eight-year ordeal and into the post-war era, he saw living conditions and human conduct steadily deteriorate. His report is of a country falling apart. But it goes to pieces in a Chinese way, with a stoic humor and a survival capacity different from the West.

There were many things for an American to do in these middle years of China's long war of resistance. After getting to Chungking, Graham Peck worked with the Chinese Industrial Cooperatives, and lived in their co-ops in the Northwest. After Pearl Harbor he joined the United States Office of War Information and became head of its office in Kweilin, the capital of Kwangsi. Here he met the problems of wartime propaganda and information work and became acutely conscious of the gap between American hopes and the realities of its China policy. Being an American official by no means estranged him from the Chinese people. Rather it gave him a further opportunity to appraise the curious inconsistencies and hidden pitfalls in the Sino-

American effort to mount a modern patriotic war on a fragmented, premodern peasant base.

After World War II he spent a year in Peking, working with a Chinese friend to cover Chinese materials and study the local scene while he also wrote his book. The second half of *Two Kinds of Time* as originally published in 1950 dealt primarily with the period after Pearl Harbor and with the American war effort in China. It made an oversized book which has long been out of print. The publishers of the present edition are no doubt correct that the latter part, written in the midst of the Communist-Nationalist civil war, is more "dated" than the earlier part reproduced in this edition. In any case, the present volume is an artistic whole that can stand alone.

Graham Peck's bitterest sense of outrage is caused by the self-seeking hypocrisy of people in the Chinese upper class and its lower fringes. The early 1940's, when Free China was blockaded by Japan with no end in sight, were an era of public corruption and personal callousness, only thinly masked by the high-sounding platitudes of a slackened war effort and an uneasy Sino-American alliance. Public spirit, generosity and even honesty were more than most people could afford. The strong not only trampled on the weak, they gouged one another. *Two Kinds of Time* is a casebook of social pathology.

In particular, it gives us a detailed portrait of the old-style Chinese ruling class in its latter days, not very long before the beginning of its systematic destruction by the Chinese Communists after they came to power. The mandarin tradition of upper-class domination had followed the ancient Confucian adage: "Some men labor with their minds, some with their hands. Those who labor with their minds govern others, those who labor with their hands are governed by others." The Chinese peasant mass had been oriented for so many centuries toward the goal of rising into the nonlaboring and governing class that the perpetual emergence of this ruling class with its habits of exploitation was indeed generated by its victims. An official removed by one generation from farming ancestors knew only how to assert his perquisites and grab his profits when the chance came. This tradition lingers on today in South Vietnam, where the local ruling elite are sometimes unresponsive to American hopes for vigorous reform and revolutionary leadership.

Two Kinds of Time illustrates another feature of the Chinese political cal scene — the importance of prestige, retaining the respect of others.

In Peck's vignettes, time after time disaster follows a loss of face. By the war's end the Kuomintang in fact had lost the Mandate of Heaven by this route. The populace no longer respected it as the government. Its days were numbered.

In the result, Graham Peck's book gives us a backdrop against which to measure the revolutionary problems and achievements of the Chinese Communist regime. By this yardstick it is plain that Chairman Mao and his cohorts had to start their nation-building at a much more backward level than we have tended to assume. Securing nationwide support and energizing a national program was in itself a great initial problem. How far the evils of "bourgeois tendencies" and "bureaucratism" that Peking now denounces are recrudescent from the past, how far they are a response to the new tyranny of new rulers, we cannot clearly tell. But China remains a crowded land. The interpersonal struggle of daily life may occur in somewhat different terms today, but it can hardly have lost the intensity that Graham Peck caught so graphically and sympathetically twenty-five years ago.

PART I
The Problem Proposed

1· *Double Exposure*

BY ONE Chinese view of time, the future is behind you, above you, where you cannot see it. The past is before you, below you, where you can examine it. Man's position in time is that of a person sitting beside a river, facing always downstream as he watches the water flow past.

I have heard that back in the more stable periods of China's history, pleasure gardens used to be designed to express this idea. They were set on slopes, and each held a stream. Little bays or backwaters were built along the shores, and beside each bay was a comfortable seat, facing downstream. At the upstream end of the garden, men were posted to place cups of rice wine on small wooden floats, then commit them to the current. Those who could enjoy the garden would sit by the shores, meditating on the scenery downstream. Never looking behind to see what was coming, they would swallow whatever cupfuls the unpredictable flow brought into their own bays, until drunkenness or the night overtook them.

When I went to China in the spring of 1940, I wanted to take that view of time. I had gone out there once before, in the autumn of 1935, expecting to spend about two weeks as part of a knockabout trip around the world, thinly financed by portraits and other pictures I had sold while in college. The fascinations of an exotic country where living was still cheap and easy for foreigners helped those weeks expand almost imperceptibly into two years. Mainly through a series of lucky accidents, I traveled quite widely in the Chinese interior, and learned enough of the language and customs to feel at home. At the end of 1937, after the Japanese invasion began, I returned to America, determined that China would be my profession.

7

In 1938 and 1939 I hoped to go back to make a pictorial record of the mountain tribes I had seen in the southwestern province, believing they would soon change because of wartime migrations into their remote country. As I had no training in anthropology, I could not get the backing I needed. I also began to realize that the tribes were going to be there for a long time.

When I did start back in early 1940, my ideas of the Kuomintang were based on optimistic stories printed in the American press, and I had some notion of looking for work in one of the relief or propaganda bureaus which welcomed foreigners. But by that time I had written a travel book about my earlier trip and had made enough money to see me through another two years and another book. My main object was just to sit by the river of Chinese life again, watching whoever happened to float around from behind, recording whatever of interest came my way.

In America and other Western countries, the commonest view of abstract time seems to be the opposite of the old Chinese one. In this, man faces in the other direction, with his back to the past, which is sinking away behind him, and his face turned upward to the future, which is floating down upon him. Nor can this man be static: by our ambitious Western convention, he is supposed to be rising into the future under his own power, perhaps by his own direction. He is more like a man in a plane than a sitter by a river.

The river-sitter can object that the man in the plane, since he turns his back on the past he can know and faces into the future he cannot know, is flying blind and that is dangerous. I quite agree.

In my later years in China, however, after America was shot into the Pacific War, it became clear that willy-nilly, no man could think of himself always as a river-sitter. Luckily I was not in Japanese-occupied territory at the time of Pearl Harbor. I was given an American government job in China and this brought some special knowledge of what was happening to China as a nation, and what America was doing to China.

At the atomic end of the Pacific war, when it appeared that the Japanese invasion had to be replaced by a Chinese civil war and America and Russia might be drawn into the results, it began to seem that everyone alive was locked in a sort of plane or rocket, embarked on a swift trajectory into the future. The one advantage of this came from the fact that all the seats in the machine were so uncomfortable. I found myself trying to peer out in all directions, hoping to see where I was going.

2 · *Uneasy Weather*

Soon after reaching China the second time, I went through a spell of real river-sitting. This took place in June, 1940, in a small junk moving up the Hsi Kiang, or West River, which leads from Hong Kong into the interior. I naturally faced forward during most of the trip, but the pirates and more mysterious types who boarded the junk at intervals were so unpredictable that I might as well have looked backward.

That June was a month of many omens in Hong Kong. The Chinese tabloids carried word that snow had fallen within the Great Wall in summer, and the sun had appeared at Shanghai with a dark iridescent halo — both signs of a bad harvest and increasing wars. Rumors spread that a two-headed baby had been born in the Kowloon suburb of Hong Kong, that the images in a fishermen's shrine near the power-house had begun to sweat. The weather, too, made it seem something was going wrong, for it was the hottest, heaviest rainy season in years. Every evening, oppressive black clouds slid up and lay over-head, sagging tier above tier in the fading green light like the torn floors of a ruined house. The pink lightning quivered and flared in the highest clouds — ghostly disturbances in the decaying attic — while the warm torrents poured down as if to stifle and destroy the pale city sunk in its cellar of mountains. The thunder crashed and rolled over the harbor like an echo of the bombs already falling elsewhere in the world.

It was a bad enough time even for the matter-of-fact, since the Nazi blitzkrieg in Europe had begun while I was crossing the Pacific. Belgium and Holland were conquered, France was all but lost, and it was feared Japan would attack all European colonies in the Orient. Communications between British Hong Kong and French Indo-China had been cut in mid-June, but the French were known to have let in enough Japanese to control their railway to China. On the twentieth of June, Japanese troops landed in Chinese territory just across the

Hong Kong border, and the government in London desperately agreed to complete the blockade of China by closing the Burma Road for three months. But the Japanese firmly continued their encirclement of Hong Kong, burning and looting in the villages on the Chinese side, driving hordes of terrified refugees into the colony. They were rumored to have nearly a hundred thousand troops on Hainan Island, midway between Hong Kong and Indo-China. Calamity was thought certain enough for the Hong Kong people to prepare talismans against it.

While they arranged the evacuation of their women and children, the British invoked their monumental calm. The English-language press all but ignored the bad news in the Orient and played down the bad news from Europe: by delay, by emphasis on trivial good news, by frequent mention of Britain's glorious past. On days of the blackest reports from France, the papers would editorialize on such matters as the fiscal problem in Hong Kong or the increasing fidelity of historical films. One published a letter from a reader assuring there was no need to worry about the defense of Hong Kong since any Englishman could learn to handle a rifle in a few hours.

Among the Chinese residents, the rich bought stronger iron doors and palings to guard against thieves, and a club of their patriotic sons sent a silk banner to Madame Chiang Kai-shek in Chungking. The middle class laid in stocks of food. The poor flocked to the fortune-tellers. Refugees who could afford it fled again, to Portuguese Macao just across the estuary of the Pearl River.

For a neutral traveler like myself, a quick departure also seemed the wise device. I had come to Hong Kong because it was the best point of entry to blockaded Kuomintang territory. I intended to go on to Indo-China by coastal ship, and enter China on the French railway into Yunnan Province; then the ships to Indo-China stopped running. I next planned to take the overland route through Shayuchung on the Hong Kong-Chinese border; then the Japanese landed and closed that route too. It was beginning to seem that the only way to Chungking was the expensive, blind voyage by air, when I met a group who planned to sail to Macao and have themselves smuggled through the Japanese-held sections of the West River delta backing that Portuguese colony.

The leader of the party was an elderly Texan missionary from Kwangsi Province, who spoke rapid Cantonese with a high Pan-handle accent and had made the trip several times before, running church literature and canned goods through the blockade. This trip, he was escorting half a dozen Chinese Christian virgins whose families had decided they would be safer in the interior even though they weren't pretty. Also with him were an English girl, an Austrian doctor, a German doctor: all in the Chinese Red Cross.

On a hot misty morning in early July we sailed for Macao on an excursion steamer packed with refugees, passing in mid-journey a sister ship, Hong Kong bound and crowded with refugees who had decided Macao was to be attacked. At Macao, the Reverend Mr. Mix went with his virgins to the Bible Boat of his mission to contact smugglers, and we others spent the rest of the day looking for lodgings in the refugee-jammed warrens of that odd and squalid remnant of Portugal's sixteenth-century empire. It was a brief return to my tourist years, and I wished I had more time to wander about the tiny peninsula with its bright, dusty streets showing most of the styles of building known to South China and Latin Europe for the past four centuries. As it was, the only guidebook spectacle I remember seeing was the gambling shop where fan-tan was so popular that holes had been cut through two floors above the table, and the game was gambled by three layers of players, the upper two circles peering between their knees and letting their bets down in little baskets on strings. In the evening we found rooms in a Chinese hotel looming over the noise and glare of the rowdy district. It was a rookery which seemed to be built entirely of varnished yellow matchwood, sharp shiny tiling, barbed wire, and electric lights which could not be switched off. Across the dark harbor, the low hills of the Japanese-occupied land lay as silent and lightless as if they had just risen from the bottom of the sea.

Next morning Mr. Mix had news that our first problem should be the worst. Several miles of open water separated Macao from the safer swamps. By day the Japanese sometimes patrolled it in launches. At night they retired to their forts, leaving the waters to the traditional pirates. Here was a choice of dangers: sun or moon. As a Japanese launch had recently caught three smugglers' junks and machine-gunned the passengers, we decided on the moon. The smugglers with whom Mr. Mix dealt promised that the pirates made only reasonable demands.

At the end of a glassy, glaring afternoon we were rowed across the harbor, into a channel between the mainland and a rocky green island. We were followed by another junk with Chinese passengers traveling through the same smuggling company, and were chaperoned by an agent of the company, a frail excitable man in a fisherman's black pajama suit. Each of us had paid the company thirty-five Hong Kong dollars — about seven American dollars. All ransom was to be included in the fare. The darkening channel was full of fishing boats hurrying back to Portuguese waters so urgently that soon the sea stretched empty ahead. Thunderheads massed over the mainland and let down veils of rain which made the whole prospect tricky and indistinct.

While there was still some light and the Mediterranean waterfront of Macao was visible behind, a sampan put out from shore and hailed us. It was sculled by a pretty Chinese girl in pink pajamas, whose only passenger was a sullen-looking young man in black pants and blue shirt. He was armed with a Mauser in a wooden holster and wore a yellow armband stating he was the official pirate here. He demanded ten Kuomintang dollars — about fifty American cents. It was readily supplied by the smuggler agent, and the official pirate pushed away with a faint smile of derision. We all were relieved, and as it grew dark Mr. Mix and the virgins played parlor games in Cantonese and sang hymns in English.

Between eight and nine, when the sky had clouded over and it was very dark, two large junks appeared and veered in. By this time the virgins had gone in under the roof of matting and built a nest in the luggage where they were playing some game of their own. They could not see out and kept clapping their hands in rotation and chanting "Pa-pa! Pa-pa-pa!" until the junks crashed alongside and grappling hooks were thrown over. Nearly twenty men jumped aboard, more conventionally dressed as pirates in ragged, tarry black pajamas, with rusty guns and large knives. After a careful flashlight appraisal of passengers and luggage, they demanded five hundred Kuomintang dollars.

The smuggler complained, and was curtly told a new system had been set up; this money would cover the fees formerly collected farther down the coast. With a theatrical display of fright, he told Mix his plans had been upset by so many foreign passengers, and he could not afford such ransom out of the fare. The foreigners had better do their own bargaining since they would have to pay themselves. Mr. Mix, the only one of us who spoke Cantonese, protested to the pirates that two hundred dollars should be enough and was roughly told five hundred was the fixed price. If it were not paid soon, our party would be taken ashore and held until a real old-

fashioned ransom could be sent from Hong Kong. When we had
collected the money and it had been counted twice by flashlight, the
junks slid silently off.

Between warm showers and spells of fitful moonlight, this kind of
thing went on all night, as regularly as if scheduled. The eleven-thirty
pirates wanted two hundred dollars. The one-o'clock pirates wanted
only fifty. They seemed less professional, for they came in a
smaller boat and as they left called back pleasantly: "We used to be
fishermen, but now we have to make our living any way we can."
The two-thirty pirates demanded three hundred dollars and while
we were assembling it, they boarded the smuggler's other boat and
looted it.

When they heard the first large group of pirates threaten to take
us ashore, the virgins had hung coats over the entrance to their nest
and changed into specially unbecoming clothes. During the later
flashlight inspections, they would squint, sag their shoulders, puff out
their cheeks and stomachs as unattractively as possible. Now, when
loud female noises came from the other boat — we later learned the
pirates were only tearing down the women's hair, looking for money
— they began to cheep and call to Mr. Mix. But, kneeling on deck
with his head in his hands, he was suddenly a helpless and speechless
old man. His breeziness had vanished after the second pirate visit and
after the third he decided prayer was better than bargaining. The
smuggler kept whispering with the pirate guards, apparently on cordial terms, and from time to time simulated alarm to the virgins,
warning us through them that if we valued our lives we would pay
everything asked. When the pirates returned and saw all this, they
upped their fee to four hundred. Mr. Mix was too lost in devotions
to hear when asked for his share.

By five the coastal hills and swampy plain of the delta were grayly
visible. Halfway to shore sat a black object which might be a rock;
then it sprouted oars and moved forward. "We will inspect your
luggage!" a hoarse voice called as the grappling hooks were thrown
over.

They came aboard in relays, the important ones first to take first
pick. All luggage was opened; when the keys to the English girl's
trunk could not be found, Mr. Mix recovered himself enough to
borrow a cleaver from the boatmen and personally hacked it open.
For half an hour we stood dumbly by, weaving to avoid the guns and
knives of the scrambling searchers, our feet caught in a rising tide of

tumbled personal belongings. Mix prayed, while the doctors muttered darkly of what they would do if they had guns. Looking very pretty in her rage at Mix, the English girl sat with some of the virgins on the side bench near the open deck; they had discovered that in the general confusion they could resteal loot which had been taken outside, then slide it back into the cabin behind them.

It was really impossible to understand what was going on in that dark boat, rocking gently in the warm shallows, the center of an uncertain, mouse-colored world of sea, swamp, and sky. Who were these pirates anyway? From what could be seen, they were very ordinary citizens; their shiny black pajamas were standard wear for almost all classes in South China. They made themselves harder to believe by the things they stole — money, watches, and fountain pens, of course, then whatever took their fancy — a cloth flower, an old magazine. It never seemed entirely clear whether this was a joke or a disaster. Only the guns were there for sure.

I had an American fifty-dollar bill in my shirt pocket and transferred it to my shoe by pretended scratching. A virgin later told me two pirates near her had become suspicious, and discussed whether or not to kill me. When they decided against it, one complained: "Don't these foreigners know we only want to rob them, not kill them? Why do they try to cheat us?"

The Austrian doctor had hidden several tins of American cigarettes in the scuppers and just at the end, when only four or five lesser pirates left grubbing about, these were found. It was the last straw for the doctor. He snatched them back. "If we can't have the tins, can we at least have a cigarette apiece?" the pirates asked agreeably, so the doctor opened a tin and doled out one smoke to each.

Before it was light enough for Japanese, the pirates left and our boatmen poled to the delta through a stretch of reedy mud flats. They dismantled a low footbridge and entered a canal as long and straight as an avenue, flanked by the greasy windmill foliage of banana trees. When the coppery sun rose over the dark leaves they anchored at a knot of smoke-blackened huts built over the bank on piles, primitive and miserable as a prehistoric lake-dwellers' village. In the filth and shadows among the piles, black hogs and red chickens wandered. Somewhere a drunkard was singing or wailing monotonously. At the waterside an old woman knelt nose-down, beating a rag between two rocks as if she hated all cloth. Hong Kong and Macao, the foreign port cities with their arcades and elevators, ice cubes and steam whistles, lobby rumors and fortified beaches, seemed thousands of miles and years away.

Cheered by a problem they thought they could handle, the virgins went off to look for food while the rest of us talked over the next step. More than half our money for the trip inland was gone. It would be a week's travel to the nearest unoccupied town large enough to have a bank, and the remaining money might not be enough. There could be more pirates ahead; there certainly were pirates behind, and it might not be wise to try to return without enough money for them. Mr. Mix had got out his Bible and was opening it at random for passages of advice when several men in white underwear peered through the banana trees, then came down carrying guns and umbrellas.

They were police, loyal to the Kuomintang, they said. They invited the foreign guests to the police station. Again there was no way of knowing who they really were. One with a bad eye looked like a pirate last seen in the confusing dawn. But again, they had the guns.

The police station was a mud-floored hut beside a swamp blue with hyacinths, and in it several familiar-looking men in white underwear were playing mah-jong, their black pajamas hung on the wall, their guns and knives stacked in the corner. They said they were Kuomintang guerrillas. When Mix explained who we were, they told him one main branch of the West River separated us from unoccupied territory and this was patrolled by Japanese launches. Since the doctors had a cargo of medical supplies for China, they said, they would help us cross. The medicine would have to be taken by itself, because it would be too dangerous if we were caught with it. This seemed a dodge to steal the medicine but again there was no choice.

Soon the virgins arrived in breathless dismay because they had failed to buy food. The villagers here were so close to starvation, they refused to sell what little they had. Our hosts gave the girls a dried fish dug out from under some bedding and a melon cut from the vine over the door, and with all their self-confidence back they set about cooking a stew.

At dusk the Red Cross cases were loaded on a sampan, covered with straw, and poled away by two guerrillas who disguised themselves as farmers by putting on their black pajamas. They would cross the big river, they said, by a safer way not open to large boats and return the medicine on the other side in the morning. After dark five armed guards boarded our junk and we set out under a clear sky and a moderate moon, with a guerrilla sampan to scout the way. The banana orchards gave way to thick mangrove and palmetto swamps, these to pale open marshland bordering the big river. Half a mile downstream, the lights of a Japanese fort glowed weakly.

The sampan crossed first and after twenty minutes its all-clear came, three tiny winks from a flashlight. The junk swung out on the wide field of water and for an age remained exposed under the moon, its bamboo sails and wire rigging clattering like a collapsing house. Then the far shore slid close and after a few straining minutes while the mouth of the opposite canal nearly slipped past, the boat was poled out of the current, into tree-shaded water where two large junks crashed into it. There was a furious outburst of duck-quacking and when the grappling hooks were secured, a Chinese gentleman in a white silk gown and black Homburg came aboard with a revolver in each hand. The sight of so many foreigners seemed to jolt him.

"I beg your pardon!" he said in Oxford English and fled back to his own boat. A Japanese launch came down the big river with its siren screaming and its searchlights sweeping the shore but it paid no attention to the three junks locked together under the trees.

The new captors were puppets employed by the Japanese fort. All night they kept us in the stifling smell of ducks while they argued what to do with us. From all Mix and the virgins could hear over the yapping of the crated birds which unaccountably filled both puppet boats, a rumor had spread that a party of foreigners were trying to smuggle half a million dollars of some kind into unoccupied China. The lesser puppets wanted to turn us over to the Japanese for a share in this, but the chief in the white gown discounted the money-rumor and thought it more trouble than it would be worth to interfere with foreigners of so many different nationalities. At dawn a puppet customs launch came down the river and moored at the mouth of the canal, where its commander was asked for a decision. In the growing light we could see well enough to wonder if we hadn't met some of these men before, either the day before or the night before that. All wore the standard black pajamas or white underwear.

Whoever they were, they decided they did not want us. As the sun rose, our boatmen were allowed to pole us westward, down a canal winding through swamps and rice fields, past sharp green hills laced with cataracts and clumps of spidery white lilies. A few miles on, the sampan with the medicine waited and all the cases were smilingly re-loaded by the two men who had taken them off the night before, helped by a third with pockmarks who was almost certainly an acquaintance from the night before that.

In the late morning the canal circled a crumbling clay pillbox guarded by a little boy with an ancient rifle. Barefoot, with purple underwear shorts instead of pants, he didn't look much of a warrior but he had a uniform tunic and was our first regular soldier. This was in fact the formal Kuomintang frontier.

Mr. Mix spruced up tremendously and took his great black umbrella to walk along the canal bank. It was his work to bargain at the toll stations set up every half-mile or so by Kuomintang troops who taxed smuggled passengers and goods. With all his old brashness back, armed with the news that the puppets had not taxed us and that we were carrying medical supplies for China, Mix got through all without paying. These Kuomintang soldiers would have lost face if they taxed us when the puppets hadn't. Other smugglers' junks were anchored at the toll stations while their cargoes of cloth and thread, canned fruit and dried sea foods, Western-style shoes, cosmetics, cigarettes and all the other things which could be sold at great profit in this blockaded and warring country were inspected and the money changed hands.

Shoals of silvery minnows splashed the surface of the canal and among the reeds small sulphur-colored butterflies chased one another. The virgins had been paralyzed and silent ever since they heard the puppets might turn us over to the Japanese, but now they gradually came alive. They bucketed up canal water and began to wash and smooth their tumbled clothes. Beside one rice field a water buffalo basked in a pool which fitted as if made to measure; around his flanks a flock of tiny ducklings curvetted in perfect formation, like a primer illustration labeled "The BIG Buffalo, The SMALL Ducks." After a while the virgins cheered up enough to sing and over the hot July waters shrilly rang the sound of Christmas carols in Cantonese.

We were all so pleased that we soon stopped wondering what had happened to us and who had done it: why the guerrilla sampan had signaled us across the big river to be captured by puppets; how or if it escaped after it signaled from the canal where the puppets waited; what indeed had been the connection between all of them — puppets, guerrillas, police, pirates, and smugglers. It was not until some years later that I could make reasonable guesses about them.

During part of the Pacific war, in 1943 and 1944, I was stationed in South China and for months worked in territory not far from the

West River delta where this charade with the pirates had taken place in 1940. I was supposed to learn what I could of neighboring provinces, and the mechanics of the smuggling business became clearer to me.

They were being exposed in gruesome fashion, for a great famine was underway in the West River delta and nearby counties of Kwangtung Province. The most important smuggling was now in rice rather than trade goods, and the food was moving in an unexpected direction. It was being taken *out* of the famine-struck sections of Kuomintang territory, smuggled into the occupied areas and sold to the Japanese enemy. For anyone who was being hustled into the future in a planelike projectile and wondered where it would land, this smuggling racket and the famine it aggravated were the kind of thing that had to be noticed. Both were encouraged by the make-up of China's traditional society, preserved almost intact under the Kuomintang government.

Until the Communists began to make changes, the country districts which formed the great bulk of China had always been controlled by tiny local minorities, the majority of people being peasant farmers. Grain was a preferred medium of wealth in this agrarian country, and the hoards of surplus grain which gave economic power were generally in the hands of a small group of landlords, merchants, and usurers. Landlords took tithes in grain from their peasant tenants in accord with China's old land-rent system which usually allowed the landowner at least half — and sometimes more — of the tenants' total crop. Merchants and usurers enforced old rules of commerce which were so hard on the ignorant peasants that many businessmen were able to become large hoarders of grain.

This minority also had political power, for most local officials, appointed from above, were members of the wealthier families — landlords, merchants, usurers, or a combination of all three. They naturally collaborated in their relatives' and friends' business ventures. They took many of their taxes from the peasants in grain rather than in money.

The grain-controlling group commonly had military and police power too. The officers in the local garrison or militia might be outsiders, but they were almost always from the same privileged background and were drawn to their own kind. Many would go into business when they were stationed in a community for any length of time. As the military could tax and control the movement of grain

and other goods, they were sought as partners by the other commercial operators. Officers could always take grain from the peasants
for their troops.

With such a monopoly of power, it was almost unavoidable that the
grain-controlling minority should be corrupt, and much of it was. Its
official members would look the other way when their friends tried to
squeeze the peasants for larger levies, tithes, or debt payments than
were justified. Officers loaned armed guards to help officials collect
extra and unauthorized taxes. When higher authorities tried to inspect,
the non-official members — all of them pillars of their communities —
would help cover up for their official cronies.

A well-entrenched gang like this would naturally muscle in on any
prosperous business within reach, and in the middle years of the
Japanese invasion, that was just what smuggling became in the West
River delta and most other frontline sections of Kuomintang territory.
In its wartime refuge in Chungking, the central government had failed
to set up even enough handicraft industries to replace the modern
factories lost in Shanghai and other coastal cities. When the Japanese
fronts became static, the products of these coastal factories — including
the puppet and Japanese ones — began to pour into the interior in
almost as great volume as before the invasion. The Japanese forbade
the smuggled export of anything of military or industrial value, but
ignored the flow of other goods. The Kuomintang taxed all smuggled
commodities but made no effort to stop even the trade in luxuries, and
its propaganda claimed this commerce was wholesome because everything that came in was of military or industrial value.

By 1940, when I passed through the West River delta, the local
grain-controlling minority had monopolized a good part of the smuggling trade. For convenience, many of its members had made contact
with their opposite numbers in occupied territory — puppet officials,
officers and so on. This was fairly easy to do, because the Japanese
had built their puppet régime out of the same privileged minority the
Kuomintang used. Many Kuomintang people were relatives or pre-
war friends of the puppets on the other side of the static front. The
mysteries of my trip with Mr. Mix and his party were certainly an
indirect result of this collaboration.

Of course the smuggling trade harmed the front-line areas of Kuomintang territory, not only because it weakened the frontiers against
Japanese spying and infiltration. Smuggled imports, being better and

often cheaper than local products, helped bankrupt local industry. So did the quick profits of smuggling, which attracted capital away from industry. Raw materials such as tobacco and cotton, which might have been processed locally, began to be smuggled into enemy territory, later brought back as cigarettes and cloth. But the smuggling-in of enemy goods was not nearly as ruinous to the Kuomintang as the later smuggling-out of rice during the famine.

The West River delta and other more crowded counties of Kwangtung Province were not self-sufficient and in normal times imported rice from Indo-China and Burma; some was still being smuggled in from Hong Kong when I went through with Mr. Mix's party. In the following year, though, when the Pacific war began and the Japanese took Hong Kong, they cut off this supply. Later, they began to offer high prices for rice in their occupied territory, buying it with cloth, thread, Kuomintang dollars and other loot they had captured in the warehouses of Hong Kong. Although unoccupied Kwangtung had been suffering from drought and was in the first throes of famine, rice soon began to be smuggled out by the grain-controlling minority in the Kuomintang areas.

Rice which had been extorted from already starving peasants by officials of their own government and officers of their own army was now — in wartime — sold to their enemy, for private profit. The trade continued through the following two years of greater drought and mass death, finishing off what was left of war morale in unoccupied Kwangtung. Perhaps this was the Japanese purpose in offering high prices for rice.

Since more than a million and a half people are believed to have perished in Kwangtung during the 1943–44 droughts, there would have been a calamity here no matter what kind of government was in power. I have never heard any estimates of the number who starved for artificial reasons, because of the sale of their food to the enemy, but even if it were only a few thousand, the damage to the Kuomintang was incalculable. Exposed in a few courageous newspapers, the scandal became a subject of talk among politically minded people all over China. For many, it completely destroyed the government's moral case against the Communists.

Reports of it also spread over the peasant bamboo-telegraph, which was very sensitive to news of the farmers' welfare. In villages hundreds of miles from the famine, it was bitterly said that the lucky peasants among the starving were the ones who got jobs as coolies for private businessmen, since they were paid when they carried rice down for sale to the Japanese. Coolies who transported rice from the hoards of Kuomintang officials or officers were taken as forced labor, under armed guard, and were not paid.

At the time this was happening, while the Pacific war was still being fought, the Japanese connection seemed the most shocking thing about it. Since then, Japan's invasion has receded into place as one incident in the course of China's long revolutionary upheaval. Another feature of the West River famine has begun to look more important. It was common to all the Kuomintang-controlled famines I heard anything of. Since it caricatures the process which wrecked China's traditional society and exposes the collapse of social responsibility which made such ruin possible, I had better describe it right here.

In all drought-threatened parts of Kuomintang China in recent years, when the sun had burned too long from a cloudless sky, the peasants would ration their daily meals of grain in order not to starve until they had harvested their weather-damaged crop. They would usually have enough to eat until harvest time, when the men who were privileged by the rules of this sick old society collected as wealth much of the grain that could have been used as food. Some few members of the grain-controlling minority were of course kindly, and reduced their exactions after a bad harvest. In the famines of which I had personal knowledge, however, most taxes, levies, and tithes were collected in full, even when that took so much of the peasants' grain that they would have to starve.

With the demand for grain growing through hunger, it was then customary for the grain-controlling minority to raise the price. Since few peasants had money reserves to buy back the grain they had grown, they would begin eating substitutes, or selling their property to buy back the grain. While there were leaves to eat, they would sell their furniture, clothes, parts of their houses. Banditry would begin, but in this mild period of hunger it was usually carried on in the stylized old way, with those who had guns as tokens of power quite politely taking only what they needed.

Usually toward the end of the leaf-eating period, the local members of the privileged minority would begin moving their families and valuables and surplus grain to safety, preferably inside a town which still had its medieval walls and was strongly garrisoned by Kuomintang troops. Sometimes they departed themselves, leaving agents to sell grain and buy whatever the peasants were forced to sell. If it was feared that the Kuomintang "Peace Preservation Corps" in the famine area was not large enough to safeguard order and profits, more troops were sent in.

If the bad harvest had been the autumn one, and the leaves soon fell and turned inedible, the peasants would begin eating bark or clay, or selling their farm tools and land to buy back more grain. Now they would eat their seed-grain, kill and eat their beloved farm animals, sell their land, destroying their hope of ever farming again without new debts. The price of grain would be raised still higher, while the grain-controlling minority offered lower and lower prices for the peasants' property, as the hunger threw more of it on the market. One mark of this stage of the peasants' descent into despair would be the period when they began saving for grain by burying their dead naked, without coffins: a shame and a torment among people who greatly revered ancestors.

The numbers who turned bandit would increase, and in their need and the haste brought by increasing competition, they would begin killing before they robbed. Of course bark and clay are not foods, only a means of postponing hunger, and soon the famine area would enter a wild period when the bandit gangs would be large enough to attack whole villages. Brutalized by their own sufferings, they would sometimes kill other famine-victims just because they found nothing to rob.

By now, many peasants would be too weak or uninterested to bury their dead at all, and would simply drag them into the fields away from their homes. Some would be lost enough to begin prowling for other families' corpses, driving away the dogs and ravens while they cut off their own food. Some would begin selling the less useful members of their families in the hope of saving the rest. Women and children were sold by the pound even when they were sold as slaves, not food, and the day the price of a pound of living human flesh sank below that of a pound of grain could be taken as the point at which the famine settled into its final stretch. By this time, many peasants who still had the strength would have taken their families in flight from such a place of abominations. Those who remained would begin locking themselves into their houses, to die hopelessly but decently at home.

Sometimes in the final stages of famine the bandit groups would become large and desperate enough to attack more than the other victims. They would threaten to plunder the towns and steal back the hoards of the grain-controlling minority. This was rare, though, partly because of China's strong traditions of social obedience, partly because of the precautions taken by those who had the grain and the power.

When the drought had run its course, many surviving peasants would increase their debts as they borrowed for the seed and tools they needed for their next crop, plus the grain to keep them alive while they grew it. They mortgaged their remaining land for these loans, or promised to repay in grain from their next crop. When they bought back their tools and other essentials with borrowed money, the cost was naturally much higher, sometimes by two or three times, than the price they had got when they crazily sold in hunger. When they borrowed grain, the value of the loan was estimated as the current money-value of the grain; it would have to be repaid with grain of the same money-value at harvest time. Interest on loans in money and grain after a drought was usually more than ten per cent a month.

The minority whose hoards let them control the price would keep it at a famine high until they had given loans, then, during the weeks before the next harvest, they would throw grain on the market, bringing the price down. It was not unusual for the price to drop by half in such a period. When this happened, a peasant who had borrowed fifty quarts would have to repay one hundred at harvest time. After the harvest, the peasants were again visited by their landlords and other masters, who not only made exactions on the current crop but collected arrears from the previous bad harvest, even when this again left the peasants with little or nothing to eat. The peasants would mortgage or sell more of their land and other property.

If the weather were kind and there was no more mass famine, the community would still bear permanent marks of the drought. A few well-to-do peasants would probably have lost enough land to be middle peasants. A number of middle peasants would certainly be poor peasants. A large number of the poor peasants would now be landless. The grain-controlling minority would be richer, in land as well as grain and money. And in the distant towns where many ex-farmers had fled, where some would aimlessly remain because they had sold everything at home, the wages paid for refugee labor could be forced down a bit farther.

I imagine the average American who reads of these cruelties must ask how any society could reach such degradation and survive a moment longer. Kuomintang China entered its extreme state of collapse or suicide only in recent years, and has not survived, despite American rescue attempts. But China has been moving towards this crack-up all through its recent century of contact with the Western world.

Until the early nineteenth century, a number of factors kept Chinese society fairly stable. Cut off from other great countries, China was usually at peace. It did not need large armies, nor a powerful government. The emperors of the successive dynasties appointed the important provincial officials, but the imperial authority rested lightly on the country, like a tiny tasseled mandarin hat topping the huge body of China. Most communities were virtually self-governing. The emperors and their courts might live in fabulous pomp, but their taxes, when distributed over the whole country, were seldom a crushing burden.

Isolated by poor communications, the separate Chinese communities were as little disturbed by outside economic pressures as by political or military interference. Most of their needs were filled by local handicrafts. There was scanty industry or trade by the Western definition, slight opportunity to amass fluid wealth. Little money circulated; the chief medium of wealth was land and the grain it produced.

Large inherited inequalities in land ownership already existed and the imperial officials were recruited from a small, distinct landlord class. As in the Kuomintang period, some eighty per cent of the people were illiterate peasants. Many were tenant farmers. All were at the mercy of the few who had the authority.

In the past, though, one check against too much rapacity among the rulers was the Confucian idea of society which China's humane culture had begun to develop long before the birth of Christ. This held that just as the father in a family was responsible for the good life of his sons, so an official was responsible for all whom he ruled. The emperor was responsible for his officials and, through them, his people. He was head of the national family.

The duties in this plan worked both ways; the filial inferiors owed their paternal superiors good behavior in return for protection. Since the emperor was also the "Son of Heaven," offspring of the most complete and abstract Good any man could imagine, this social system strengthened, and was strengthened by, all yearnings toward morality and a decent life.

Though ancient China had many tyrannical or foolish emperors and corrupt officials, except in the periods of chaos at the end of dynasties they usually preserved in some form the concept that all Chinese were one family, in which no members should too grievously harm the others. When a dynasty allowed its government to become too oppressive, it was thought to have lost its "Mandate of Heaven." The emperors had offended their abstract father by allowing cruelty to their own national children, the people. The revolt which brought a new dynasty to power was believed inevitable and justified.

The emperors were so shut away in their palace-capitals and the spread of news was so limited that many communities might enjoy good government and decent human relations during periods of national decay and change. Combined with the fact of China's sluggish, non-modern economic life, this generally meant that the rich just stayed rich and the poor stayed poor.

When China's isolation from the West ended, however, the country fell victim to a series of wars and invasions and other impositions brought by the colony-minded Western powers. The foreign inroads exposed and increased the weakness of the Manchu Empire and its successors, the warlords and the Kuomintang. China was racked by a series of internal wars and revolts which required large armies and increasing taxes. Security and stability were lost in a period of boundless disorder.

Even in quiet times, Western industry and trade helped destroy the old balance. The interior was opened to new supplies and demands from the West, upsetting the old local markets and crafts. Railways and modern shipping lines made close neighbors of distant communities within China, creating bewildering new economic pressures. When modern industry began sprouting in the coastal cities, China's static economy was laced with areas of fiercely competitive commercial life in the Western style. More money and other forms of fluid wealth came into circulation.

Improved communications helped corrupt the old paternalist government and its morality. When the emperor in his distant capital had been fairly unknown, more of a symbol than a ruler, his presumed virtue had restrained local officials. In the last half of the nineteenth and first half of the twentieth centuries, however, the spread of news let all communities know that their national leaders — in the Manchu, warlord, and Kuomintang régimes alike — were of questionable virtue. Many were racketeers and profiteers. Naturally the local authorities followed the new example.

Western ideas and education were another confusing influence. Too many new meanings and values were presented at once. The Western standards most widely adopted were naturally those most often shown in China, in the cutthroat free enterprise of the Westerners who were vying with one another to get the most out of the country in the shortest time.

In the larger treaty-ports which the Westerners opened along the China coast, modern industry and trade did produce a small new wealthy class of Chinese — compradores and others who helped or imitated the Westerners. Some of them developed into a middle or upper class quite similar to the Western model. They invested their fortunes in their businesses, and sometimes learned more from the West than commercial savagery. In the rest of China, however, including the rural areas which were the important part of the country, it was generally the old grain-controlling minority that could learn, invest, and profit by the new ways. This was the only group with education and spare capital, however meager. As soon as members of the minority gained new wealth, through industry, trade, squeeze, or embezzlement, they commonly bought land, the traditional investment for their class.

Because of a rapid — and as yet unexplained — rise in population, China had entered its trying modern century of confusion and Western-influenced change with far more mouths than could be supported by an old land which was already seriously deforested, eroded, and exhausted. The difficulty of survival, and the latent panic, encouraged rapacity and dog-eat-dog individualism in all dealings outside the family, the last surviving unit of mutual benevolence and responsibility.

Thus, from a little before the middle of the nineteenth century until the present, the rich in most parts of China began to use new and often unscrupulous ways to get richer. Hamstrung already by their ignorance and inherited inequalities, the poor peasants were in no position to resist. They were handicapped by the disastrous increase of mouths in their own families and by the burden of all the new wars, a load which the privileged had naturally put on peasant shoulders. Slowly and more or less humanely at first, then more rapidly and cruelly, the wealth of China — including the land itself — began to change hands. The poor got steadily poorer, until the methods and results of change reached the insupportable stage I have described as part of a Kuomintang famine.

3 · The Threatening Sky

AFTER THE last pirates or smugglers or guerrillas bade their polite farewells to Mr. Mix, we sat for a tropical week in the junk from Macao, as we were poled through the delta network of tidal streams and canals, on our way north toward the main body of the West River.

Before the Japanese invasion, when the coastal areas were the most prosperous and modern, a trip inland had been a slow farewell to Western-style comforts and the sophistications of urban Chinese life. From the great, complete metropolitan centers near the ocean you went inland by gradual stages, first to the end of the railway, then to the end of the motor road, then to the end of the telegraph line. Typical landmarks would be the last city rich enough for theatres, the last town with a clean hotel, the last village with a roofed restaurant. Out beyond the last little path-side stall which sold Shanghai cigarettes, you could feel you had really arrived in the archaic, impoverished interior.

In my wartime entry in 1940, this pattern was reversed. We struck the most primitive conditions right on the coast, the first morning out of Macao. Going inland, into the Kuomintang's blockaded hinterland, was a gradual journey in from the wilderness, past such welcome landmarks as the first real footpath, the first path wide enough for rickshaws, at last the first motor road; the first little restaurant, the first big hotel, at last the first town with electric lights. The first railway, at Liuchow, was some three hundred miles from the coast.

In that week of junk-travel across the delta, we slowly zigzagged back and forth among sun-struck, jungle-fringed swamps and fields, fretting out whole days in detours around the Japanese forts and patrolled waters. Later I tried to trace this voyage on a map; I could not find any of the waterways, but believe the week's result, measured in a straight line, was less than forty miles. It was an eerie time, silent

28

except for the constant chatter of the virgins in the junk. The parts of the delta that were not occupied or semi-occupied were always in danger of Japanese raiding parties. Most of the wealthy had fled, and the peasants were struggling with the first of the bad years which were to culminate in great famine three years later.

In the heat and glare of the July weather, the emptiness gave the journey the quality of a dream — a sinister one since each clump of trees, each bend of the stream, might disclose something black for unarmed people. We would glide between the luxuriant banks for hours with no glimpse of human life except an occasional farmer in a field, who ran and hid when he saw us, or a quiet watcher in a thicket, staring out with enigmatic face. Sometimes, above the trees, the towering masts of other smugglers' junks on parallel canals slid soundlessly and mysteriously past. Once a column of smoke wavered across the plain not far ahead, accompanied by the hysteric tootling of a motor launch, whether Chinese or Japanese we could not tell. Whenever we floated by a village, it was a little like passing a tableau of horror in a tunnel ride at an amusement park. The walls of mangrove and palmetto would fall away, revealing the decayed houses with their shabby people caught half in, half out, frozen in attitudes of surprise and apprehension, no sound or motion except the scuttling of the giant scavenger crabs on the garbage heaps edging the water.

We saw few soldiers other than the Kuomintang troops at the toll stations, but the material relics of war were scattered everywhere. At

the entrance of the large waterways, lines of rusty mines floated like the knobbly snouts of submerged monsters. Along the shores, the bombed, bleached hulks of passenger steamers and launches wallowed, usually beneath overhanging trees where their pilots had hoped to hide them from the Japanese planes during the great flight from Canton two years earlier. The Chinese themselves had blasted all bridges and torn all roads back into fields at that time, as part of their "Scorched Earth" policy, and more than once we passed the strange ruins of filling stations, flanked by derelict gas pumps and the carcasses of gutted trucks, but standing in open farmland, incongruous as a sewing machine on a beach.

Even after a week of this tranced landscape the first real town, Tam Shui Ko, where we left the Macao junk, was a shock. Out in the country the evidence of war had been surrounded by miles of unblemished, fertile-looking land. I had convinced myself that any city here must be a little like Hong Kong or Macao — full of giddy architecture, lively crowds, colors, noises, and smells. But Tam Shui Ko was a tomb of a city. Though it had not been invaded, it looked as a colonial Roman settlement in outer France or Britain must have in the early Dark Ages, after the barbarian invasions swept through. Most of the inhabitants, poor as well as rich, had fled during the panic following the fall of Canton; weeds and bushes were growing in the little white-colonnaded streets. The town had been heavily bombed before it was deserted and the windows and doors which were not bricked up gaped upon the blackness of charred rooms or the dazzle of the open sky. The deadness of the walls was broken only where the sides of public buildings were scrawled with huge, savage, anti-Japanese murals from the young years of the war, smeared and fading now. In most streets the only living creatures besides the wild dogs and cats, and strangely tame rats, were a few ragged sidewalk peddlers with trays of flyblown wares. In the misty mornings, though, the peasants still brought their vegetables and crude handicrafts to sell to one another in the city; on the market corners they squatted, bargaining clamorously in rough raincoats of palm fiber, like a herd of shaggy beasts among the ruins. The fine hotel near the river had somehow escaped the bombing and at night its roof-garden restaurant was the only other scene of vigorous life and exchange. Here the big merchant-smugglers gathered to feast with the officers and officials who were becoming their colleagues. Over the silent town where only a few weak vegetable-oil lamps flickered, the roof garden floated like a hallucination, a garish island of green radiance pumped from smuggled Japanese pressure-lamps.

The night of our arrival, we foreign travelers were invited to a banquet in the roof garden by the general of the Kuomintang garrison. It was a sumptuous meal of sharks' lips, shrimp, chicken, duck, pork, in pungent sauces, and it tasted fine after a week of dried fish and melon. It was almost cool in the roof garden, between the rockery and the aviary, and there was considerable drinking and jollity among the other guests, stout officers and merchants. They had as much fun as children, comparing the new trinkets their smuggling had brought them: fountain pens, thermometers, watches, pedometers, metal belt-buckles stylishly inscribed in English with such mottoes as "Modern Times" or "Welcome." Among the guests were all the Kuomintang faces which were to become so deadeningly familiar to me — the sly triangular ones, the brutal square ones, the round ones of the fat fellows who would laugh uproariously without the slightest trace of amusement.

The general and his aides had been fascinated when they learned that the European doctors in our party were in the Chinese Red Cross; they had never heard of it before. They were also interested to know that the two doctors had worked in the Spanish Republican Army before coming to China, and asked many questions about comparative conditions in Spain and China. The good food had only slightly filmed the doctors' sarcasm.

"How does the strength of our Chinese soldiers compare with that of the Spanish?" asked the general.

"Chinese soldiers can endure conditions no other army would tolerate," said the German doctor.

The general looked flattered.

"Do you think China can ever be defeated?" he asked.

"Never!" cried the Austrian doctor waving his hand over the table, deep with the rich débris of the banquet. "China's resources are limitless! Even at the beginning of the Spanish war, the highest Republican generals did not eat like this!"

The general was flattered again. He and his plump young aides speculated about this strange Spanish failure.

"Faulty distribution," they decided at last, with crafty laughter.

Beyond Tam Shui Ko we traveled on foot, in a long, ragged procession. The virgins trotted ahead in a tight little group, their maroon

parasols held straight over their heads, their knees working like pistons under the bright print dresses they had put on as soon as we were out of reach of the Japanese. They chattered as tirelessly as they walked, and ended each blazing day as fresh as when they started. Far behind them, the Reverend Mr. Mix flailed steadily through the layers of heat in his thick canvas suit and heavy white sun helmet, with his black umbrella rolling to his stride. Much farther behind, the rest of us straggled among the baggage coolies, hurrying, stopping in the shade, hurrying again.

If it hadn't been for the heat and the haste, this trek would have been a perfect return to the surprises of travel in rural China. In one series of villages the women twisted their back-hair into long conical buns, elegant and cruel-looking as the abdomen of a wasp. In another they wore silver chains on their dark blue aprons. In one stretch of plain, the villages had the look of medieval Italy, built around clusters of tall, square gray towers which were the forts of the usurers. In another, the richest houses belonged to returned emigrants and were built in as much of a Californian or Indonesian style as the owners had been able to shout into the heads of the local carpenters. In the hills, the villages surrounded pools where carp were farmed; the communal latrines were thriftily built over the pools and the villagers took Rabelasian delight in a diarrheal traveler's first fright at the ravenous

fish. All the way, we walked along what once had beer
road. In the flat fields no sign of it remained except the s
telegraph poles, chopped away for firewood. In the grassy
course was marked by a line of tank traps, so wide and deep that if a
highway were ever to be built here again, it would be easier to build
it along another route.

Shiuhing, where we reached the main body of the West River
above the delta, was a town half of bone-colored ruins and deserted
buildings like Tam Shui Ko, half of inhabited houses painted black
in camouflage against air raids. The bigger buildings had dark cages
of bamboo on their roofs, to serve as bomb-baffles, it was hoped. The
main streets at noon held as many people as might have been found
in peacetime at eleven-thirty at night, and a few shops were open,
largely stocked with smuggled goods. There was still no sign of local
industry except peasant handicrafts.

Here the smuggling traffic which had seeped through the front along
countless byways came together as the delta streams did, and we
were able to travel upriver by public carrier, a junk the shape of an
Elizabethan galleon, large enough for nearly three hundred passengers
and a thousand or more ducks. For two weeks we sat on this hulk,
ascending from the jungle-tufted plains of Kwangtung Province to
the severe, grass-covered, pinnacle-strewn plateau of Kwangsi. Slowly
the river changed from muddy red to clear lime green, and the weather
from moist, sweltering glare to dry, breezy heat. One by one the
virgins debarked at towns where they had relatives, and so at last did
Mr. Mix.

Because the front and the Japanese airfields were so close, the huge
junk traveled only at night, swinging in the current behind the fountain of orange sparks which sprayed from its towboat, a tiny wood-
burning launch. At the stern of the junk, the second-class cabin
towered above the third, and the first above the second, in tiers of
latticework and carved wood, but in the heat all classes sat on deck
for the night voyages. By day the junk was hidden under the giant
bamboos which overhung the shore, and the passengers scattered into
the fields and citrus orchards to sleep.

Besides local traders and casual travelers, most passengers were
small-time smugglers — "guerrilla merchants," as they were facetiously
called — each returning from Japanese territory with a suitcase or two
of stockings, cosmetics, fountain pens, and other light merchandise. I
also remember four young soldiers traveling as bodyguard-servants to

a general's wife who was on her way back from a vacation with her husband at the front. As members of an officer's household, they had better equipment than the average Kuomintang soldier and seemed to have more to eat, for they frolicked like truants all the way, chasing and swearing at butterflies when they went ashore, sitting in the tender and splashing their feet when we were traveling. Their most prized possessions were pillows and towels, fashionably embroidered in English: "Good Night" on the pillows, "Good Morning" on the towels. Since they knew no English, they tried to get full value from the linen by having their foreign fellow passengers read the mottoes whenever the articles were used, then repeating the words to each other, with mocking laughter, as long as they could remember the pattern of sounds. In the mornings they went ashore shouting "Good Night" and in the evenings, as they washed their faces, they shouted "Good Morning."

Each town farther up the river was a little fuller, a little busier. At Wuchow on the Kwangtung-Kwangsi provincial border, the outskirts of the city had been savagely bombed but the four- and five-story buildings in the business center were intact, all of them camouflaged with black paint as if this were a city for bats. At dusk, when there was no more danger from planes, a few feeble electric bulbs glimmered in the shadowy canyon-streets and a dingy crowd roamed in the half-light: haggling, quarreling, jeering, with just enough tigerish vitality to suggest the swarming life of pre-war days. Though most goods for sale here were smuggled, a few small shops were open, manufacturing luggage, wicker furniture, and other small-investment urban wares. At Wuchow we began to feel the central authority of the Kuomintang, for our passports were examined and we had to fill out entrance papers for the first time, more than a hundred miles in from the frontier. There were also heavy timber and barbed-wire gates erected across the main streets, to "control the people" in case of panic or riot.

Above Wuchow the junk made its nightly stops at little settlements which had been fishing villages before the war, when the important river traffic by-passed them in the big steamships which had been bombed or "scorched." Now they were boom-towns, packed with new restaurants and hotels, noisy all night with the gambling and drinking games of the new-rich "guerrilla merchants" who traveled by junk. But Liuchow far up a tributary river, where the railway from Kweilin and the other unoccupied cities of southeastern China met the mountain highway to Chungking, was the first really normal-looking place. Even in daytime, its crowded streets resounded with the sounds of a full commercial life, with the clatter of building and rebuilding, the roar of motors, the cries of newsboys, and the rolling songs of marching soldiers, who had become steadily more conspicuous as we came inland. Liuchow had been bombed, but in most places the ruins were already hidden behind a rash of new houses. There were small factories on the outskirts of town, prosperous banks in its business district, many well-dressed people among its crowds. This was beginning to look like the warring China I had read about.

I had come back that summer with a full set of standard ideas about the Kuomintang's war, acquired from the American press: the gallant losing battles, the brave and clever guerrillas, the millions of determined refugees fleeing west; later, the firmly held fronts beyond which there would be no retreat, and behind them a new country a-building; the factories in the caves, the busy Co-ops, the new roads and schools and hospitals, and looming over the whole united land, the massive figure of the Generalissimo, his attractive wife only slightly in the background. As a pre-war visitor to China, when I read about such things in America I had also marveled: "How different from the place I knew!" The idea that a new China was emerging from the war was one reason why I returned.

Naturally the queer events of my first thirty-six hours out of Macao

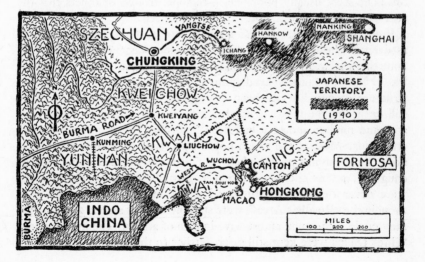

had not fitted into these glowing preconceptions, but I could dismiss them as accidents of time and place, part of the haphazard nature of any front. In the following weeks, though, as I traveled through the wide belt of diseased territory backing the front, it became harder to believe that everything I saw was unusual. Years later, when I had visited front-line areas in northern and central China, I began to understand that the southern front in 1940 was typical not only of resistance in those slack middle years of the Japanese war, but of the qualities in the Kuomingtang which impelled it — in peace or war, invasion or civil war — to make weakness out of strength.

The government's withdrawal into western China at the beginning of the Japanese invasion had been one of the heroic episodes of modern history and was certainly a major reason why Japan failed to conquer China. Later, however, the epic scramble into the western mountains, and the fortress psychology it engendered — of cautious, withdrawn, passive resistance — ruined the front-line areas where the war would logically be decided.

Behind all Kuomintang fronts stretched "Roadless Areas" such as we had passed through in the West River delta; they were usually ten to fifty miles deep, depending on the Japanese raiding habits. Here all communications, even the wide footpaths, had been destroyed or left to decay. The cities and towns had been deserted. Nobody lived here except the peasant farmers and a few members of the grain-controlling, smuggling minority or their agents. The armies stationed in this zone were usually poor ones — regional troops, or others that the central government was willing to have reduced.

Inside the "Roadless Areas" lay a belt of partly deserted territory, as deep as the danger of sustained invasion was thought to extend. Sometimes it was a hundred miles wide, sometimes more, sometimes less. Here the villages lived quite normally but most of the superstructure of city life had been dismantled. The country roads were still open, but the railways had been destroyed if there ever had been any, and modern industry had been "scorched" or removed to western China. Most of the urban upper class, with their businesses, their skills, their buying power, their money to invest, had gone west or emigrated across the front into the Japanese-occupied cities which were never threatened with invasion. More and better armies than those in the "Roadless Areas" were stationed in this second zone, where they could manoeuvre and survive in case of attack. The most favored "élite" troops were kept still safer, farther to the rear.

Even in the latter stages of the Japanese invasion, when most fronts had been static for years, little effort was made to connect these outlying territories to the life of the western fortress. They were left crippled and abandoned, with no large business activity except the smuggling arteries along which enemy goods moved to the richer markets of western China. Economic distress was allowed to create the political uneasiness which must lead to military weakness.

It was natural enough that private interests should be reluctant to stay in exposed areas, but it might be supposed that the national government would have tried to fight their timidity, setting an example by taking necessary risks. Instead, the government led in safeguarding private advantage, to the detriment of the country and its capacity for resistance.

This was most clearly shown in its placing of troops, with the poorer armies at the front, the better ones in the rear. The government of Kuomintang territory was of course a one-party affair, completely run by the Kuomintang Party, and by the time I came to China in 1940 it was recognized among politically minded Chinese that this régime was hoarding strength for a war against the other major Chinese party, the Communist one, which had its own territories and armies in the north.

Since the Communists also seemed to be planning on a post-war civil war, perhaps this was justified. Other aspects of the Kuomintang's caution were not. The five great state banks, run by Kuomintang appointees, were notoriously shy about making loans for any kind of constructive activity near the fronts; the private banks were usually more willing to take risks. In government bureaus engaged in public work on a national scale, there was a pronounced distaste for "wasting" valuable equipment or personnel by assignments to frontline territory. High Kuomintang officials set their example by taking their personal wealth out of endangered areas and reinvesting it in western China or sending it abroad. Indeed, the Kuomintang's wartime withdrawal into the mountain-walled west was quite like the flight of landlords from any local community threatened by calamity. During the Japanese invasion, the peasants and other less privileged people in the front-line areas were left as much to their own devices as were the farmers at the height of a famine, after the grain-controlling minority — supposedly the responsible core of society — had withdrawn to the safety of the nearest walled town.

The national government's likeness to a local grain-controlling minority was to become clearer in the final war years. As the rural landlords exploited the passing of a famine to increase their monopolies of land and other wealth, so the Kuomintang used the Japanese invasion to increase its nation-wide monopolies, of economic, political, and military power. Even before the war, this régime had shown that it wanted most of China's basic industry and trade to be controlled by monopolies belonging either to the government or its state banks. Later, it used the dislocations of war to give its monopolies such a stranglehold on China's economy that private business was plunged into a state of extreme depression and began to die out. In the same way, the emergencies of war were exploited to reduce the political and military power of regionalists and all others outside the central Kuomintang group.

These tendencies reached their climax after Japan's surrrender when we Americans tried to guarantee the Kuomintang as the government of all China, transporting it down to the Japanese-occupied coast, and giving it so much general aid that it began to think Chinese popular support less necessary. Then it increased its monopolies to such a fantastic degree that all China became as ripe for revolution as the neglected front-line areas had grown during the years of Japanese invasion.

Before the war it had been hard for a casual foreign traveler to talk or listen to a wide variety of Chinese; usually you knew only the rather special and often disagreeable types who associated with foreigners, plus chance acquaintances from public vehicles or places of entertainment. Everyone else was too busy, or their lives did not touch on a foreigner's sphere of activity. Wartime China was very different, as I found in Liuchow where I waited for a sunny August week before getting a place on a truck for Chungking.

The hotel at Liuchow was in a suburb ringed on three sides by conical little Kwangsi peaks. In the center of the open side stood a shorter, sharper pinnacle, like a conductor's podium in a theatre, standing before the banked seats of the auditorium. At dawn my first morning in the hotel, thudding strokes on a heavy temple bell sounded from among the trees covering the small pinnacle. Then a megaphoned voice, huge and hollow, spoke through the leaves:

"Shih-BA Chia TI-I-I CHI-I-I-I," it boomed. "TAU KWANG-Si Lai-i-i-i!" Eighteen enemy machines have come to Kwangsi.

Intoned with the exaggerated, emotionless singsong of an announc-

ing robot, the giant words rolled out over the roofs raising a storm of
human cries. Through the hotel the clerks and porters streamed,
knocking on doors and shouting "Ching Pao." Warning news. Air
raid. Liuchow was famous for its panics because it had been badly
bombed a few times, but never regularly enough to make its people
nonchalant.

Down the stairs and into the garden the hotel guests tumbled with
suitcases and bags and wicker hampers which they piled around the
lotus pool or the magpie cage. Then they pushed through the gate
and joined the crowd streaming across the square. The long tree-lined
road to the country flickered with those who ran out through the
bands of sun and shade. Closer by, the lower slopes of the peaks were
already engulfed by a tide of climbing figures.

The fields between the square and the peaks were swampy, the
paths wide enough only for single file. Here the shouting was shriller,
with running fights where slipper heels had been trodden, or slow runners pushed off into the mud. A scaffold topped one summit overlooking the fields and a red lantern had been hung from its crossbar
at the time of the first alarm. Suddenly a second lantern was hoisted,
and the giant voice from the little pinnacle-podium rolled out over the
crowd in flight, booming the news that the enemy machines were
within thirty miles. Its slow robot tone changed to the voice of an
excited man. "K'uai, K'uai, K'UAI, K'UAI-I-I-I!" it screamed. Hurry,
hurry, HURRY, HURRY! With shouts and wails and curses, the long
lines of runners jigged and stumbled in double time, fanning out on
the drier ground near the peaks, scattering into a single wave of climbers.
Perhaps a third went into the limestone caverns at the foot of the
peaks, Liuchow's natural air-raid shelters, while the rest hurried up
where they would have fresh air and a view; these hills had never
yet been strafed.

On the heights the thousands settled like an audience in a theatre.
Beyond the podium the dappled midsummer sky stretched empty for
the performance, and beneath it the city lay as handy to the eye as
a scene on a stage, a compact patch of silver-gray buildings on gray-
green uplands, circled by dark triangular peaks. A cloud of dust from
the running feet lay over the houses, and from it yellow tentacles
lengthened out into the country, over the roads where the cars were
escaping.

"TI-I-I CHI-I-I-I Dau LIU-Chow LAI-I-I-!" boomed the megaphoned voice with icy slowness. The enemy machines have come to
Liuchow.

On the hills, cigarettes were stamped out, parasols furled, children called to their parents. Those with white clothes were warned to cover. All talk died away. From the abandoned city below, no sounds rose except barnyard noises, and in the sunny streets the animals could be seen in possession: dogs sniffing along the boarded shop fronts, a flock of geese waddling importantly to water. Then the silence began to hum, and every fan stopped, every eye turned upward, as the droning deepened. That morning the planes passed south of the city in groups of three, little black seeds streaking through the luminous clouds beyond the podium. In a few moments they disappeared to the west, where the road from Indo-China crossed the Kwangsi plateau. As a wind begins sweeping through a field of wheat, the sound of voices mounted on the slopes surrounding Liuchow.

I was sitting in a cranny with two officials in Kuomintang civil uniforms of good smuggled material, and though neither spoke to me in English, my presence reminded the younger of his trip to America. He began describing New York to his companion — the skyscrapers, very high; the bridges, very long; the tunnels, very deep. His friend was bored. Then he told of a bird he had seen when he ventured into the American interior. With only a little exaggeration he explained how tiny and brilliant it was. He fluttered his hands to show how its wings vibrated. He made a beak of fingers and hummed so forbiddingly that a woman farther down the slope squawked, "The flying machines have come back!" and hastily collapsed her white parasol.

But now the older official was not bored.

"I wouldn't mind going abroad to see that bird," he said.

The people of Liuchow might not have been bombed enough not to panic, but they were experienced fugitives. Instead of the calendars, vases, or albums which novices clutch, they had brought with them things to eat and drink and sit upon in the hills. They spent the first ten minutes after the planes passed in making themselves comfortable, improvising sunshades from boughs, weaving nests of grass as carefully as if they were going to lay eggs. When everyone was content, the noise of conversation increased to a roar. Vendors of noodles and bean-milk and corn-on-the-cob set up their stoves near the mouths of the lower caverns and did a rushing business with those who had been planning on a late breakfast at home. Ragged little boys wandered up and down the hills like candy butchers in a theatre, selling newspapers and peanuts.

After a while some leisure-class children came down the hill behind me, playing the air-raid game, zooming their hands about and shouting "Boom!" as they tried to slap each other's scalps. Naturally when they saw the foreigner they abandoned their game to twit me with their idea of "Djeedee-gooloo-gooloo Talk," as outland languages were onomatopoetically called in Chinese slang. In cities where English was well known, the children usually mocked foreigners by crying something like "Aberessuh! Essuh! Essuh!" which seemed to be derived from A B C and "Yes, yes, yes." But these Liuchow kids kept fluting "Hr-r-r-r! Tr-r-r-r!" like a flock of wrens. I later learned that Russian was the foreign language more often heard in Liuchow in 1940, because of the Soviet advisers attached to the local Kuomintang army schools. The children may have been trying to say "Herosho," the Russian word for "Fine."

The officials in my cranny were soon annoyed by the kids and ordered them away, but continued with their own tart talk about foreigners. Both came from coastal cities, and were old enough to have grown up in the days when foreigners in China often behaved as if the country were already the colony it was expected to become. As the two men discussed the "No dogs, No Chinese" signs and the other dreary classics of discrimination, they used the classic derogations for foreigners, calling them "kao pi-tzuh" — high-noses — and "lao mao-tzuh" — old hairies. So much of their bitterness was reasonable that it made uncomfortable listening, except for one story told by the old hummingbird fancier:

"On the edge of the town lived a female high-nose, a missionary, and when her houseboy died she got a secondary hairy (Chinese Christian) boy from the country and tried to train him. You know, missionaries say they hire Christian servants for religious reasons; it also seems the meekness they teach helps them get their Christians to work for less money.

"This high-nose had a great deal of trouble with her new boy, teaching him the old hairies' ideas of cleanliness. After she had Chinese visitors, she wanted everything they had touched either boiled or scrubbed with medicines, and the boy could see no sense in that. Worse still, she wanted him to wash his own face and hands five times a day. He was afraid the skin would come off, and disobeyed her as often as he dared. One day when he brought her lunch he had a smudge of good clean Chinese coal dust on his face. The old high-nose lost her temper and told him to bring the mirror from her room. When he brought it, she held it out and shouted:

" 'Do you see anything wrong?'

"It took the sensible boy only a glance. 'It's cracked,' he said."

As the morning wore on and the clouds burned away, the clear heat descended and the long shadows began to contract to the base of the little peaks. The crowds on the hills grew restive, squabbling when those above moved around and showered dust and pebbles on those below. They laughed constantly and invented extravagant public conversations when the slightest irregularity met the idle eye. Once it was a dog fight, once a quarrel between peanut-vendors, once a frightened little boy who was not allowed to relieve himself on the shaded heights where everyone was sitting — "Not here!" "Not here!" "Not by me!" they shouted humorously at him as he went weeping down into the sun and, he thought, the danger. He accomplished his errand in view of an audience of several thousand who guessed about his health and diet with loud amusement, then he stood up and howled; he was too young to wipe. Finally a soldier went down and fixed him with leaves and he scampered up the hill again amid sarcastic applause.

Later a little funeral appeared in the empty streets below, on its cautious way around the edge of town. When the megaphoned voice boomed that one plane was returning to Liuchow, the whole procession sprinted for the hills, complete with the coffin and the traditional red-and-green scalloped banners. For some reason the coolies carrying the coffin on shoulder-poles tried to lug their burden up among the living. On the hills the wags called, "Leave him down there. He won't mind!" and the peaks echoed with sardonic laughter.

The single plane flew over Liuchow very high and fast. Just as it passed, a foolish man on the opposite hill took off his shirt with much flashing of white cloth. A growling reverberated over all the crowded slopes as a cascade of angry people covered the place where he had sat. He ran wildly down and out of sight around the base of the hill, his lynching party close on his heels. The growling on my hill changed to a humorous public conversation on the most suitable and painful ways to kill traitors who seemed to be signalling to Japanese planes.

Toward the end of the morning, the people around me began looking at me and hooting with laughter, then pointing toward the foot of the hill where those who had grown tired of sitting were walking around the edge of the flats. I saw another foreigner, a small man in a large white sun helmet. He was surrounded by a crowd of laughing people who were pointing at me. The whole hillside began to buzz with anticipation and we foreigners had no choice but to approach each other, sheepishly. The buzzing increased to general mocking laughter ("Look! Now they see each other; they are smiling; each walks to the other, each silly-looking in his own way. Do you suppose they both speak the Russian of the same country?") which culminated when we two outlanders shook hands and sat down side by side on a rock. It was clear this was the most richly ridiculous event of the morning.

"I sometimes wish I had never left Switzerland," the other high-nose said, mopping his face with his handkerchief in a hopeless attempt to look as if he really were sitting cool on an empty Alp. He said he was a doctor, a specialist in plague control, sent to China by the League of Nations, and illustrated his plight with a story.

He had to have lots of rats, he said, for his laboratory. He had trained two coolies to help him catch them in the streets at night. One carried a flashlight to dazzle the rats, the other a net to sweep them in. One night in a poor alley, crawling with rats, they bagged a huge one. Before they could make off with it, an old pauper woman burst out of her hovel.

"That's our rat!" she screamed. "It's been eating our food for years!" The doctor had to give her some dollars before he could take it quietly away.

By this time the sun had passed overhead, the shadows were beginning to creep out from the opposite side of the peaks, and there was more restless climbing and moving about as the crowds tried to get out of the new stretches of sunlight. Since public business was suspended during alarms, most men were content to sit and gossip on the hills until the all-clear, but the thought of unfinished housework seemed to trouble the women, many of whom started back into town.

Suddenly the megaphoned voice rolled out, announcing that the other planes were returning. As the bright sky began to tremble again with noise, those on the heights crouched among the bushes and crannies and fell silent, and those who had been heading into town ran silently back to the hills. Even after years of routine air raids, it seemed that airplanes never quite lost a supernatural quality for many provincial Chinese. There was a persistent superstition that the pilots could hear everything on the ground and it was dangerous to speak above a whisper, even in dugouts. On the other hand it was not generally known that a moving target was easier to see than a still one.

Always, when the planes were finally coming, there was a rush of stragglers. As they made themselves perfect targets by frantic running, in a fearful and needless silence, they seemed the most pathetic and typical citizens of this country perpetually threatened by forces which it not only could not resist but sometimes did not understand.

That morning's eighteen planes had evidently dropped their load on the highway from Indo-China, a popular target that summer since it was crowded with trucks bringing up the supplies which had been rushed over the border just before the Japanese forced its closure in June. Again the bombers passed south of Liuchow without swerving from their course. As they droned by, the crowd on the hills focused its attention on a little knot of people in the swampy fields on the edge of town. Walled in by houses and trees, they could not know they were already safe, but their flight on the narrow path was blocked by an old bound-footed woman bobbing and lunging like a fish trying to run on its tail. Those behind her were skipping and prancing with fear, but only the old woman was terrified enough to break the silence. "Faster! Faster!" she kept shrilling, as if she herself were not the obstacle. On the hills, as soon as the planes had disappeared, the laughter began to mount again.

Before Pearl Harbor, though I saw only a few dozen completed air raids, the cities and towns and villages where I was living went through hundreds of alarms. Landscapes covered with people who had run away from their houses are the chief part of my remembered country and weather of that war. I also recall them as the most heartbreaking tableaux of a people who had found themselves subject to cycle after cycle of victimization. The planes seemed a symbol of all the other forces which were ravaging the modern Chinese: the interests of stronger nations, and of powerful and self-devoted groups within China. When the noise of the planes deepened in the sky, the families sitting on the hills or in the fields and groves would briefly interrupt their jokes and small-talk and turn upward the completely expressionless faces of accepted habit.

And as I listened to the endless talk which went with these futile, humiliating occasions, it often struck me that in coming from America to China I had traveled farther than from a country at peace to one at war. I had come from an active, self-contained land, confident that its fluid future was to be shaped by its own competence and strength, into one of the outer limbos of the world, a country where every man who knew anything about politics was conscious that he and his nation were at the mercy of outside forces. Indeed, you could make quite a case that many of the traits, particularly the unattractive ones, that we Westerners have come to think typically Chinese, are simply the natural human reactions for any people who are temporarily victims. Most of our evidence about China comes from Westerners who were in China during decades when the country was almost colonially at the mercy of the West; the dealings these outsiders had with Chinese had to be corrupted by the unequal positions of their countries. As this was also a period of increasing inequalities within China, the behavior to be seen among many Chinese must also bear the stigmas of weakness. Trickery, malice, cruelty, triviality, delight in petty triumphs, fear of petty defeats: all were the marks of habitual victims. So was that incessant, exasperating laughter, used as a bandage, a crutch, a drug.

One morning as I sat out an air alarm on a Liuchow hillside — I sat near some girls from the red-light district by the river — quite a bit of the surrounding masculine conversation was of sex. One plump gentleman in Western clothes, who held a banana leaf as an umbrella, told of a Lama abbot whose family had entered him in a monastery when he was a very small boy. He spent all his life in Lamaist seclusion, earning a great name for pious austerity. When he finally took to his bed to die, his disciples came and asked him if he had any last wish.

"Yes," he said, "I want to see a naked woman."

They sent down to the town for a girl who wouldn't mind, and when she stood without clothes by the abbot's bed, he raised his head

on the pillows and his old eyes sparkled. Then he sank back, all his interest gone.

"But she looks just like a nun," he complained.

Oh-ho-ho!

Another morning a cheerful young man whose shabby semi-Western clothes and official badge showed he was a clerk in some government office, who had the air-alarm hobby of spitting on leaves and pasting them on his arms and legs to make sunburn patterns, told of two clerks in love with the same girl-clerk. To get rid of competition, each went privately to the bureau head and denounced the other as a Communist. Though spies were set to watch both, neither denouncer had been able to supply enough proof for the other's arrest. Then the girl announced her engagement to a third clerk. The two earlier suitors went to the bureau head and denounced *her* as a Communist, and it landed her in jail.

The laughter following this story had the same uncomfortable edge as that which rippled over the hills when the planes had flown directly overhead. Then there was a pause, while everyone within earshot looked uneasily at each other; in 1940, anti-government talk among strangers was still unusual, though the secret police were so inefficient that it was usually safe. This province of Kwangsi had always been somewhat hostile to the national Kuomintang and a man whose civil uniform of gray homespun cotton in the Nanning style established him as a Kwangsinese, advanced the delicate conversation one step farther.

He told of an official high in the Chungking government whose limousine broke down in the Kwangsi mountains north of Liuchow. When the chauffeur confessed he had sold his tool kit, the official haughtily ordered a farmer in the neighboring field to go to his village and bring back enough men to push the car. The peasants of rocky Kwangsi had always been notoriously tough and stubborn, and their sense of independence had been increased by the political and military education they had before the war, under their own provincial régime. The farmer refused to go. In Chungking style, the Kuomintang official ordered his bodyguards to beat him up.

This was seen by a farmer in the next field, who hurried home and reported to the village chief. He rang the gong of assembly and with their spears, pitchforks, and bird guns the villagers marched down the road. They forced the official to apologize to the bruised and angry farmer, then they pushed his car.

The pleasant laughter which followed this story emboldened another of the audience, a "guerrilla merchant" of the poorest kind, though he explained proudly that he had been an independent farmer on the western edge of Kwangsi, above Indo-China, until bad crops and debts forced him to give up his land.

Last year, he said, there had been so little rain in his home valley that the poorer farmers, with bad land high on the hills, had their rice paddies go dry and began to starve. The good easily irrigated fields down by the river, belonging to the richer landlords, yielded normal crops, and when the hill farmers grew hungry enough, they began to creep down into the valley at night, to steal unripe grain. The landlords posted guards. The oldest son of one hill family decided the only way he could help his people was to go down into the valley and work as a guard. He did so, but secretly, since the guards were considered enemies by the starving. He was hired by a landlord who was also a Kuomintang official and was able to outfit his guards with guns from the local garrison. The first night, the nervous boy heard a rustling in the field he was watching and fired wildly into the darkness. He heard a cry, then the wallowing of a wounded man taking himself off. Next day he returned to find his father had been fatally wounded in the fields this boy was guarding. The boy committed suicide, throwing himself into the river, and the rest of the family soon followed his example.

There was not even any of that painful, druglike laughter after this story.

During my week in Liuchow, an air alarm sounded every day but one. One day there were two, and once a light bombing by half a dozen planes. In many ways the attack itself was harder to realize and fear than the human tumult which began every alarm. From the hills, the brown fountains of smoke and dust on the other edge of town seemed less the action of hostile men than a natural phenomenon. The noise of the falling bombs was mainly perplexing, a hurling or rending or shaking sound, as if strips of the sunny sky had been torn off and were being rattled like sheet metal. The noise of the explosions, vibrating as much through the earth as the air, seemed like a splitting and sliding in the core of the rocky hills. Down in town the dogs raced in terror through the empty streets but on the hills the people sat with the detached expression of men whose talk has been interrupted by thunder.

When the planes left, up and down the hills rippled the pattering sound of one question asked again and again:

"Pa-bu-pa? Pa-bu-pa?" Afraid or not?

Then came the replies, from the children, the old people, and the invalids.

"Bu-pa! Bu-pa!" Not at all! Not at all!

"Pa i-tien!" Just a little.

Or the saddest and most frequent of the cheerful answers:

"Pa! Mei-yo ban-fa." Yes, afraid, but there's nothing to be done about it.

When the great voice from the podium told that the planes had left the province, a murmur swelled over the hills, as in a theatre where the lights have failed for a while, then been reconnected. Laughing, brushing the leaves from one another's clothes, picking flowers as they went, the people flowed in a tide down the hills and repossessed their town.

4 · *Around and Around*

IN THE SUMMER of 1940, with the London blitz just beginning, Chungking was still the most-bombed city on earth and the Red Cross truck which took me there at the end of August passed hardly a dozen other northbound cars in the week's journey up from Liuchow. Southbound travelers reported the usual late summer clouds were lying over the capital, but the last raids before the weather changed had been experiments with incendiary bombs, burning out more than a square mile in the heart of the city. The clouds would lift in September and Radio Tokyo had promised that Chungking would then be razed.

In the last miles outside the city, where the road wound down from the mountains into the moist, semi-tropical basin of Szechuan Province, I felt all the government authority which had been so lacking near the front. Among the truck-parks and flimsy, black-painted suburbs lining the approach to the temporary capital stood many customs and police stations, each with its own tests and paperwork for passengers and cargo. The wartime confusion of dialects slowed all parleys, and it was the end of the afternoon before we reached the southern brink of the Yangtse's mountain-bordered trough. Here the chief in the ferry ticket office shook his head and said it was too late to cross. He showed his watch, which read five minutes past six. Three outraged truck passengers dug full-size clocks out of their suitcases, one reading ten before six, one reading twenty before, one reading five before five. After the neutral watches of several passersby had been appealed to, the official angrily began making out the forms for the ticket. A quarter of an hour later, when the truck had slithered down the muddy track to the ferry landing, it was stopped by a whole team of gentlemen with badges, canes, and briefcases: standard equipment for Chungking's notorious petty bureaucrats.

"You can't cross now. It's past six."

51

"But we bought the ticket before six."

"You have to be here before six. You can't cross now. It's nearly eight o'clock."

After a half-hour of tangled argument among the ferry staff, the full complement of the truck, and many of the idlers and junk-coolies on the beach, the officials triumphantly pointed with their canes. "Look! Now it doesn't matter what time you got here. Now it really is too late to cross."

Darkness had begun to settle over the river, coiling in the first strength of its brown autumnal flood, and even the shallow, agile sampans had been sculled to safety near shore. Downstream, the stricken city on the other side spread high across its soiled cliffs. Under the protecting roof of clouds, its weak electric lights outlined sprawling dead patches in their pinpoint net. When the ferry officials had walked contentedly away, swinging their canes, and the shouting among the junks anchored by the ferry-landing died, the tiny ringing of thousands of picks echoed across the water. We truck passengers tried to sleep under our car, the nearby inns being full, and all night the massive river valley reverberated with a muffled blasting as the dugouts of Chungking were lengthened deeper into the rock.

Next day, when the truck was ferried over to the city, I got a room in the Press Hostel on the edge of town, and spent most of the following week walking around and looking at this strange capital,

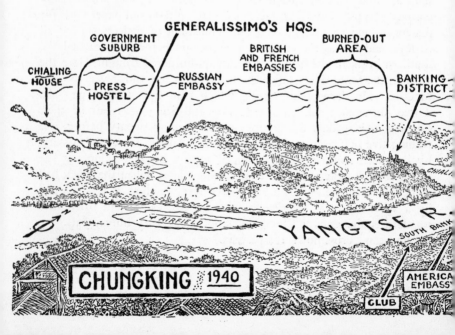

GENERALISSIMO'S HQS.

GOVERNMENT SUBURB

BURNED-OUT AREA

BRITISH AND FRENCH EMBASSIES

CHIALING HOUSE

PRESS HOSTEL

RUSSIAN EMBASSY

BANKING DISTRICT

AIRFIELD

YANGTSE R.

SOUTH BANK

CHUNGKING 1940

AMERICAN EMBASSY

CLUB

perched on its towering rock between the Yangtse and the tributary Chialing River. The marks of three summers of bombing lay everywhere but the clouds stayed overhead and I saw nothing of the way the ruins were manufactured until I crossed the Yangtse again to spend the weekend on the South Bank.

The businessmen in the tiny pre-war foreign colony had lived on this southern shore, in a treaty-port section downstream from the ferry-crossing and across from the center of town. Their houses were still the best Western-style ones in Chungking. Since the American Embassy was on the South Bank, and the American, British, and French gunboats were moored along it, the Japanese had hinted it was neutral territory, not to be bombed. About half the 1940 foreign colony lived here, oddly packed together in the moldering old commercial houses. Social life centered around the Chungking Club, with its crumbling tennis court, scuffed billiard tables, and library littered with ancient magazines: a melancholy relic of the semi-colonial years in a minor treaty-port. Chinese were still barred from the Club as members and were not welcomed as guests.

I went to the Club on Saturday night, to a farewell party for one of the American Embassy staff. Following cocktails of raw Chungking vodka, then a buffet and more drinks, the rather flushed crew of foreigners was herded into camp chairs in the lounge. The guest of honor was to run off the movies he had made during the summer.

After the customary false starts and homely jokes, the screen flickered into enough clarity to show a group of people in white clothes, fumbling with a picnic among trees by a brook. There were humorous cries from the audience: "Uff! I looked terrible that day!" "Godfrey really had a skinful, didn't he?" Two girls on the screen had begun a parody minuet by the brook when, without warning, the scene changed to what seemed another grove of curiously black, misshapen trees, wavering on a mound beside a wider brook. A row of shrubs sprang out of the ground and with puffing motions soon grew into trees. This new brook was the huge Yangtse, the trees were explosions, and the mound was Chungking.

The audience was silent for a moment, then began to murmur technically: "That looks like the June twenty-ninth." "No, I think it's one of the July ones." Abruptly the screen showed a group of foreign young men on ponies in a quiet valley, laughing and pointing offscreen the way people do in home movies. Then came another bombing, then a porchful of foreign women putting potato salad in their cheeks, then another bombing, on and on. Drinks were brought into the lounge and the jollity during the personal sequences overlapped into the footage of destruction. "Where did you take her after we left the ponies?" or, "I'll never forget the way he looked when we pushed him in!" they would shout in the darkness, as the screen filled with the towering white pillars of explosions among clustered junks, and flames ate away the lower half of the city. Later the camp chairs were swiftly folded by the Chinese servants and there was dancing in the room overlooking the river and the cliffs and the ruins.

In the bare little bar, after the dancing:

"Oh, so you're another of these journalistic bastards, are you? Come to write about our darling war, have you? Well I hope you'll be different from the others over at the Press Hostel; tell the people back home what's really going on out here."

"God yes, from what we read in the state-side magazines, back home they're forgetting China is still full of Chinks. 'China's War of National Regeneration'! 'China's Spiritual Rebirth'! The crap is unbelievable."

"Sure, but you're all missing the point. That baloney in the American papers is for a purpose. These Chungking people are building up their propaganda so they can ask for the end of 'extrality' and all our other good treaties. With that parlor-pink in the White House, I wouldn't be surprised if they get it. Then they're going to boot every foreign businessman out of China."

"Here's one that won't wait to be booted. I'd rather give all my money to the blind than try to do business under *their* laws. Not even our lives would be safe. They just don't value human life the way we do."

"Nuts, have another drink. Why do you think about Chungking when you aren't paid for it? Do like me; I've moved my office into my house on this side and except for the days when I've gone over to get snapshots after the raids, I haven't crossed the river more than six times in the last year. I keep myself healthy by thinking when I'll be transferred back to Shanghai. Mmmmmn-mh! Cathay Tower, the French Club, Farren's, Ciro's. . . . I'll go over into Chungking only once again, the day I get my transfer. Then I'm going to make a special trip, just to spit on the place."

A few days after I had seen and heard Chungking attacked at the Club, a night wind slid the roof of clouds off the city. All through

the following month of hot autumn sunlight, the bombers came, usually in squadrons of twenty-seven, sometimes every few days, sometimes every few minutes. From the South Bank, the raids were a super-spectacle with yellow blasts and scarlet flames in lurid technicolor, but they were even harder to recognize as a danger than the little Liuchow attack had been, when watched from some shaded porch or terrace full of other foreigners busy with their cameras and cool drinks.

Perhaps the most awesome moment was the one just before the planes came. When the urgent sirens howled out, baying up and down the city's peninsula like a pack of nervous wolves, the last of the little figures on the reddish cliffs across the river vanished into their black cave-mouths, like fleas into the fur of an animal. Chungking on its long humped rock was shaped like a beast crouching to be whipped, an enormous one thinly covered with a pale scurf of houses and ruins. When all human noises died in the green amphitheatre of mountains the flooded Yangtse could be heard slithering over its rocks like a huge brown snake. Nothing stirred except the dark scavenger hawks circling over the roofs. Then, from the burning indigo sky far down the river to the east, came the roar of the approaching mechanical birds. It was as if a crevice had been opened into a primordial world of myth and behemoths, where tiny men had always to hide from their monstrous flying gods.

Over in the city, the attacks were pure routine. The orderly crowds filed into dugouts with time to spare, sat quietly in the darkness listening to the familiar noises, then filed out again. Of course these autumn raids did not raze Chungking. They did not even disturb it much, for everyone now knew their dugouts and alarm system were quite reliable. Each bombing might destroy a score of houses, but there were seldom more than fifty casualties a day, usually among rickshaw men, boatmen, and others of the poor who had no way of locking up their property and risked staying in the open.

I later learned that businesslike but not too disastrous raids were common all over China at that time. After Pearl Harbor, I heard some U.S. Army officers in Chungking speculate that the earlier bombings had simply been target practice for the Pacific war. Cruel as the idea seemed, it may have been partly true during those middle years of stalemate.

The raids had little military use, for most were on civilian targets far from the fronts. Even in Chungking, they were never heavy enough to throw the city out of operation; after the Japanese made their successful trial of incendiary bombs in August of 1940, they never again used them on a large scale over the capital. In other cities, the raids were spaced too widely in time and place to destroy industry or trade. It was true that since the cities of western China had a good warning net but little air defense, a few Japanese planes could cheaply interrupt the urban life of several provinces; in all threatened towns, business would stop from the first alarm to the all-clear. But work lost during alerts was always made up in the evenings or on cloudy days.

Furthermore, the political effect of the raids spoiled any other value they could have had to the Japanese. By 1940, the spirit of patriotic enthusiasm and all-out resistance which had apparently swept Kuomintang China in the first two years of the invasion had been dead for almost as long as it had flourished. Dissatisfaction and internal discord were increasing. The air raids were of constant value to the Kuomintang, as a reminder of the national war, channeling popular resentment away from other problems. Since the fronts corrupted by smuggling made spying easy for the Japanese, they must have known this.

If the raids were indeed practice, they take a specially ugly place in the cycles of injury which have been the fate of the Chinese people in modern times. The years of unresisted air attack gave them renewed schooling in endurance or passivity. A whole generation learned to accept, in one of its most outrageous forms, the proposition

that no man's life or propery could be secure. Though the threat was
the work of other men, they knew there was nothing they could do
about it. They learned how to escape or, if caught, to suffer philo-
sophically. They practised jokes about the whole thing, if it did not
touch them too closely.

The Kuomintang's benefit from the raids did not end at the beginning of the Pacific war, when the routine attacks stopped and some
features of its own rule — artificially enlarged famines, non-resistance
to new invasions on the ground — began to cause a greater loss of
Chinese lives and property than the Japanese bombers ever had. The
fact that there had been raids, and were now no more, gave a tremen-
dous boost to national morale. A new supply of sufferance was found,
a new determination to wait the war out, no matter how the country
seemed to be falling apart. After the Japanese surrender, this terrible
patience was to be almost as important as American aid in allowing
the Kuomintang to survive long after it would have been overthrown
in a country where there was less tolerance for the insupportable.

In my later years in China, I began to think most other disasters
which have befallen the modern Chinese interlocked just as the Japanese air raids and the overlong death throes of the Kuomintang seemed
to. The recent weakness and unimportance of China apparently forced
other nations to treat it with indifference and implied contempt. No
matter what their intentions, this could lead them to damage the
Chinese people. The Chungking raids I remember most vividly are
still the first I saw, in the amateur movies at the Club, for that tawdry
evening was a key to the cycle of victimization which we Americans
have unwittingly contrived for the Chinese.

Most of the men I heard shouting drunken pleasantries during the
bombing movies, who later carped so stupidly at the Chinese in the
bar, were Americans. They were fitting spokesmen for us in 1940 —
more truthful than our press, which was then picturing Chungking as a
beleagured and indomitable capital, a pillar of strength in Asia, a
center of admiration for all freedom-loving nations. I think those
Chungking Americans also felt, at least subconsciously, that they were
expressing our real national attitude; they knew that America had
sold more aid to Japan than to China, that the bombers over Chungking flew on American gas and sometimes dropped American explosives. It was a little as when children who had been taught to
address all adults respectfully as "Mr. or Mrs. So-and-so" could sense

that their parents thought poorly of the neighbor who was a failure. Then they would feel free to run past his house shouting: "Yah! Yah! Old Man So-and-so! Old Man So-and-so." I am sure Americans in London during the 1940 blitz did not talk like the Americans in that South Bank bar.

As I had begun to learn in my first week at the Press Hostel, there was an even stronger reason why Americans and other foreigners in Chungking should show contempt toward the Chinese. No matter how much the friendly nations praised the Kuomintang, they showed that the part of China which really interested them was the richer and better-known coastal area, then controlled by the Japanese. America's trade with aggressive Japan before Pearl Harbor seems to be still remembered — "Oh yes, those were the days when the earnest girls wore cotton stockings to boycott Japanese silk. Their legs looked terrible" — but our share in this other indifference to China was more important, since it laid the groundwork for so much that followed.

When the Japanese invaded in 1937, there were about ten thousand Americans in China. By 1940, the Japanese had captured the big cities and coastal land where more than seventy-five per cent of them lived. Most of the Americans who did not go back home stayed where they were. While the American government gave abstract rebukes to the Japanese invaders, most American business with China was with the sections they had invaded. A similar amount of relief and missionary money went to occupied territory. Everything Americans living under the Japanese did to preserve "normalcy" in their own affairs, doing the Lord's work or turning an honest penny, helped the Japanese restore "normalcy" among the conquered Chinese. Furthermore, almost all American organizations in China kept to their pre-war headquarters, in Shanghai, Peking, or the other big cities of the coast. Their top men were stationed there and made trips to Chungking only occasionally, to save the face of the Kuomintang. Second-raters were commonly the ones stationed in Chungking and the lesser cities of Kuomintang territory.

Chungking was a backwater if not a doghouse for the Americans who were sent there on regular jobs. The South Bank businessmen might live in the remains of nineteenth-century treaty-port grandeur, complete from frogged liveries for their sedan-chair coolies to a pantry supply of BB shot to roil sediment out of their bottles for boiled drinking water, but they were little more than caretakers for their firms' property. The State Department men might enjoy the protocol and prestige of station in an alleged national capital but they could not avoid the uneasy feeling that the real work was done, and the careers made, down in the greater occupied cities. It was the same with the correspondents; there was a certain glamour to be had from residence in the most-bombed town in the world, but they knew they would not really be getting ahead until they were called back to the coast.

Except for Russia, which was then giving the Kuomintang military aid, the other Western nations seemed to evaluate the various parts of China in the same way. This was certainly the reason for the sense of frustration and futility which marked the life of the Chungking foreign colony. Few people felt fully occupied. Much of their time was spent in "Pure Discourse."

This was a kind of ritual behavior which must have been invented in many countries in prehistoric times, but I think it was first given the right name in China, several centuries ago, when a group of Taoist intellectuals started a splinter movement or cult to protest against the state religion — Confucianism — which was passing through a very formal and corrupt phase. According to the *China Handbook*, the Kuomintang's package of facts suitable for foreigners, the "Pure Discourse" movement was marked by "excessive drinking, nihilistic behaviour, and the ridiculing of all the peoples of the earth." The foreigners in Chungking naturally chose the Chinese people as their particular butt. Sensing that they themselves were a little contemptible, many of them were bitterly contemptuous of the Chinese.

The failure of the American press and State Department to establish less superficial contact with Kuomintang China was later to result in so many Chinese deaths that perhaps it should be explained in more detail.

The Chungking Press Hostel was two or three miles from the treaty-port section of the South Bank, out at the other end of the wrecked city, on one of the hills where the offices and barracks of the refugee government spilled out over the truck gardens and cemeteries of the pre-war town. It was a semi-official place itself, in the compound of the Kuomintang Party Ministry of Information. When I went to live there in the early autumn of 1940, it was a sort of field, fenced in with bamboo palings and fringed with banana trees, holding two little timber and wicker dormitories from which the summer bombings had blown so much of the mud-plaster that the correspondents liked to mutter they were going to send down to Hong Kong for a goldfish bowl — "So we can get some privacy around here, dammit." Except for a couple of Russians from the Tass News Agency, who had a house of their own near the Soviet Embassy, and one senior American newsman who lived with his wife in a mission compound, all foreign correspondents stayed at the Hostel. There were less than a dozen at that time. Two or three were Chinese, and some others were stateless European refugees. The Americans were mostly young beginners in newswork, who had wandered to China for reasons of their own.

Discounting the Chinese correspondents, who were believed to have been bought by the Kuomintang, they were a terribly frustrated group. Almost all realized the Kuomintang war differed tragically from the flattering propaganda picture presented abroad, but it was hard for them to do anything about it. Honest news was easier to gather outside Chungking, in the provinces where less effort was made to hide unpleasant facts, but the correspondents could seldom travel; they were not allowed enough funds by their employers and, as sole representatives in unoccupied territory, had to stay close to the capital for official releases. Also, the Kuomintang was slow to give visas to foreign observers who wanted to travel outside Chungking.

The correspondents might have collected unofficial and more honest news from the independent Chinese newspapers and other sources in Chungking, but they were not often allowed the funds to hire translators, researchers, or leg-men. Their contacts with unofficial Chinese were limited because the Press Hostel was watched by the secret police, and it was thought risky for "unauthorized" Chinese to visit there often.

In moving about to gather news, then getting it past the censors, the American correspondents were in a poor bargaining position with Kuomintang officials because so many were obscure, junior employees of their papers. The position of the stateless correspondents working for American agencies was worse, as they were technically subject to Kuomintang laws. The presence of pro-Kuomintang Chinese correspondents, also employed by Americans, hindered any group protest against restrictions. The China bureau heads and most correspondents with the experience and prestige which would have helped them get more news and get it out were kept where they had always been, in the big cities of the coast. Their flying visits to Chungking were so brief that they could not see far behind the window-dressing. Kuomintang China was admired in the American press because it was being ignored. It was not important enough to be debunked.

While I was living in or near the Press Hostel in 1940, a series of prima-donna correspondents dropped from the sky on the Hong Kong plane and got the quick treatment, which included a lunch with the Generalissimo or his Madame, a visit to a "warphanage," a descent to a model factory or hospital in a dugout. Then off they went into the clouds again, to write their flattering stories. For the rest of the time, much of the news which went out to the world was cooked up in the Kuomintang propaganda offices right behind the Press Hostel, mimeographed on green paper, carried over to the Hostel and tossed into the correspondents' rooms, retyped by the correspondents on white or yellow paper, carried back and passed across the desks of the Kuomintang censors who worked upstairs from the offices where the news had originated, then sent to the telegraph office. A number of other stories wired abroad came from Central News, the Kuomintang Party monopoly which had already driven all the major private Chinese news agencies out of business. Central's main work was to supply "authorized" news to the Chinese press, but it also published an English-language service in Chungking, on brownish paper, which was tossed in through the Press Hostel windows.

Obviously the American press's part in this situation did not fit with its claims to public responsibility. The State Department's failure seemed greater, for all its responsibilities were to the American public.

Until Pearl Harbor, we had six consulates general in China, including Manchuria. Between 1931 and 1938 the Japanese took all the cities where they were located but these offices stayed on. We had seven consulates in China proper, and in 1937 and 1938 the Japanese conquered the cities where all but two of them were. The consulates stayed on. No new consular offices were opened in Kuomintang-controlled West China, not even in Chungking. By lucky chance the Japanese did not take Kunming or — until 1941 — Foochow, which held our last two consulates. As the only ones in unoccupied territory, and undermanned at that, their work was largely with passports, visas, and other desk matters.

Because we recognized the Kuomintang as the legal government of China, our Ambassador was often in residence at Chungking in the last couple of years before Pearl Harbor, but our diplomatic outpost there was of such a sketchy nature that it was not even listed in the State Department Register. Our China Embassy officially remained at Peking — which had not been the capital for nearly a decade — with an ambassadorial office at Nanking, the puppet capital. Most of the personnel who made up a functioning diplomatic mission stayed on in Peking or Nanking.

In 1940, our rather anomalous State Department office in Chungking had the courtesy title of Embassy, but the indifference to the Kuomintang which shaped its real nature could be seen in its physical location, on the South Bank where Western-style living was more comfortable. Since it took about an hour to reach it from the center of town — you had to climb down a long flight of steps to the Yangtse, cross on the ramshackle passenger ferry, then climb another steep staircase alley — this was like a location some thirty miles out of the capital by train. The British, French, and Russian Embassies were accessibly placed inside the city.

When I came to Chungking the current Ambassador, Nelson T. Johnson, was there. He spoke Chinese, of course, but he was not young, and except for the most essential state calls, seldom made the tedious trip across the river. He was aided by military and naval attachés who also spoke Chinese. While these officers lived on the South Bank, they did get around quite widely in Chinese military, and some political, circles. But of nearly twenty China career officers in our diplomatic service, trained in the language and political reporting, only one was then in Chungking. He lived in a bungalow in the scenic mountains behind the South Bank, about an hour uphill from the Embassy or the equivalent of sixty miles out of the capital by train. He was also contentedly uncritical of the Kuomintang, apparently because of deep admiration for Madame Chiang, who had given him a setter pup. There was very little contact between American officials and Chungking's nonparty political figures — professors, writers, newspapermen, and others who were part of the independent intellectual life of the capital.

A year later, at the time of Pearl Harbor, the State Department had had some four years for readjustment, but only four China career officers besides the chief of mission — then Ambassador Clarence E. Gauss — had yet been sent to Kuomintang territory. More than eighty per cent of the State Department personnel in all China were still in the Japanese-occupied cities. A Military Mission under General John Magruder had been belatedly established in Chungking in the latter half of 1941 and some of its officers made hurried survey trips out near the fronts. For more than two years, no other official American observers had gone out to study conditions in the provinces which were really Kuomintang China.

The conservatism of the State Department at that time, its hostility to change even in its own operations, had helped create this failure. I don't think all the blame can be put on the Department, though. Many of the State Department men I later met in China knew the need for expansion in research and intelligence. But they were hampered by the traditional American attitude towards them, which considered the State Department a minor branch of government, limited to the care of American citizens and business abroad.

This attitude had been sensible enough when America was a merchant nation which preferred political isolation. It survived too long, and the State Department did not begin getting the funds and authority it needed until we were already awash in the problems of world leadership. In China before Pearl Harbor, even if the State Department had wanted to send more men to find what was happening to the Kuomintang and its war, it could hardly have done so, since there was too much work for it in occupied China, smoothing relations between the resident Americans and the Japanese. However the blame should be divided, when Japan brought war to us, we acquired in Kuomintang China an ally which had been disastrously ignored and was now dangerously unknown, to both the American people and the American government.

During the Pacific war, our confusion led us to accept the Kuomintang at its own face value. We became overindulgent, giving it lavish military aid which weakened it politically. After the Japanese

surrender, American arms and the hope for more of them encouraged
the Kuomintang to risk a civil war which it could not win because its
popular support was lost. This plunged the Chinese people into years
of extra, American-supplied, conflict.

In 1946, while that civil war was beginning, I lived in Peking. It
was a curious place then, for the city was controlled by the Kuomintang, while the surrounding country was in Communist hands. The
Executive Headquarters for the Sino-American Truce Commission,
formed by General Marshall in his attempt to stave off civil war, was
in Peking; so were American military advisors, working to strengthen
the Kuomintang for civil war. The fact that we should be working
for peace and war simultaneously, and in ways that ensured our failure
in both, was based on our ignorance of Chinese conditions, which in
turn had been produced by our earlier indifference and implied contempt.

The only consistency in our behavior seemed to be that we had to
victimize the Chinese people. While our peace effort was still in
process of collapse, American equipment supplied to the Kuomintang
through our advisory groups was sometimes used against Communist
territory; the bombers which now killed Chinese not only flew on
American gas and dropped American bombs but were American ships
with American-trained Chinese pilots.

Some of these attacks occurred not far outside Peking but no movies
of them were shown at the elegant old Peking Club. Even if the planes
had been close enough to photograph, the raids were supposed to be a
Kuomintang secret. Nevertheless, while I listened to American chatter
at the Club that year — often between officers on the Truce Commission and those in the military advisory groups — I had the feeling that
I had gone around a full circle, or cycle, and this was where I had
come in before.

" . . . And as I was saying, these Chinese just don't value human
life. Only the other day we found another of them in the gutter,
starved to death and frozen, right out by the gate in front of our PX."

" . . . If those Commies ever get here, you won't see me around.
First thing they'll do anyway is boot every foreigner out of China."

" . . . Ah, what the hell! Why do you have to talk about China out
of working hours? The way I figure it, we're doing the world a
favor, helping these goddam Chinese kill each other off."

For a journalistic bastard like myself, there was a certain advantage

in beginning to watch the sad merry-go-round of modern Chinese politics in 1940, during the pre-Pearl Harbor period of stalemate and slack American indifference to China. It was a more objective time than later years, when the machinery was hidden behind banners for Democracy or Communism, and so many famous Americans were circling about as painted wooden horses. During my first stay in Chungking I studied some of the early history of Chiang Kai-shek's Kuomintang and found that many things this government did later were foreshadowed by the way it had been founded.

Originally, the Kuomintang — or National People's Party — had led a coalition and the program of its first leader, Dr. Sun Yat-sen, who ran the revolt that overthrew the Manchu Dynasty in 1911, planned for complete political and economic democracy. These were radical aims since economic democracy called for the reform of the old inequalities in rural land ownership, but the Kuomintang also had nationalist hopes which appealed to conservatives; it wanted to win China's independence of the territorial concessions and unequal treaties which were making the country a colony of the Western world. The Chinese Communist Party — which had been founded in 1920, by a group of Marxist intellectuals — joined its coalition in 1923 and most other small modern parties supported it. So did some of the regional generals, or warlords, of South China, where the coalition was organized. Members of the Kuomintang included businessmen, army officers, professors and students, labor unionists, intellectuals, even some peasants and landlords. It was the nearest thing to a popular movement yet seen in modern China, involving most progressive or patriotic Chinese.

Ranged against the Kuomintang were the warlord generals of northern and central China, and the great landlords, industrialists, and bankers who thought Kuomintang reforms threatened them. Japan and the Western Powers were also hostile, apparently thinking their interests were based on an inert China. Soviet Russia, at that time the only foreign power which professed to want a unified and independent China, had sent to the Kuomintang the political and military advisors it requested. Partly because of the presence of these advisors, who derived much prestige from the recent success of the Communist revolution in Russia, the Chinese Communist Party began to expand rapidly, attracting many types besides intellectuals.

In 1926 – after Dr. Sun's death – the Kuomintang coalition armies from South China broke north into the Yangtse Valley, led by Chiang Kai-shek, their Commander-in-Chief. Setting up a capital at Hankow, they advanced toward the coast and threatened to take Shanghai, China's greatest center of new commercial wealth and Western-style industrial power. Many foreign warships and several thousand troops, mainly British, Japanese, and American, were assembled in a show of force at Shanghai. Thousands of Chinese who opposed or feared the Kuomintang sought refuge in the protected foreign concessions in the center of the city.

The Kuomintang assault on Chinese Shanghai – outside the concessions – was to be a double one. When the regular armies neared the city, the Shanghai underground of the coalition would attack the city police and the warlord garrison. In mid-February, 1927, troops under Chiang Kai-shek came within twenty-five miles of Shanghai. The labor unions which were the backbone of the underground called a general strike as a first step toward taking over the city. On Chiang's orders his troops stopped advancing and the strike was a bloody failure, broken by street fighting and police terrorism.

A month later, the Kuomintang armies marched into the Shanghai suburbs. The underground ordered another general strike and an insurrection. The uprising was well planned, largely by Communists and labor-union leaders in the Kuomintang coalition, and after a day and a half of battle, all of Shanghai outside the neutral foreign concessions was taken; the police were overcome and disarmed and the last of the old garrison was in flight. The vanguard of the Kuomintang armies entered the city, against Chiang's orders, and there was wild celebration. With the wealth and industry of Shanghai captured, the Kuomintang's ability to keep its promises seemed assured.

Then Chiang Kai-shek arrived in Shanghai, and moved his headquarters into the foreign concession, technically neutral ground but actually the stronghold of the enemies of his movement. He opened negotiations with its enemies: the big Chinese bankers and industrialists, the secret police of the concessions, and, indirectly, the foreign interests. He received money from them; the exact amount will probably never be known, but its total value is believed to have exceeded ten million American dollars. He conferred with the notorious gangs of Shanghai, the most powerful armed Chinese opposition left in the city.

In a few days he declared martial law in outer Shanghai, now garrisoned by his troops. He began to remove members of the coalition underground from the positions of control, replacing them with his own appointees. He closed down the headquarters of the real General Labor Union and gave its powers to "Moderate Labor Unions" largely recruited from the criminal underworld and the plain-clothes detachments of the concession police. On the night of April 11, the police of the foreign concessions began rounding up members of the Kuomintang coalition underground in their neutral territory; Chiang had given them lists of those he wanted. The captives were turned over to his troops, and taken off and murdered on Chinese soil. Next morning, the "Moderate Labor Unions" sallied out of the neutral concessions, fully armed, and in co-operation with Chiang's soldiers attacked what remained of the coalition underground. The men who had captured the city for Chiang were killed at their posts or rounded up and herded off for massacre. There is no full record of how many of the betrayed lost their lives in the next few days, but the number certainly ran into thousands.

Shortly afterwards, with Shanghai in his pocket, Chiang proceeded to Nanking and announced he would form a new national government with a Kuomintang of his own there. By personal fiat he ordered the disbandment of the coalition government in Hankow, which had in good faith raised him to the post where such a monumental double-cross was possible. He ordered the Soviet advisers to go back where they came from, and decreed Communism punishable by death. Most of the coalition armies had gone over to his side, following the old paternalist tradition that the soldiers go as their commanding officer goes. Bereft of power, and torn within itself by varying reactions to the Shanghai coup, the Hankow government soon dissolved. The hunting and murder of the Communists and other leftists and liberals formerly in the coalition spread from Shanghai to all the territory Chiang controlled and in the next few years took the lives of tens of thousands.

In describing 1927, apologists for Chiang and his Kuomintang have made much of communism and his hate of it, democracy and his desire for it. They have said that he was indeed a revolutionist, but a democratic one, not a radical. They have said his treachery at Shanghai was a public-spirited act, prompted by a belief that the policies of the coalition Kuomintang were too extreme to be practical. They have explained that his negotiations with the Shanghai interests, and the bribes he took from them, were only tokens that China's reform should proceed along American-British rather than Russian lines. More recently, they have begun to say that his whole object was to keep Russia out of China.

But no matter how righteously anti-Communist Chiang's new Kuomintang might be, it had been founded through opportunism, treachery, and murder. Though many men who had been double-crossed and massacred were Communists, the men who did it became cheats and murderers. Their future behavior was as likely to be corrupted by their own past acts as if their victims had worn any other political label.

All important members of the small group who helped Chiang rule China after 1927 — the Chen brothers, Ho Ying-chin, H. H. Kung, T. V. Soong and others — took part in the Shanghai coup. The way they came to power determined the personnel, techniques, direction, and final destination of their government. Shorn of the ideological words, this coup had been no different from China's other classics of warlord trickery and cruelty, motivated by greed for power and profit. Expecting the men who pulled it off to act out of character — progressing towards democracy, for instance — would be as naïve as hoping that a group of men who had picked each other to collaborate on a bank robbery, and by the successful robbery had won appointment as a Committee for Civic Beautification, should seriously set themselves to planting flowers.

The later development of Chiang's Kuomintang did proceed logically along the lines forecast by the coup d'état which gave it birth.

With power in the Shanghai-Nanking area, he and his group were just at the beginning of their problems. They could not rest for a moment in their search for more strength with which to survive. China was still dangerously subject to coercion from stronger neighbors. Internally, power was disputed by warlords and regional governments in almost every province outside the lower Yangtse Valley. In

South China there were Communist armies which had grown out of the break-up of the Hankow coalition. Even in the areas Chiang controlled, popular support of his Kuomintang was shaken by the treachery of the Shanghai coup. By Western concepts, the new Kuomintang had the choice of two ways to strength. It could move toward Democracy or Fascism, toward the decentralization or centralization of economic and political advantages.

Chiang's Kuomintang wanted the prestige it could get as heir of the earlier, democratic, Kuomintang of Sun Yat-sen; to the majority of Chinese who know of it, democracy was still the most intoxicating political word. It wanted the friendship and support of the Western democracies which were the masters of the Pacific world. Automatically, therefore, it declared itself for Democracy.

Among those who described China to the world in following years, it was generally said that until the Japanese invaded in 1937, the Kuomintang was leading the country toward democracy. New schools, hospitals, industries, and roads were built, particularly in the big coastal cities. The capital at Nanking was decorated with wide cement avenues and modern government buildings. Plans for elections, a national assembly, a constitution, were committed to paper. Chiang Kai-shek announced himself a Methodist, and the "New Life Movement" for "spiritual regeneration" was publicized by his American-style wife.

But in the provincial areas seldom noticed by those who reported abroad, the real nature of this government could not be mistaken. From the first, it was a government of repression and exclusion.

To be democratic the new Kuomintang, like the old, would have had to include spokesmen of the peasants, the regional factions, and all minority parties. But because of the violence and treachery of the Shanghai coup, members of the earlier coalition could not be admitted to the new circle of power except as turncoats who would swear loyalty to the clique of their betrayers, and become their "men" or filial dependents in the old Chinese paternalist style. If they were admitted otherwise, they would work against the centralization Chiang and his clique had achieved by the unpopular coup. A new coalition could not be formed without endangering the absolute power of the small inner group.

According to the earlier plans of Sun Yat-sen, the middle stage of the Chinese revolution was to be a "Tutelage Period" of Kuomintang one-party rule, preparing the country for constitutional democracy. In the years after 1927, Chiang and his group naturally claimed that a "Tutelage Period" was what they had brought about. Certainly many Kuomintang members believed this was so, perhaps the leaders did. But once any group has tasted absolute authority, a voluntary relinquishment of power is unlikely. It is so easy for authoritarian government to become a racket.

Instead of moving toward democracy and decentralization, Chiang's government began to move further away from it. Its most serious early step was the abandonment of land reform. The promises of political voice and economic improvement which the earlier Kuomintang had given the peasants were kept on paper but jettisoned in deed. Instead, the traditional rulers of the rural areas — members of the grain-controlling minority — were endorsed again by official appointments. With the rural economy in the corrupted state it had reached by 1927, this meant that the Kuomintang's policies of exclusion and repression must operate against at least eighty per cent of China's people.

The abandonment of land reform may have been one of the points for which Chiang Kai-shek received bribes before the Shanghai coup. It was certainly congenial to him and his group, most of whom had a landlord background. But the new Kuomintang had no choice but to suppress such reform. The rural mass movements which the coalition Kuomintang had formed through its program of land reform had been a source of strength for the liberals and leftists who opposed Chiang and his clique. If continued, the program would be a loophole through which they might crawl back into power.

Since the grain-controlling minority had regained the saddle, the decade before the Japanese invasion saw no halt in the collapse or suicide of the rural economy. Instead, the rich began getting richer and the poor getting poorer more rapidly. Though the peasants got little benefit from the new motor roads and government buildings, it was on them that the new taxes which paid for the Kuomintang's surface modernization were levied by the landlord-officials, and from them that the men and money for Chiang's new national armies were collected.

Aside from the growing misery, the most important change in rural areas was the establishment of tighter political controls, allowing the misery to increase. Chiang's Kuomintang soon revived the Pao-Chia system of mutual responsibility, the classic tyranny for policing and extortion which had been outlawed after the fall of the Manchu Empire, as a system unfit for free men.

In the Pao-Chia system, every ten to fifteen families were a Chia in which all were responsible for any crime committed, or anything owed, in any one family. Every ten to fifteen Chia formed a Pao in which all member groups were accountable for any single one. The Pao were organized into a Lien-Pao or district group. In some places, the Chia and Pao were allowed to elect their own leaders — Changs — but usually the system was appointive. The top official, the Lien-Chang, was appointed by the county magistrate and picked his Pao-Changs, who in turn named their Chia-Changs. As the Lien-Chang had almost automatically been a member of the grain-controlling minority, most of the "men" he appointed, and the "men" they in turn chose, represented privilege.

The very make-up of the Chia and Pao was often unfair. Each Chia was supposed to be responsible for an equal amount of taxes and requisitions, so wealthier families were put into Chia of their own, the poor into others. The wealthy Chia were sometimes big fifteen-family ones, while the poor were in ten-family Chia, in which the burden on each family would be heavier.

I believe the Kuomintang had paper plans for developing the Pao-Chia system into a channel through which suggestions, complaints, and demands could move upward from the people to the authorities. As it worked in every rural community I knew, however, it was just an

exploiting device, a machine through which official demands — for money, grain, conscripts, labor, building-materials, whatever the government wanted — were extracted from the people. Furthermore, its nature as a personal hierarchy made it usual that the demands would be filled unfairly.

If troops came through a village and their officer had permission to get grain or conscripts from the local Lien-Chang — or if he could persuade, bribe, or bully him — the Lien-Chang could decide what amount of grain or men should come from each Pao. Each Pao-Chang could decide how much or how many to take from each Chia. Each Chia-Chang could decide what or who to take from each family. It was one of the theoretic virtues of the system that in abnormal times, drought or flood, the personal touch could exempt families in difficulty. Some Pao-Chia officials did use their authority this way, but their power was tempting to tyranny and discrimination. The heaviest demands were too often made upon those least able to fill them.

As the greatest victims were the most ignorant and timid, it was also easy for the Pao-Chia officials to turn the system into an outright racket, requisitioning more material than was demanded and keeping the balance as squeeze, selling exemptions to whomever could afford their price. Because of the helplessness of their victims, their only danger would have to come from above. Since they were the "men" of the higher authorities who had appointed them, and it was a loss of face for a superior to impeach one of his own "men," they were quite safe from penalties.

The Pao-Chia system was a source of great strength and wealth for the Kuomintang, temporarily. Since the Pao-Chia officials could often exempt themselves from disagreeable exactions, they were willing to collect from others whatever was demanded from above, even when the demands were unreasonable and ruinous. But the system was essentially suicidal. By placing so much of the burden on those least able to carry it, and sparing the privileged, it helped increase the inequalities which were dooming China's old social structure.

Above the village level, the Kuomintang's drive toward power in the decade before the Japanese invasion smacked no more of democracy or any other Western-style ideology than the Pao-Chia system did. In a less backward country, a "Tutelage Period" of one party, controlled by one clique, under one man, might have resulted in a

government like European fascism. Enough details of Kuomintang
rule — leader-worship, élite armies, the political police — followed
fascist models to raise the suspicion that the Kuomintang was fascist
in spirit and would like to be fascist in structure. But in China, the
foundation for a modern fascist state did not exist. The rural landlords,
the majority of the middle and upper class, were by tradition too
devoted to personal or family interests to support a public movement
of any strength. Poor communications, lack of the means to produce
modern weapons, low rate of literacy, lack of a tradition of efficiency
(by Western definition) were other handicaps.

Unwilling to accept democracy and barred from fascism, the Kuomintang fell back on a method of control that was as old in Chinese
history as the Pao-Chia system. It made its own adaptation of the "law
of avoidance," which had been used by many emperors and warlords.
Through it, an unpopular or anti-popular ruler might create a balance
of weakness in which he — while still weak — would be relatively
strong.

Before the Japanese invasion, the classic example of this had been
the Kuomintang's handling of the Communist "Long March," the running campaign between the government forces and the Communist
armies which had grown up in South China after the Shanghai coup. In
the mid-thirties the Communists were forced into a two-thousand-
mile retreat through all of southern, western, and northwestern China.
Communist historians may claim that the route of the "Long March"
was set entirely by Communist strategy and bravery. I cannot believe,
however, that it was either Communist effort or plain accident which
time after time let these outnumbered and poorly equipped troops

break through the Kuomintang encirclement and march in just the direction most favorable to the Kuomintang: namely, through the provinces ruled by regional factions which were still independent or semi-independent. As the Communist armies went into each province, the Kuomintang strategists were able to send their pursuing forces into areas where, if it hadn't been for the Communist threat, they would never have been allowed to come without local opposition.

While their armies were there, the Kuomintang leaders did what they could to reduce the regional factions. When the Communists went on to another province and the Kuomintang forces followed, they would take away as many of the regional troops as they thought their superior strength would let them demand, and leave as large a garrison of their own troops as they could spare. By that measure, the invaded province would be a Kuomintang conquest.

Through this technique an American state, say California, would have been brought into our union in the following way:

To fight the Indians, enough federal troops would be sent in to outnumber the California militia. Then several hundred of the Californians most likely to take the governorship and other important local posts would be moved east and given such jobs as the Secretaryship of the Bureau of Printing and Engraving in Washington, Directorship of the Highway Commission of Connecticut, Chairmanship of the Committee for State Parks in Virginia. It would be announced that no California elections could be held at present, lest that "make the people restless," and meanwhile the central government in Washington would appoint a variety of Ohioans, Vermonters, Georgians, and other outsiders to all the posts in California which controlled the key government functions: taxes, police, and so on. The top operators in this appointed bureaucracy would be from the home states of the President and his Cabinet, and the very highest would be friends or relatives or business-associates of the important people in Washington. To prevent unpleasantness, the California Militia and Home Guards would be split up and sent to preserve the federal régime in Florida and New Hampshire. A garrison of Pennsylvanians would be moved in to safeguard law and order in California.

In its attack on provinces it could not invade, the Kuomintang's centralization relied on the old tricks of warlord politics — bribery, treachery, intimidation — to get central "men" into positions where they could begin to divide and rule the local groups. Largely, it seems, because of the personal astuteness of Chiang Kai-shek, this was done so successfully that when the Japanese invaded in 1937, the central Kuomintang had some control over every province south of the Great Wall. This was hailed as the "unification" of China but since unity implies compromise and coalition, that seems hardly the right word. Until the invasion crisis forced him into it, temporarily, Chiang did not allow remnants of the regional régimes to enter his government except as turncoats who would become the "men" of his own group.

Some regional governments were old-fashioned warlord satrapies and little could have been salvaged from them by any modern administration. A few regional generals, however, such as Li Tsung-jen and Pai Chung-hsi of Kwangsi; Chang Hsueh-liang, the "Young Marshal," of Manchuria; Feng Yu-hsiang, the "Christian General," were at least as modern-minded as Chiang and his group. If their régimes had been assimilated instead of excluded and reduced, they might have added a progressive influence as well as more genuine unity and strength.

Furthermore, in filling the vacuum created by the destruction of these regional powers, the Kuomintang had to begin destroying itself. The very top group around Chiang, for whose benefit this chaos was planned, was a tiny minority in its own government. To ensure that its own feebleness would be comparative strength it had to create a balance of weakness even there. In central government posts, men from all parts of the country, men of many shades of political thought, representatives of all the lesser cliques in the Kuomintang, were mixed together to create a balance of power, lack of power. "Men" of the central group held the positions of balance everywhere, but this could be neither a strong nor efficient régime. It was also as easy to turn into a racket as the Pao Chia system had been. On a national scale, official corruption hastened the concentration of too much wealth in too few hands.

In December of 1936, the Kuomintang's planned chaos had been briefly threatened by the Sian Incident, when the person of Generalissimo Chiang — the tiny pebble on which the inverted pyramid of government by patronage was balanced — was kidnapped by two regional generals, Yang Hu-cheng of Shensi and Chang Hsueh-liang of Manchuria, and held hostage for the promise of a United Front against Japan. These regionalists were supposed to fight the Chinese Communists, but as the Japanese had already taken Manchuria and were openly infiltrating North China, they preferred to ally with the Communists against the foreign invaders.

The Generalissimo was soon released after making only vague promises for a United Front. A few months later, however, when the Japanese invasion began in the summer of 1937, the crisis forced him into accepting one. For roughly two years — the period of rapid Japanese advances — there was no more Kuomintang-Communist fighting and the two factions even co-operated in battle. The Kuomintang also halted its campaign of exclusion and repression against non-central groups in its own territory.

Regional generals were allowed considerable independence in their campaigns against the Japanese; some even commanded their own armies in defense of their home provinces. This resulted in stubborn resistance and a few victories. In the national capital — which was then being moved from Nanking to Hankow to Chungking — a "People's Political Council" was formed to include some of the regionalists, the small parties, non-party figures, and a few Communists. All Council members were Kuomintang-appointed, its majority were Kuomintang men, its function was purely advisory, but it was the first step toward decentralization of power since 1927. At the same time, the Kuomintang relaxed its persecution of liberals and other dissidents, and seemed to encourage any social unity which would help the war. It even placed on paper new laws and taxes which could divert part of the burden away from the peasants. The patriotism and feeling of hope caused by such steps had a great deal to do with the heroism of the withdrawal into western China.

By the time I returned in 1940, however, the phase of partial coalition and unity was long finished. For the two past years the Kuomintang had been entrenched in mountain-walled Chungking; it could hope that the Japanese had reached the limit of their threat to it.

Behind the brief United Front period lay a decade of precedent impelling the government back to its earlier policies. This racket had been too good for too long. The temptation to make it better was irresistible. The stresses brought by the invasion, the retreat to the west, and the blockade, rendered all classes more vulnerable to unscrupulous officials. The machine of Kuomintang development was thus in motion again and its direction, fixed by the Shanghai coup, was more evident. It was heading neither towards democracy nor towards fascism. It was simply going in a spiral, increasing the area where those who were to be excluded and repressed stood, decreasing the circle of privilege. The peasants had already been saddled with heavier taxes than ever before, and those who protested were crushed with unprecedented savagery. The Communists had been dropped from the Kuomintang's plans for resistance and the northern area their troops controlled was blockaded. And now the passive state of war against Japan was being used to debilitate and destroy the non-Communist opposition. Non-central military and political figures would accept any assignment, any diminishment of power, when they could be denounced as traitors if they refused.

The Kuomintang fronts had been made into a hodge-podge of mutually suspicious or hostile units, so entangled that their commanders could not unite against the central group of the Kuomintang, or against the Japanese. Non-central troops were given the more dangerous frontline positions, while the "élite" troops, commanded by central "men," were stationed behind them as a sort of police. Usually the front-line armies were regional troops from the most distant provinces — western troops were sent to the seaboard, southern troops to the north, and so on. This not only cut down regional strength in the home provinces, but prevented the growth of strong regional armies at the front, as might have happened if the troops were defending their homes, instead of provinces with whose people they hardly shared a common language. When, despite all handicaps, a non-central commander showed signs of becoming too strong, he was commonly taken away from his own troops and put in another army where he would be a mistrusted outsider.

The civil government was in similar confusion. The "People's Political Council" had proved a stooge assembly, its advice no longer heeded, and new allocations of official posts clearly aimed to increase the dominance of the central group rather than build an effective state. During the United Front period, a number of organizations for social unity had been founded. The patriotic student movements, and the Kuomintang's own Political Department for popular mobilization were examples. They were now being neutralized, with central "men" placed in them to divide and rule, sabotaging any real movement toward unity.

The trend toward personal monopoly, the reason for all this artificial disunity, was perhaps best shown in the economic field. Kuomintang apologists have always liked to point at the Generalissimo's personal frugality and apparent lack of money as proof that at heart his government was not corrupt and greedy. The signs of such evils on lower levels were supposed to be accidents. I believe it is true that the Generalissimo never stooped to personal graft. Even the bribes he accepted at Shanghai in 1927 were apparently put into his government, not his pocket. But his clean hands were also part of a tradition reaching back through the warlords to the emperors. Since money was considered a second-rate material in ancient China — land was the wealth that carried prestige — it was thought rather soiling for a man in public power to deal with it directly. An officer or official who wanted to do well by himself would put his friends in a position to make money, with the tacit understanding that they would look out for him if he ever needed anything. More particularly, he would put his wife's or mother's relatives in the way of enriching themselves; their fortunes would be indirectly his, owned by his family unit.

In modern times, this custom has persisted on all levels. At one point during the Pacific war I roomed with an American officer in the U.S. Army Services of Supply. I remember an evening when he came home livid, after seeing a Kuomintang officer in a bureau which sold gasoline to the local American forces. Although the gas was Lend-Lease, and quantities of it were appearing on the black market after it was turned over to the Kuomintang, the U.S. Army was allowed to buy back only an officially set amount. This American had been arguing that his allotment should be increased. "Officially I can't

allow you any more," the Kuomintang man had replied blandly, "but my wife can sell you what you want on the black market."

Certainly the Generalissimo's brothers-in-law, H. H. Kung and T. V. Soong, were among the leading profiteers of the Kuomintang period. Many believed them to be the two greatest, since for years they managed the two largest state banks, the Central Bank and the Bank of China. In such a personal and paternalist institution as Kuomintang banking, in which filial inferiors could hardly question their superiors, it was impossible to know where the line was drawn between the bank's assets and the private fortunes of the managers.

Minor members and friends and connections of the Chiang, Kung, and Soong tribes — and of the Chens, the Hos, and the other top families — were profitably placed in these and other official banks. Their "men" and the "men" of their "men" were also scattered in key positions through the various Kuomintang monopolies. Some monopolies, like the Natural Resources Commission, were government bureaus superimposed on private business; this Commission could buy and sell, at its own fixed prices, the produce of private mines. Other official or semi-official monopolies, like the China Merchants Steam Navigation Company, competed with private enterprise, very successfully, since they often could get official subsidies and tax exemptions. "Men" of the central group who went into private business could usually get similar advantages, as well as informal official help in getting around the laws which restricted ordinary business.

By 1940, either through the monopolies or private investments, the top ruling group had a stranglehold on practically all national businesses which were still profitable: transportation, mining, munitions and other heavy industries, plus the marketing of many daily necessities such as tea, matches, and salt. Private enterprise was sinking into the depression from which it never did recover; the national economy was beginning to resemble the land and grain economy of any rural community.

Among non-Kuomintang Chinese it was generally feared that from the profits of even the most official monopolies, large sums were being deflected into the private pockets of the corrupt. These fears seemed to be corroborated in later years, after the Japanese surrender, when the amount of money sent abroad by wealthy Chinese, especially members of the Kuomintang inner circle, was estimated by U.S. officials to exceed a billion and a half American dollars. Private estimates were higher. A U.S. Treasury man once told me unofficially he believed the Chiang-Kung-Soong family unit had at least one hundred million banked abroad.

In other fields, the decreasing circle of privilege was becoming almost as obvious by the time I came to Chungking. The government's wartime taxes and levies had drained the peasants first, now threatened the petty middle class, and were already reaching higher. Political repression which had first operated against the Communists and others of the far left was now moving in on more conservative liberals. With most regional groups fairly well absorbed into the balance of weakness, marginal cliques inside the Kuomintang were beginning to lose their positions of power and profit. It sometimes seemed as if all these spirals of monopoly would go on fining down until the Generalissimo himself was the one man who got benefit or satisfaction from his régime.

The most foolish part of this whole governmental mechanism, of course, was that while the Kuomintang was decreasing its base of popular support, the Chinese Communists in the northern provinces where they had settled after the Long March were increasing theirs. Ironically, the Kuomintang itself may have been partly responsible for this.

Until 1937, the Communists appeared to have run a rather severe form of class war in their territory, confiscating large land holdings and businesses, sometimes executing the owners. This could cause uneasiness even among poor peasants, who were by tradition conservative and thought themselves in the propertied class if they owned only the tiniest patch of ground, too little to live on.

When the United Front alliance was made in 1937, on Kuomintang insistence the Communists agreed to abandon their more radical practices. They would still take action against landlords who were also absentees or puppets, but would merely reduce the tithes the peasants owed to the others. Private enterprise would be allowed to continue, and the local governments were to be coalitions; one third Communist, one third Kuomintang, one third independent.

From all I heard, I would judge these governments were somewhat rigged, with Communists or their "men" usually in positions of control, but the Communist Party did adopt a more moderate policy toward non-Communists. Partly because it operated so much in guerrilla districts behind the Japanese lines, where the people desperately needed help in organizing against the Japanese, partly because of its new moderation, it began to expand more rapidly than ever before. Between 1937 and 1940, its armies — and the area and population they controlled — increased by at least ten times. Among Chinese, the Communists were already the strongest force opposing the Kuomintang's monopoly of power, and they were steadily growing stronger.

In the many dull periods of travel in the Chinese interior, where I often had to wait as much as a week for a bus or a boat or a change in the weather, I used to invent similes and parables about the politics of this unhappy country. When I knew only enough of the Kuomintang to be puzzled by it, I thought of calling it the "Four Not Likes," after a game animal said to be found in the swamps along the lower Yangtse. The beast got its name because it was not like a deer, not like a horse, not like a cow, not like a goat, though a little like all of them. In the Kuomintang there were some pretensions to democracy, some to fascism, some resemblances to monarchy, some to anarchy, but it was not really like any of them.

Later, I thought I could describe the Kuomintang with a parable called: *"The Leopard who said he was not only going to change his spots but would become a Vegetarian."*

The scene of the story was a park where birds and animals up to the size of a leopard lived. When the leopard appeared, young and small, he made the other sizeable creatures uneasy by his appetite for mice and sparrows and squirrels. But the leopard reassured the bigger ones, saying that when he got the small ones where he wanted them, he was going to change his spots and become a vegetarian. Happy to hear it, the others went on devouring their own victims.

By the time he had eaten all the small things, the leopard was bigger, so he started on the rabbits and ducks and woodchucks. Naturally the foxes, wolves, eagles and other largest birds and animals became uneasy again. They asked the leopard what he intended, got a reassuring answer, and went about their business.

Finally, a large fat leopard was the only creature left in a blood-soaked, bone-littered park. He settled down in the center of the park and began chewing up his own paws, tail, and other parts of himself he could reach.

"Hey!" called a passer-by. "I thought you were going to change your spots and become a vegetarian."

"Sure I am," said the leopard's mouth. "Soon as I finish eating this critter."

After Pearl Harbor, when China began to fill with American GI's and their cheerful legends, I decided the Kuomintang more closely resembled a bird in the American mythology. This one was called the "Swamp Swivel" because it lived in the murkiest swamps and flew around and around in ever-decreasing concentric circles until it disappeared just under its own tail-feathers.

5 · *That Secret Smile*

DEEP in the Szechuan basin, Chungking has an evenly humid and almost windless climate, but the year is sharply divided between summer and winter. From May through October, the sky is generally clear and the sun boils the inert air into tropical heat. From November through April, fog covers the city, raining or drizzling much of the time. There is no frost, but the dampness makes a penetrating cold. On the rare days of winter sunlight, the air can be uncomfortably warm. Under the few summer clouds, it can be unpleasantly chilly. The only winds are violent ones, heralding a change of weather.

In 1940, on a muggy midnight towards the end of October, an autumn storm fell on Chungking like a bomb right down from the top of the sky. The furious wind lashed heavy gouts of rain about with the force of stones, and flushed the last pools of fetid summer weather out of the alleys. Amid cries and the cracking of bamboo timbers, it toppled dozens of cliffside houses into the Yangtse; casualties equaled those of an ordinary air raid. Next morning the sky was blue with desert clarity and the city lay exposed to the bombers in microscopic detail, every bleached brick and jagged pinnacle. The weather remained dangerously clear for nearly half a month, and the expectation of planes was replaced by uneasiness because they no longer came.

In the brisk sunlight, cooler each day, the city murmured strange stories. Central News, the Kuomintang monopoly, claimed that Chinese troops had retaken Nanning in southern Kwangsi Province; the public rumor was that the Japanese had mysteriously packed up and moved out of their own accord. It was rumored the Japanese had set fire to Hankow and Canton and were evacuating both cities. A ship from Chungking was said to have ventured down the Yangtse Gorges, out through the wall of rock above Ichang, and come back to report that Ichang, too, was in flames and the boats of the retreating Japanese filled the river. There were whispers of peace, and in mid-November, when Radio Tokyo revealed that Japan would recognize the puppet Wang Ching-wei's Nanking régime as the government of China, since the Generalissimo remained "unreasonable," it was believed there must have been overtures. The source of peace rumors was suggested when some fifty Chinese and several Japanese were arrested as fifth-columnists in Chungking.

The winter fog tentatively hid the capital in late November, but December 1, the date of the formal Japanese recognition of the Nanking puppets, was a day of watery sunlight and there was an alarm. Already Chungking had lost the habit of raids. Few people went to the dugouts until after the urgent, then there were fumbling panics, followed by self-conscious laughter when no planes came. Bombers visited the outlying military airfield, but only a few fighters came near the city, to make indecipherable smoke scrawlings and drop illegible leaflets. In the next week the fog thickened into a solid mass in the river-troughs and slowly rose to cover the houses with safety and gloom. The days turned dark, the nights pale. With relief and a little regret about the lost chance for peace, and great boredom with war, Chungking settled down to a routine winter, the fourth of the invasion.

Even during my first trip to China, I had sometimes suspected that everyone I watched was obscurely engaged in an enormous practical joke. Then, a great deal of the effect had come from my tourist unfamiliarity with the country. To a newcomer, the remains of old ceremonial ways and superstitious rites — the oblique politeness, the stylized arguments, the shrines, the festivals — could appear irrational to the point of prankishness. Until the reasons were explained, some Chinese customs in eating, sleeping, building, marketing, seemed so contrary that they might be kept for the fun.

In Chungking on my second trip, I began to feel more strongly than ever that the people I saw on the streets knew about a pork chop that would turn out to be rubber, or a cigar that would blow up in somebody's face. Meanwhile, they made a great show of their busyness; like people who were in on a joke, they seemed determined to look plausibly matter-of-fact, with just a hint of a knowing smile. Because so many odd things had to be done in the wartime capital, they often seemed victims of their own amusement.

Of my early Chungking contacts with run-of-the-mill Chinese, I remember best a December morning when I went to take a bus out to Sapingba, the university suburb. The yellow tinge in the fog promised this would be another unusual winter day of pale sunlight, and soon after I left the Press Hostel, triangular red lanterns were hung on the air-alarm scaffolds to warn that a Japanese scouting plane was overhead. But everybody now seemed to assume they would not be bombed again before next summer, and went on with business or pleasure as usual.

The bus station was in-town from the Hostel, near the top of a hill on the one motor road winding out of the city above the Chialing River on the north side of Chungking's peninsula. As I climbed toward it, the city itself seemed a sort of practical joke, a semi-modern, semi-ruined capital crammed up on cliffs which had suited a medieval fortress town. It was also a weirdly beautiful place, of course, for its stunning location on a great boulder between two rivers gave its worst slums the look of a mirage. The road up which I walked circled through several bays in the side of the rock, and wherever the bordering houses had been bombed away, I could see down into the huge river-troughs and up to the ridge of the peninsula, its face covered with sagging, galleried tenements. Above and below, the steep sides of the city were gashed with staircase streets, teeming with people like blue maggots in long irregular wounds. Chungking had few motor noises in those years of blockade, and the chattering, bickering, bargaining of the crowds floated up through the melting mists. From the beaches far below came the wolfish howling chants of the boat trackers dragging junks against the current.

Perhaps this unearthly background had something to do with the fantastic effect of the tumult on the motor road. The yellowish-gray fog certainly did, for it made the distance insubstantial; people and things in the foreground stood out as distinct as the colored pictures of exotic fish or flowers scattered on the white page of an encyclopedia.

At several points along the road, the smaller wartime shacks, knotted together with withes of split bamboo, had been so loosened by rains that they slumped sideways and were sliding into the valley. The men who lived in them were pulling them up into proper shape and firmly retying their timbers, much as a man will adjust his clothes and tighten his necktie after a nap or a fight. The women and children from the shacks had moved their furniture onto the narrow sidewalks and were placidly cooking, sewing, sleeping there, although this forced pedestrians into the street where they blocked the wheeled traffic. Everybody in the rather unnecessary mêlées seemed to wear that look of half-concealed amusement.

The rickshaws threading through these tangles had been designed for level country. Going uphill on steep grades, the pullers had to bend so far forward that their faces nearly touched the road. They crept upwards at much less than a walking pace but their fares stayed sitting in the carts, lolling contentedly as they smiled that smile. Going downhill, the rickshaw men would balance deep between their shafts, tipping their carts so steeply backward that there was danger of the sitters' landing in the road on their scalps. Then the pullers would speed alarmingly down the slope, their wide-swinging feet touching the ground only now and then. They smiled at their passengers' screams.

The results of bombing definitely added an air of cruel joke. In a few places the road passed through a stretch of ruins as flattened as the burned-out center of town; the crowds in the traffic flowing through these gray wastes looked like people pretending to be city-dwellers in a desert. In one field of ruins lay a big bomb crater which the rains had turned into a pond. A dozen or more neighborhood women crouched around its lip, rinsing vegetables and spanking clothes as if this were the most natural body of water in China. They all wore that smile.

The blockade, which made so many things hard to get or repair, was another part of the peculiarity. Automobiles going downhill coasted to save gas. As their horns were too broken or too valuable to use, the chauffeurs, their aides, and the other riders would thrust their heads and arms out the windows, shouting and beating on the outside of the cars in warning.

Several automobiles coming uphill were too weak to make the whole slope in one frenzy, so the chauffeur's aides would follow on foot with large rocks to stuff behind the rear wheels as brakes. When the chauffeur had tickled the machine back to life, he shouted and his "men" would pick up the rocks and trudge on with their secret smiles.

Near the bus station a Kuomintang mint was working twenty-four hours a day, printing money to keep up with the inflation which had recently taken its first upward lunge. As I passed, some men from the night shift were amusing themselves with a rat before they went to bed. They had it strung up by its tail and were holding lighted matches under its nose. They smiled quietly, as if they knew of a joke much bigger than the one they were playing on the rat. Behind them, the mint thundered with the presses turning out the Kuomintang's unbacked paper currency, which was money only as long as it was believed to be.

The inflation also furthered the air of fantasy because it made the hoarding of objects more sensible than the saving of money. Sapingba, the suburb where I was going that morning, was thought quite safe from bombing and was a popular place for storing investments in goods. When I reached the cavelike wooden shed which served as a bus station, among the people waiting there I found a dignified old gentleman with a garland of bicycle tires around his neck, a girl with a gross of cotton gloves and half a dozen dried pressed ducks, a young clerk with a pair of old-fashioned tin alarm clocks in ornate glass-fronted boxes, and an army officer with the porcelain bowl of an imported flush-toilet. In the style of the mysteries which had alarmed me in my tourist years, another man was an undertaker with two large

effigies of servants made out of twigs and gaudy paper, to be burnt on somebody's grave with the hope — which nobody really credited any more — that the dead one would get good service in the afterworld. Others in the crowd carried bouquets, one had a little olive-colored songbird on a leash, and one — a soldier — had a big gray monkey.

Though there was plenty of room in the shed, these people were densely wedged around the ticket seller's cage, and it took some elbowing and apologizing to get through to the window. There I found the ticket seller theatrically relishing a Szechuanese breakfast of rice porridge, pickles, and red-pepper sauce. He refused to sell any tickets until the bus came, if it did. He stuck his right arm out through his window and clattered his chopsticks mockingly under my nose, like the beak of an exasperated heron. The smiles of the waiting passengers broke into open laughter.

At first I thought it was because I was a foreigner that none of them had warned me I could not buy a ticket. In a moment, however, a fat man in brown civilian uniform, with a basket of green vegetables and a pink kite shaped like a phoenix, entered the shed. He had to push and squirm through the faintly smiling people just as I had. Since he pompously told the ticket seller not only where he wanted to go, but why he had to go there, on official business, and thus had to have a ticket before anyone else, the other passengers were specially pleased to hear the chopsticks clattering under his nose. Later, when an old bound-footed lady with two yowling cats in a bird cage tried to get to the window, he made himself the greatest block in her path.

It seemed that here, on a tiny scale, one of the unique qualities of life in China was being shown. Sometimes it was consciously arranged but usually not. It was the habit of making any situation complex, calling for attention and talk.

I had already learned that personal affairs, business, politics, and war could be more complicated in China than elsewhere. This was a leading cause for anti-Chinese feelings among foreigners. ("These goddam people always have to do things the slow, hard, silly way.") It was true that human relations in China were sometimes marked by customs which had become impractically elaborate and corrupt through centuries of use. The savage individualism which had grown so strong during the recent century of national disintegration could make for anti-social behaviour. But there were reasons for enriching every situation, no matter how small, with overtones of intrigue, conflict, or sheer nonsense.

The formal entertainments in China were few. The old theatre, literature, and other arts were pretty much the monopoly of the well-to-do minority, and in the modern period of collapse had begun to decay. Western mass-entertainments — the movies and radio — had been introduced only in the largest cities. The Japanese blockade had slowed or stopped their spread in the interior. Most Chinese had to get their amusement from daily life.

But I do not think they did this just because they had to. The richest Chinese in the coastal cities, who could spend their lives going from theatres to night clubs to dog races to *jai alai* tournaments, did it too. It seemed part of a basic Chinese philosophy, to be valued equally with the Western idea that all work must be real and earnest, and recreation should be an escape from work.

In the Chungking bus station, the waiting passengers knew that it might be an hour or two before the wretched old Sapingba bus came to pick them up. They could have regarded their trip as a serious workaday matter, and waited as aloofly and self-effacingly as Westerners daydreaming of their favorite movie stars. Instead, they chose to thrust themselves upon one another, if only in inconvenience. Theirs was a civilization based on the belief that the interplay of personalities was most important.

If they had waited as chilly strangers and later parted with no sign that they saw each other as humans, it would have been a small defeat. It was a little triumph when they could make each newly arriving stranger reveal himself by turning towards them a face on which some emotion flickered, even though this be rage, and the strange face should cry: "Roll away, you turtle's egg, that's my foot you're stepping on."

Before I reached the bus station, the triangular lanterns had been hauled down from the air-alarm scaffolds and replaced with round red ones, warning that Japanese bombers had taken off from the Hankow airfield. For half an hour, though, traffic kept pouring along the street in its normal volume and raffish diversity. Housewives stumped by on their way home from market: one with a paper full of live eels, one with a bloody pig's ear dangling from a straw handle, one with a silver mesh purse full of garlic. Shoals of petty bureaucrats

hurried to their offices with their badges and canes and the sun helmets they wore through the coldest weather. More important officials were carried by in litters, belly up, like the squealing Szechuanese pigs borne past them to the butchers.

After a while a line of shabby soldiers in gray cotton uniforms and straw sandals came slogging up the hill, technically in double-time, but really mocking the quick step. For all their jogging up and down, they moved forward less rapidly than the burdened housewives. Like soldiers all over China, they were chanting numbers to keep in pace: "One, two, three . . . (step, step, step) . . . FOUR!" When their officer screamed at them to hurry it up, they began chanting faster and faster, out of time, while their feet pounded the road as slowly as ever. They all wore that smile. In the bus station, the waiting passengers began to beat each other over the head with their air-raid anecdotes.

One was an elderly countryman in blue homespun clothes and a white Szechuanese turban: a wealthy peasant or a petty landlord, for he wore a pair of shiny black rubber galoshes — smuggled goods, and very costly in Chungking that winter. He valued them so much that he wore them next to his socks — over them he had tied decayed leather shoes, to keep the rubbers out of the mud. He carried a small frog woven of reeds, and had a red spot painted on his forehead to cure his headache. In a tone of mild outrage he told what had happened to him during one of the autumn bombings.

He had been in the country north of the Chialing River, hiding by himself in a hollow between two rocks. When a stray bomb scaled a third rock over him, he had not been hurt but was as trapped as a crab in its shell. After the all-clear, he asked the first passing farmer to help him out. The farmer asked what it was worth to him. They argued prices, until the old man in the rocks decided to wait for cheaper delivery.

"Why didn't you tell him you would pay as much as he wanted, then you could say you didn't have any money when you got out?" someone in the bus station asked.

This was plainly a new idea, for the country gentleman thought it over slowly and craftily. Then he replied with a transparent blend of bluster and dismay, "I had to keep my name as an honest man!" Everyone laughed happily.

Out on the street, a ragged old woman marched past with a tray of brightly painted dragons and other toy monsters made of sticks, feathers, and lumps of clay. She had a whistle hidden in her mouth to make the advertising noise of her trade, and out of her impassive wrinkled face came a shrill "Twee-e-e-e-e twah-twah-twah-twah! Twee-e-e-e-e twah!" A younger woman sitting in a rickshaw creeping up the hill balanced a bed frame in her lap. A man walking past her carried a fish the size of a two-year-old child. By this time the passing crowds were noticeably thinner and a few people in the bus station uneasily left to go to their home dugouts. Most stayed, though, sure that the bus would come to carry them as far as the public dugouts on the edge of town.

Towards ten o'clock, a second round lantern was hoisted on the air-alarm scaffold across from the station and the sirens began to howl, warning that the bombers had entered Szechuan. The sky was almost clear, so the shopkeepers began to dismantle their sidewalk stalls and board up their windows. A number of families with dugout baskets full of lunch and valuables started down the stairways which led from the motor road to the riverside caves and the ferries. All talk in the bus station was now rather sketchy, because the suburban buses were beginning to return from their dawn trips to the country. Whenever one labored up the hill, trailing a black cloud of greasy smoke from the vegetable oil it burned, with its windows bulging with heads and elbows and tails, the passengers by the ticket window would fling themselves into motion. Each time, their exercise was so much the same, it almost seemed rehearsed.

Sparring and feinting with their bundles, they would crowd together on tiptoe, in a tight knot before the ticket window. Each rustled a handful of the dubious banknotes overhead, like a ceremonial cluster of leaves. All began chanting the names of the places they wanted to go. Inside his cage, the ticket seller had finished his breakfast and was mending his own torn paper money with bits of newspaper and porridge paste left from his meal. With a great pantomime of annoyance, he would seize a handful of newspaper scraps, poke them out through his window, and wave them sarcastically above the bobbing tufts of banknotes. When the passengers saw the approaching bus was not the one they wanted, they instantly subsided.

The soldier with the monkey, who had been waiting when I arrived, kept himself haughtily out of these scrimmages. He was a tough and humorous type, with leather shoes gleaming below his cotton puttees, and looked like one of those rarely lucky veterans who had survived his conscript years in good shape and had turned professional, in the household or business firm of an officer. He had a rosy flush around the eyes, suggesting a good deal of ta chu — raw grain liquor — with his breakfast. In a pause between buses he looked at the Kuomintang New Life Movement posters above us, and pretended to read from them in a scolding voice. He was illiterate, but the posters on good behavior for passengers had pictures to prompt him.

"It seems the people have forgotten their New Life!" he began with pomp, and all in the bus station turned toward him, fixing their faces to see this eccentric as no stranger.

"They should not scratch, bite, or goose one another!" he reprimanded those on his right.

"They should not push, shout, or tear clothes!" he intoned to those on his left.

"The people should stand in line as if they were dead and dressed up!" he declaimed. "And, if their hands are dirty, they must wash them," he added softly. "No tickets will be sold to people with unclean hands."

The smiles of his audience gave way to delighted but slightly alarmed laughter. This kind of fun was subversive, for the New Life Movement was a cherished ornament on the government's façade of Western-style progress.

When I traveled in China before the war, I had seen that the Movement was then cleaning up the surface of life in the big cities. Its campaigns for neat streets, hygienic habits, and orderly behavior had results among those of the small new commercial and industrial upper class who wanted to make China like the West. In the countryside and the smaller provincial towns, however, its work was irrelevant to the point of comedy or tragedy. Uplifting wall slogans were posted in villages where nobody could read, and peasants who could not afford soap were lectured on the duty to wash.

On my trip up through the southern provinces in the past summer I noticed that even the superficial work was slackening off; most posters were weather-ruined and indecipherable. In Chungking the Movement was still eagerly conspicuous — fresh posters were always appearing, and there was a New Life Center for inspirational rallies — but the old spirit seemed to be gone. There had been only a tiny pseudo-Western class in Chungking before the war, and those who came in later were members of the refugee government, now following their leaders into more cynical opportunism. Madame Chiang, the original patroness of the New Life, had lost interest; she spent much of her time in self-imposed exile, in her comfortable villa in British Hong Kong. Behind the modern buildings on Chungking's few newly widened avenues, the steep alleys were as filthy and turbulent as they had been in the Middle Ages.

And as the New Life Movement decayed, and the country it tried to surface sank toward ruin, its remaining work seemed to become more unreal and hysterical. It was as if the Kuomintang leaders realized they had so confused and weakened their country that they themselves were now impotent; they had to grasp at straws to assure their people, and perhaps themselves, that they still had authority. I think it was no coincidence that more stringent New Life rules against permanent waves or dancing parties commonly followed some disgracefully unresisted Japanese drive, or that an artificially enlarged famine in the provinces should coincide with a ban on ice-cream parlors in the capital.

The soldier in the bus station must have been drunker than he looked, for when his New Life speech was applauded, he stared impudently at a poster of the Generalissimo which topped the others. Chiang was pictured in dainty military regalia, standing sidewise with a hand on the hilt of his tasseled sword as he gazed into the distance with a blandly pleased air of decision. Below him some slogans were printed and the soldier did not need to read these either. He started on a rash parody of a Kuomintang speech, the empty kind heard at the Monday Morning Memorial rallies.

The more Chiang's Kuomintang differed from the earlier one of Sun Yat-sen, the more fervid had its lip service to the dead democrat become. Memorial services for Sun were held on Mondays, by order, in every school and government bureau. They featured speeches by local Kuomintang leaders, grotesque when delivered by men in government as a racket. Even if a speaker had sensible ideas about Dr. Sun's "San Min Chui Yi" or "Three People's Principles" — National Independence, Democracy, and Improvement of the People's Livelihood — his approach had usually been deadened by all those other Mondays of parrot repetition. To hide the lack of meaning, an oratorical style based on the thunderings of heroic generals in the old Chinese opera was favored.

"Why do we have THREE PEOPLE'S PRINCIPLES in our national life?" cried this tipsy soldier with a stagey vehemence which established the party and government flags behind him, the platform and the bored people below. "Why don't we have TWO or FOUR?" He put his monkey on his shoulder and glared, clasping his hands over his stomach.

"I will tell you," he said smugly.

"If we had TWO People's Principles, well TWO wouldn't be quite enough." He sipped invisible tea from his invisible lecture stand. "If we had FOUR People's Principles, FOUR might be a little too many." He cleared his throat as if to bring up his lungs too, and popped his eyes horridly.

"THAT'S WHY WE HAVE THREE PEOPLE'S PRINCIPLES!" he bellowed, like a stage general demanding the surrender of a city.

The laughter from his audience now had that uneasy edge I first noticed on the slopes above Liuchow.

On those hills I had begun to think the Chinese laughed so much in their touching and annoying way because they sensed they were always victims of forces they could not control. At Liuchow the most oppressive forces had seemed to be non-Chinese ones — the Japanese planes. In Chungking, though, bombings were so calmly accepted that they could explain only part of the defensive mirth and self-mockery which added to the city's air of an enormous practical joke. The internal problems of China seemed to affect the Chungking people more than the Japanese attacks did.

The New Life Movement could help them wear a secret, pained smile. So could the government's other propaganda. While many official statements were as abstract and meaningless as this soldier's gibberish, their basic line often gave a picture of the Kuomintang which was the exact opposite of the facts. I have no idea whether this propaganda hiding the trend toward monopoly was made consciously or unconsciously, but would imagine the latter. It was based on the old Confucian paternalism which had shaped the ancient imperial governments and still colored much modern Chinese thinking.

It said in effect that Generalissimo Chiang was the national father, the new Son of Heaven. His people owed him the obedience small children owed their father. They must be good children because their virtue reflected on him and helped make him a good parent, as well as a good child to his own Heavenly parent, the virtue which lay somewhere in all men's hearts.

Under the old emperors, when the national children were righteous and loyal, nothing better than peace and prosperity resulted. But to explain its onerous "Tutelage Period," the Kuomintang claimed that Chiang had a special new reward for his kids. It was a valuable gadget called Democracy which he was keeping in a safe place — in a sort of box, apparently, with plenty of locks on it. As soon as all his people had proved their worth by making themselves totally subservient, he would take it out and give it to them.

Even if the Kuomintang propagandists were sincere in their claims, of course, it was unlikely that the Generalissimo could, or would, single-handedly bring democracy to China. Apart from the fact that any nation grew ready for democracy only by having it and using it, perhaps misusing it, China was already in a state where such drastic changes were needed that the longer democracy was withheld, the less ready for it the Chinese people would seem. They would show less "virtue and obedience," and eventually might look for other solutions.

Since the Generalissimo was not only human but was beset with the increasing nervousness, crotchets, and tantrums of advancing years, he must believe that his national children were growing irresponsible, nothing like what he had been when he was young. He would keep postponing the gift of democracy. Also, it would be natural for him to want to keep it in that box as long as he got the slightest prestige or pleasure from having it there. After so many years of power, it would be an indirect loss of face for him, as well as a direct loss of authority, if he ever took it out.

Some four hundred and fifty million Chinese were thus expected to kick their heels while they waited for the death or deposition of Number One. The Kuomintang's misleading propaganda might be patterned after "The Big Lie" of Western fascism but this government itself was "The Enormous Practical Joke."

I had already seen that all over wartime China, the principal rooms of schools, theatres, hotels, restaurants, and government offices, were dominated by posters, photographs, or plaques of Generalissimo Chiang's shaven pate and placidly determined, slightly self-satisfied, smile. Even on the clay walls of roadside villages, crude pictures of the leader were daubed by propaganda teams; these usually emphasized his bullet head and grin to the point of caricature, and I did not know what they looked like until years later, when Al Capp invented Shmoos. And Chiang, of course, occupied as large a place in the minds of his subjects as his pictures did in the decoration of their country.

His harsher critics have called him a bloodthirsty, selfish tyrant but I doubt if the explanation was ever so simple. Technically he *was* a tyrant, the founder and head of a government which ended up oppressing almost all of its people. In private life, though, except for brief spells of shouting anger, he seemingly was quite decent. Perhaps the worst that should be said of him was that he was not a modern man. He had some Western education, at a military school in Japan, but almost all his successes and failures could be traced to his inheritance as the son of a well-to-do country landlord family. He came from a small village near Fenghua, in Chekiang Province, south of Shanghai.

I think he did believe the mumbo-jumbo about being a national father; Confucian paternalism survived most strongly in families of the rural grain-controlling minority. In his later years of power he also seemed to have succumbed to the mysticism surrounding the earlier emperors and began to believe he was not only head of the state but *was* the state, was, in fact, China.

Perhaps this could be seen in his relations with the Chinese Communists. In the latter years of the Pacific war and the early post-war period, when it became plain that the only way any part of the collapsing non-Communist section of China could survive was by a truce or compromise with the Communists, it was Chiang's personal decision to press on with the civil war which had to be fatal to him. Overestimation of the value of American material support may have helped him decide this, but I think in all seriousness that he was also unable to deal with the Communists because he held them responsible for his kidnaping during the Sian Incident, when he was chased up a hill in his night shirt and lost not only face but his false teeth.

Chiang's tendency to confuse himself with the state could also be seen, especially during his final years, in his way of interfering in all branches of government, including the trivial. He liked to read the newspapers of his capital in detail, and would make policy decisions when he saw a scrap of news which hinted at some minor irregularity. Since he could not be well informed of the problems on which he acted, his meddling was often silly or harmful. It also stifled initiative in his "men". They never knew when his snooping might reach them and his lightning wrath strike them. Since his powers of punishment were unlimited, they feared to do anything contradicting his imagined book of rules. When in doubt, they did nothing. His tampering with the chain of authority he had forged helped destroy it. Perhaps this is a failing of all personal dictatorships.

Another weakness of his government which was abetted by Chiang's idea of himself as a superman was its corruption. He no doubt wanted his government to be efficient and honest in its lower levels, but as he was above the law, he could not see the wrong in his own relatives and friends piling up fortunes through official work. Ordinary standards could not be applied to him.

Such an idea would also have been nurtured by his landlord background. In pre-modern China, where government was as much by patronage as Chiang's own régime, there was little legal tradition in the Western sense. The government was by men, not laws. It was customary for those with power to flout the regulations which applied to others, if they could arrange the personal "deals" which would allow them to do so.

Chiang's success with the "law of avoidance" was another landlord heritage, for the old ruling class had used divide-and-rule tactics to balance all its affairs. I think it has been one of the most extraordinary feats of modern times, that this poorly educated man who was beginning to be blinded by delusions of moral grandeur should have been able to use an ancient and very obvious method to centralize control of most of his country, then keep it in one piece for two decades of slow collapse.

But his success with the "law of avoidance" also showed his ignorance of the modern world, where another law — that of diminishing returns — operates. He didn't know when to stop. In present-day China, where misery was increasing, and new ideas of freedom, equality, democracy, communism, were spreading, the tolerance for frustration had limits. In the end Chiang was faced with the fact that the only way to have a strong modern government is to let one grow, which he had refused to do.

One final failing — the one which at last precipitated his downfall — stemmed directly from his landlord background, for it was his inability to understand China as a peasant country. To him the important Chinese were the ten to twenty per cent who were middle and upper class — city-dwellers and members of the rural grain-controlling minority, literate people. He never made any serious effort to gain support except among this group. His military methods of static, positional warfare were to defend the cities which were the homes or refuges of his minority support. The cities were only specks on the vast peasant countryside. When the Communists began taking over the Chinese revolution, they captured the support of the peasants first, and that gave them the countryside. The cities could not survive.

Thus, Chiang's subjects were children whose parent was always lecturing them on how to improve their lot by being moral and refined, while he indulged in questionable, perhaps criminal, and certainly self-destructive behavior. Many Chinese acted as if they understood this. They naturally wore secret smiles.

On that December morning in Chungking, when the Sapingba bus at last heaved up to the station, the ticket seller went into business so quickly that some outbound passengers got their tickets and began beating in through the car's one door — in the middle of its rear — before the inbound passengers had fought their way out. The harassed little bus conductor, dressed in blue pants, gym shirt, and official cap, darted in and dragged the interlopers out, one by one, explaining the rule that all the old passengers had to be out before the new ones got in.

When the old ones were out, the new ones surged in again, carrying the shouting conductor on their tide. He fought them out a second time, saying it was bus company law that nobody could get in until the bus was turned around. Then he found several others behind him, who had dived in the windows and were now sitting on the coveted bench seats, examining their nails or picking their noses in elaborate poses of leisure and unconcern.

He threw them all out, one by one, with special arguments for each. They had flashed through the windows like salmon up a dam, but several began moaning and imitating great decrepitude, complaining they could not possibly get down the ladder because they were sick or their luggage was too heavy. One plump and rowdy-looking girl, whose red underpants had been thoroughly shown as she squirmed across a window sill, claimed with the most plausible innocence and pouting refinement that she should not move because her uncle was a director of the bus company. When all were out, the conductor unhooked the entrance ladder and held it triumphantly over his head, a symbol of the emptiness of the bus. There was murmur of applause, as if he were a vaudeville strong man and the ladder weighed a thousand pounds.

When the bus was turned around, the passengers flowed in its door and windows like water into a car which had plunged off a bridge. The soldier with the monkey jabbering on his shoulder won a fine seat far in the forward end. With great skill the undertaker got his effigies in unharmed, then held them up and with one hand on the stomach of each, pressed them against the ceiling, where they floated like magically levitated strangers, looking down with painted smiles at the turmoil below.

Though it was nearly eleven o'clock and the urgent alarm should sound before long, this crowding was not a panic; the commotion was about seats and good places near the windows. As soon as the contests were over, the thirty-five or forty passengers, laced together so that they filled all but a few cubic feet of the bus's interior, became calm and good-natured again. When the conductor went off to help the driver fix the motor with string, several men wormed their heads out the windows to jeer. The standees by the door began congratulating the army officer with the imported toilet-bowl, who had got aboard last with his treasure and was sitting in it.

After the driver had finished with the motor, the conductor came to the rear door, flexed his arms and legs, took a deep breath, sprang into the bus, beat his way to its deepest interior, and began to collect tickets. Immediately there was an uproar. The soldier with the monkey had neglected to buy one. Officers commonly forced their way into buses, trains, and theatres without paying, but soldiers rarely did, except in large armed groups. This one's breakfast brew must have made him feel he had higher rank or more pals.

When the conductor's protests amused the other passengers more than the soldier's replies, the latter was defeated. Next he had arguments with all who had to move to let him out to buy a ticket. The final explosion came after he returned, his monkey chittering and blinking nervously on his shoulder. When he squeezed his way forward to his former seat, he found it hopelessly lost under a mass of bodies. By this time the bus was jouncing down the hill and out of town, through the fast-emptying streets.

The soldier cleared his throat oratorically.

"This country is hopeless!" he shouted, sounding as if he really meant it this time. He had a good deal of face to recover.

"The people in this country have no order, no discipline, no obedience! They have forgotten the teachings of their ancestors! They are always trying to cheat each other!"

The monkey on his shoulder hunched forward and peered into his angry mouth with comic alarm. As his neighbors adjusted their heads in the web of arms and torsos, they looked at him with far from secret smiles. He seemed to know his case was shaky, for he muttered "Hopeless!" a few times and made a great show of stooping to look out one of the low windows. In the town behind us, the urgent sirens began their baleful music.

The soldier suddenly straightened up and gestured about the quaking, bounding vehicle with its load of disheveled, poised people, each with an individual smile.

"This kind of disgraceful conduct could never happen in Japan!" he thundered.

The crowd roared with gratified laughter.

At the Press Hostel that autumn and winter, despite the segregation of the correspondents, there was a constant flow of news, gossip, and rumor — tiny mechanical details in the mean joke of a decaying war which shadowed this capital. They were tantalizing fragments, drifting isolated in the unknown as sometimes, on cold mornings, odd roofs and corners of Chungking would emerge briefly from the fog eddying around the city's rock.

. . . "Even at Madame Chiang's warphanage, they had a tough time finding orphan kids who looked healthy and happy enough for magazine pictures in America. The others were undernourished or had skin diseases . . . "

. . . "Yes, Thanksgiving dinner at the H. H. Kung's. He boasts there were sixteen guests, and the turkeys and most of the trimmings were cooked in Hong Kong that morning, flown in over the lines in special thermos containers . . . "

. . . "I hear the Americans down in Kunming expect a provincial Yunnanese revolt against the Chungking Kuomintang, if and when the Japanese start a drive up from Indo-China . . . "

. . . "She works here in a government bureau but her salary is so small, now that prices have gone up, she's decided she will have to go home and sit out the rest of the war with her parents in occupied territory . . . "

. . . "The Szechuanese aren't too fond of the Kuomintang either. Last summer a couple of the generals up the river disarmed some central reinforcements who were trying to march through their bailiwick. They released them only when bombers were sent up from Chungking . . . "

. . . "Sure, in the hills right behind the university, the students found it. Kuomintang officials in a village there have been arresting the beggars and peddlers who come through. They keep them in a cage. When wealthy villagers need substitute conscripts for the army, they can buy them out of the cage . . . "

One event of the winter which did loom out of the mists of secrecy was the New 4th Army Incident. Because news of it reached the world through still-neutral Shanghai, the Chungking censors had to allow fuller reporting of it than was usual for events outside the capital.

When the Japanese had invaded the lower Yangtse Valley early in the war, the Kuomintang pulled its best troops to the rear, and garrisoned the exposed areas with inferior non-central forces. Later it neglected the politics and economics of the front-line areas in usual style. Towards the end of the United Front period, however, it had agreed that the Chinese Communists could organize a guerrilla army there, the New 4th. This soon grew into a force of nearly a hundred thousand men, controlling large stretches of territory on both sides of the Japanese lines.

It was disagreeable to the Kuomintang leaders that the New 4th was active around Shanghai and the other Yangtse cities which the Chungking people hoped to make their headquarters again, if and when the Japanese left. In the summer of 1940, Chungking opened negotiations with Yenan, the Communist capital in North China, aiming to have the New 4th withdraw from the Yangtse Valley and move above the Yellow River, to the other side of the blockade line already sealing off the Communist 8th Route Army in the North. All through the Japanese invasion, the Communists were technically under Kuomintang military command.

After months of pronunciamentos and dead-lines, a compromise was reached whereby the New 4th would move north of the Yangtse. By the first week of January, 1941, less than ten thousand of its number, including the headquarters detachments, and wives, children, wounded, and other noncombatants, were left south of the river. The Kuomintang then ordered its surrounding armies — most of them Szechuanese warlord troops — to attack the remnant. In overwhelmingly greater numbers they ambushed it, killing or capturing most of its members.

The Kuomintang claimed the New 4th had to be "liquidated for insubordination" because it had not moved sooner and farther. By Western standards, this made sense. The idea that any army could argue with its national command for half a year in wartime, trying to reject a new assignment, would be strange to Westerners. By the traditions of Chinese military politics, however, generals could ignore orders, feign illness, or go home to sweep the tombs of their ancestors, when faced with tasks they did not like. During the Japanese invasion, Kuomintang armies with no Communist ties had been known to act against central commands, and in no case had this resulted in a massacre, only a new layer of intrigue.

I well remember the day the story of the New 4th ambush was published in the Chungking papers. At the Press Hostel, the Ministry of Information people were excessively chipper and businesslike, as if nothing had happened, but the Hostel servants kept gathering in corners

to whisper. The official announcement tried to put the best face on
the matter, but anyone who read it had to suspect that an understanding with Japan was printed somewhere on it in invisible ink. The
Kuomintang seemed too weak to fight both the Chinese Communists
and the Japanese at the same time. It was likely, by the way, that the
Japanese learned this incident was brewing and had launched their
November peace offensive — just before they recognized the Nanking
puppets — as part of a final attempt to persuade the Kuomintang
itself to take the role of an anti-Communist puppet government.

That afternoon I went to call on some missionary friends and
found them entertaining a group of Chinese Christians at tea. These
middle-aged guests, with their flawless American English, their quiet
Western clothes and conservative Western names — Grace, Thomas,
Harriet, George — were typical of the small number of mission-edu-
cated Chinese who were patriotic and idealistic. They were doctors
and teachers and engineers who had long ago decided the Kuomintang
was the hope of China, and their public-spirited work had helped
build the government's façade of progress, on the pre-war coast and
in publicity abroad.

Their careers made them anti-Communist, but that afternoon they
were distressed and confused. Official phrasing could not hide the cruelty
and treachery of the Kuomintang's part in the incident. It was not
Christian by any current definition. As they drank their tea and ate
cookies, their talk echoed the points made in the Communist protests.

"If the Generalissimo really had to move the New 4th, he should
have given it more time. After all, the guerrillas lived at home, supporting their families when they were not fighting. They had to make
many arrangements before they could leave."

"Why move them north anyway? They can't be good guerrillas
away from home, in country they don't know."

"And why move them when it means so much land must be given
back to the Japanese? Chinese should not fight Chinese."

Looking back from the present, the most serious result of the "New
4th Army Incident" may have been the uneasiness and dissatisfaction
it caused among so many non-Kuomintang, non-Communist people
in Kuomintang territory. The government was soon forced into a
new campaign of repression and "thought control." Some non-Communist liberals were arrested while others fled to Hong Kong or to
Communist territory. Censorship was tightened and several free-
spoken publications were closed down. Many people who had until

now been pro-Kuomintang turned cool towards it because of the new restrictions they felt upon their own lives. The government's spiral of self-destruction tightened by another loop.

In the Chungking fog:

. . . "That is a clever notion the Kuomintang has been spreading, claiming it is forced to become more reactionary because of the influence of local warlords in its wartime refuge in the western provinces. Actually the warlords — like everyone else outside the central group — are being steadily weakened. Many are now simply tools of the central group . . . "

. . . "I hear one of the Szechuanese generals who helped ambush the New 4th is a fine figure for a cartoon, a real old-style warlord. He lives in a fancy villa beside one of the lakes down there, and has several hundred soldiers chopping out an inscription on the cliff behind it: "Great Peace Rules the Eastern Sea." He's crazy about pictures of himself and his official photographer goes everywhere with him. He also has an adopted son, a waiter he picked up in a restaurant. The boy has two thumbs on one hand and the general's personal wizard told him this was a sign of good luck . . . "

. . . "Remember young Shih, who used to be such a ball of fire in that official relief agency? He's quit; thought he'd better, to keep out of jail. He overheard his boss saying: "If Shih is willing to work so long for such a low salary that he can't buy decent clothes, he *must* be a Communist . . . "

A second event of that autumn and winter, which the veils of propaganda could not hide at all, was the beginning of rapid inflation. As soon as the bombing season ended, this became a central problem in the lives of all Chungking people.

Within a few weeks, the price of rice more than doubled, and the price of everything else followed it upwards. The haggling at the morning markets grew shriller and the shopkeepers rewrote their price tags daily. In front of the rice stores waited long queues of people who wanted to hoard before the cost increased, and on moonlit evenings, in the misty fields on the edge of the town, the young lovers wandering hand-in-hand talked of high prices and the impossibility of marriage.

Compared with the stratospheric inflation of later years, when so many millions of dollars were needed for a day's expenses that it was awkward to carry them even in ten-thousand-dollar notes, the price rises of 1940 were nothing. For a foreigner living on American money exchanged at the official rate of twenty Kuomintang dollars for one American dollar, it only meant that things which had once been very cheap were now cheap. A restaurant meal of simple Chinese food which had cost the equivalent of ten American cents in September would cost twenty-five American cents in December. But for Chinese who had nothing to do with American dollars, the price rises were disastrous. And the inflation was a self-perpetuating process which would surely lead to prices in the millions unless it could be checked.

The government's first reaction had been to ignore it; for weeks after it began, no mention of it was allowed in the press. Then it was recognized indirectly, with news of anti-inflation plans committed to paper; this was in the style of the Kuomintang military communiqués which would admit the loss of some new city by claiming "our troops are counterattacking it from all sides." Later the government tried to fit the problem into its pattern of paternalism. It was said that prices were going up because the people were too disobedient and greedy, buying and eating too much. They had forgotten the frugal ways of their forebears and were distressing their national father. How could they expect to get peace and democracy unless they showed — by voluntarily reducing prices themselves — that their hearts belonged to daddy?

At last the Generalissimo personally tackled the inflation. In a fierce speech to an assembly of Szechuanese county magistrates, he condemned rice-hoarding landlords as the cause of it, and asked that the biggest be reported to him so he could have their rice confiscated. He had an ex-Mayor of Chengtu executed as a hoarder and a few token confiscations of rice were carried out on the Chengtu plain, the richest rice-growing area in the province. Prices halted their upward curve for a week or two.

But no systematic confiscation of landlord rice followed. It could hardly be expected, since so many of the magistrates were themselves landlords and hoarders. The bamboo-telegraph soon reported that the ex-Mayor of Chengtu had been killed less as a hoarder than as a member of the Szechuanese regional clique which was still too insubordinate to Chiang. In the same way, landlords from whom token confiscations had been made were personal rivals or enemies of the confiscating officials. Prices started rising again. At about this time wooden hurdles covered with barbed wire were stacked near several Chungking corners. They were claimed to be a precaution against Japanese parachutists at first, but it was later admitted that they were to "control the people" in case high prices led to social unrest.

There had been natural reasons for the start of this inflation. The past two years had been dry in West China and there was some shortage of rice. Smuggling had not yet expanded to fill the demands of the western provinces, and there were shortages of manufactured goods. The Kuomintang's prospects were shaky enough to make investments in grain or goods more attractive that those in its paper currency, which was known not to have gold or silver backing.

But soon after prices rose a little for natural reasons, they began to rise higher for artificial ones. Conditions were perfect for making a racket out of the crisis. On a national level and in the separate communities so much surplus wealth was already monopolized by a minority which could profit by inflation, buying up more grain or goods, hoarding them against a rise in price. They need not fear government interference, for they or their friends were the government. Because of the blockade, there was little outside competition to bring prices down. The minority had a grip on the smuggling which had replaced free international trade, and could manipulate imported goods to hasten the rise of prices. West China's poor communications and lack of industries — whose products would have limited the shortages — made the cornering of goods easy as well as profitable.

Thus, as soon as prices started to rise, and those who had grain or goods found themselves richer than those who had only money, the wealthy rushed to put more of their money into things. Hoarding created more scarcity, greater inflation. Investors in the few productive enterprises began to withdraw their capital to purchase hoardable things. The decline in production increased scarcity and inflation. Another spiral had been established.

Once again, instead of setting an example of risk for public benefit, the Kuomintang showed that it valued its own security above all. Officially it made repeated attempts to enforce price ceilings and other anti-inflation measures. Unofficially, Kuomintang "men" and even government bureaus were often the first to break or bypass the laws and profit by a new rise in prices.

In the autumn of 1940, just as prices were beginning to soar dangerously, a government edict from the top level revealed that in future all national taxes collected in rural areas would be taken in grain rather than money. I think this clearly showed the government's basic attitude toward inflation and may be taken as the most important cause of all that followed. The collection and use of the rural taxes, paid mainly by the peasants, was the largest annual financial transaction of the Kuomintang. In deciding to take grain instead of money, the government not only made itself the country's largest hoarder, but declared that it did not trust its own currency. No citizen smart enough to have got a little money of his own could fail to take the tip.

In the years after 1940, the inflation was to be a great factor in the demise of the Kuomintang, undermining the value of money so completely that it created a financial vacuum in which no government could operate. It was an appropriate death-agony. Just as this régime hurried the trend toward collapse or suicide which had been growing in China's ancient society for decades, so the inflation hastened the Kuomintang's own drive towards self-destruction.

Since officials already had such a grip on the economic life of the country when prices headed upward, the inflation aided the Kuomintang's centralization of all profit. It helped ruin the middle class, especially salaried people, for wages were almost never adjusted in time to keep up with rising prices. The group alienated from the Kuomintang in this way included many with the modern training and skills the government needed so badly. Even fairly wealthy members of the middle and upper class, merchants and industrialists, were damaged unless they had official connections. With prices skyrocketing, it became impossible to carry on normal business without government subsidies or official help in getting around the various anti-hoarding, anti-inflation laws. Throughout all the Kuomintang cities, a mood of demoralization and passive anarchy developed, favorable to revolutionary change.

But perhaps the most serious effects were felt in the countryside, among the peasants. While the farmers grew the grain which was now more valuable than money, few of them could keep enough of it to profiteer by its rising price; the benefits of inflation were harvested by the grain-controlling minority. The farmers were further damaged by the rising price of cloth, lamp oil, salt, and the other things they had to buy. More and more of the poorest approached bankruptcy.

When they had to sell their land, it was often the richest, the official or semi-official profiteers, who bought it. The basic spiral of monopoly — that of the wealth in land — began to tighten more rapidly.

In the Chungking mists:

. . . "Have you heard the latest anti-inflation plan? One of the Kuomintang spokesmen has advised the people to chew every mouthful of food thirty times before swallowing. Then they will get more nourishment out of what they eat, they will have to eat less, there will be no more scarcity of rice, and prices will go down . . . "

. . . "You remember we were wondering what had become of those beggars downtown? I drove to Koloshan last week and saw them out there, starving along the road and in the air-raid shelters for official limousines. Seems they were driven out of the city to clean up the streets, part of the New Life Movement, I believe . . . "

. . . "He says he will have to close his factory. To keep it running at a profit he has to buy half a year's supply of coal now, before the price goes up, but he can't get a loan from any of the government banks. They prefer to lend to the factories they control themselves . . . "

. . . "One of those Free French fellows who escaped from Indo-China tells me that on this side of the border-river, rice is so much more expensive than it is on the Japanese-controlled side that the Kuomintang troops row across to buy food there. The Japanese seem to encourage it; it gives them a good chance to find out what is happening on this side . . . "

. . . "Wang says some of the higher-ups in his bank have been called over for conferences with the Generalissimo, to discuss the inflation. They report that nowadays when the old gander hears something he doesn't like, he won't even listen. He just goes to the window and stands there looking out, in that pose you see on all the posters . . . "

Although I stayed at the Press Hostel off and on throughout my first visit to Chungking, I also moved around to sample other ways of living in the city. My first shift was to a Chinese hotel downtown, near the shed where I waited for that Sapingba bus. The accommodations here were neither better nor worse than those I was used to at provincial inns — bare, whitewashed rooms with little furniture and privacy, and no modern conveniences, but with plenty of willing attention from a swarm of servants, plus the casual geniality of the other guests. It was in this hotel that I began to recognize one last feature of life in the capital which added almost as much to the air of charade or masquerade as did the bombings, the inflation, or the government. It was the variety of Chungking's population, which in wartime included citizens from provinces as far apart as Sweden and Egypt, and classes which were really living in different periods of history, ranging from the prehistoric squalor of the scavenger coolies to the modish pseudo-Americanism of the official profiteers.

My hotel window was at the back of the building, on the third floor, and from it the compartmentation of life was physically visible on two planes. About a hundred feet away stood one of the five- or six-story semi-Western apartment houses built during the great boom which had followed the influx of government refugees. On the side facing my hotel, it was covered with a net of balconies and galleries where much of the life of the crowded flats overflowed; the building had also been damaged by bombing and many of its rooms were as open as a stage. Below, between the apartment house and the hotel, were half a dozen old-fashioned one-story houses built around unroofed courtyards where the occupants were fully visible as they worked and played.

From the hotel window at first, the impetuous life of every porch and court seemed very much the same, but within a few days each household in its own roost began to take on its special character. In the cooking pots of the well-to-do, meat was placed for every meal, while in others none was used. Some families, Mohammedan, ate no pork while others preferred to eat no beef. The Northerners ate wheat

noodles, the Southerners ate steamed rice. The lines of washing in one courtyard would include silk girdles and detachable collars from Hong Kong; in another would hang hand-loomed aprons and baby clothes with cross-stitch designs common before the Roman Empire fell. The father in one family would call down from his balcony when a newsboy went shouting by with the *Chung Yang Jih Pao*, the Kuomintang paper; others bought the Communist paper, the *Hsin Hua Jih Pao*, or the semi-liberal *Ta Kung Pao*. In one apartment they collected rubbings of ancient cave sculptures, in another machine embroideries imitating photographs. The occupants on one floor seemed to be Christians; they played hymns on a violin and the flowers on their balcony were kept in empty Klim cans. On another floor they were bachelors, young bankers or businessmen. The chant of drinking games came from their windows at suppertime, and sometimes late at night there was the muted sound of tiles furtively shuffled for mahjong, illegal by the rules of the New Life Movement.

Even on the main streets at noon, in the full blast of business, Chungking was a city of infinite differences. There were people in fur hats, in turbans, in Western-style tweed caps with the visors worn rakishly backwards; people without shoes, with straw sandals, with embroidered silk slippers, with two-color sport shoes from the Bata factory in Shanghai. A man carrying a chicken to sacrifice on the rafters of a new house would be followed down the road by a man carrying a carburetor, and he by a man carrying a volume of Swedenborg. The Buicks of the officials' wives, in town for shopping and tea, threaded past air-raid caves where the last and most unlucky of the refugee tide lived as crudely as Australian bushmen. Advertisements for American-trained dentists and local necromancers were pasted on the same hoardings.

Years later, after the Japanese surrender, when I went to Peking, I talked with an expatriate friend who had enlarged his taste for China's visual diversity into the philosophy which made him like to stay a spectator of life in the Orient. His theory applied not only to the behavior of individuals, but to groups of all sizes: families, clans, tribes, cults, and other regional and religious bodies; also economic classes, political parties, nations, and races.

In the Occident, he claimed, the individuals or groups in any given place were pretty much the same in what they thought and did and were. Those who differed kept to the compartments of their own kind. These Occidental enclosures — metropolitan suburbs like Scarsdale or Lake Forest were the best example — were so large, and their walls of tradition, prejudice, and physical segregation so high, it was hard for any person or group in one compartment of life to see into any of the others. In each enclosure the dogma naturally grew that everything thought and done there was reasonable.

In the Orient, such tight compartmentation was impossible. People of every degree of civilization, many races, religions, and political creeds, swarmed together in the same cities. The compartment walls were there, of course, but they had to be flimsy and low. Thus the Orient had great advantages if you wanted to live as a spectator. Coming into it from outside, an Occidental had to chose his compartment and put himself into it, or build one of his own, if he wanted to be enclosed. Otherwise he was in a vantage point like my Chungking hotel window, able to compare what went on in a variety of cells: small ones belonging to individuals or cliques; big ones for races and nations. In small and large, the occupants huddled in a circle, with their faces turned away from their own walls of prejudice and tradition, intent on their own enclosure's special dogmas and styles. Seen together they were a pleasure to watch. If their behavior was believed reasonable only because of the lack of contrast or contradiction from outside the compartment, all its rich unreason would be clear to the detached spectator.

My friend may have been right. My sharpest recollections of my years in China are of the fantastic activities of people, as individuals, groups, or nations. And certainly all those varied garments and gestures and manners of speech, those superstitions and scepticisms, would not have seemed so absurd or sinister if it had not been for the bizarre juxtapositions.

The Shansi farmer in his sterile valley might think if he could migrate to Szechuan he would find land so rich that for electric light he need only plant a pole and tie a bulb to it; the passenger reading a magazine in the plane directly over the farmer's head was persuaded he could be loved if he bought a different mouthwash. The guerrillas on the East China coast thought bullets could not harm them as long as they believed themselves invulnerable; the correspondent who visited them was sure he could write a novel about them if he kept himself drunk. The sacrificial chicken's blood on the rafter and the holy water on the forehead were for the same hope of immunity.

"If I am still a dictator when I die I will go down into the oblivion

of all dictators!" Chiang Kai-shek announced in Chungking before
the Japanese surrender.

"Russian troops are now liberating Manchuria . . . " rumbled the
Moscow Radio at the time of the surrender . . . "The Soviet Union
wishes only to see a strong, unified, and democratic China."

"America's first wish is to see a strong, unified, and democratic
China," said the San Francisco Radio a little later . . . "American
troops are in North China only to protect American lives and
property."

"Certainly you can't sleep here!" a white-bearded missionary recluse
in an isolated provincial town once shouted in my face, as he slammed
his front gate and cut off my query about a night's lodging. "We're
all women here!"

6 · *Some Compartments*

THE TRIBE or cult I learned most about in Chungking in 1940 was the small one of my own foreign kind. I soon moved out of the Chinese hotel and rented a room in a big oil-company residence in the old treaty-port section of the South Bank. The only regular tenant here was the oil-company agent, a young American, forever pulling his pale mustache as if to make it grow faster, while he nervously plotted how to get rid of his other informal tenants before the arrival of his "Dad," a missionary. The squatters were summer bomb-refugees from the city, lazy about moving out. One was Anna, a daughter of the East Prussian Junker aristocracy, married to a Chinese who did foreign liaison for the Chungking office of the Chinese Communists. The other was Maria, from still farther east in Europe, who worked as foreign-language secretary for Dr. Chu Chia-hwa of the right-wing Kuomintang and was rumored to be in Dr. Chu's fascist-style Gestapo. Luckily the Burmese leopardess which later bit so many people in the garden was not yet living there.

"If! If! If!" Anna would roar like a grenadier, flailing her spoon over the breakfast table when the houseboy tried to explain that the cook would have made the porridge softer if the coolie had built the fire sooner. "*If!* My God, if my grandmother had wheels she would be a bus!"

She would continue with her breakfast and her autobiography with equal gusto. Before she became Mrs. Wang and came to China, she had worked in the anti-Nazi underground in Berlin, where her aggressive Valkyrie handsomeness and her maiden name, von Kleist, gave her many uses. One of her frequent jobs, she enjoyed recounting, was as a messenger; she would wait on a park bench until a stranger she could recognize as her man by his red necktie would sit beside her and embrace her so overwhelmingly that it was safe to transfer the hot papers from her purse to his pocket on the off side of the bench. She

116

had come to China just before the war and fled up the Yangtse with her husband and child, from Nanking to Hankow to Chungking, as the government moved. Her favorite story of these days told of the time her ship was bombed, while moored by the shore above Hankow. Like the cautious German hausfrau she wasn't, she had evacuated with a basketful of hard-boiled eggs and when the planes came back again and again, the basket was the thing she blindly clutched as she ran through the fields, looking for cover. She scattered hard-boiled eggs over the landscape, and was loudly amused that she had recovered them all later, since the peasants thought they were embryo bombs and ran away from them.

In Chungking, of course, she had been followed by Kuomintang agents as soon as the United Front began to weaken. With her armor-plated sportiveness she claimed she had soon found them out, and got rid of them by insisting that the man assigned to shadow her should walk beside her. "Come on! Come on!" she would command, leering at him and waving her handbag like a sword. "We are going the same places, so we might as well amuse each other!" Anna thought, the outraged secret agents — notoriously conservative types — invented such favorable reports about this embarrassing woman that their agency soon relieved them by dropping her.

Maria had received her education not from a military caste but from a French governess in her Balkan country. She used to get up very late and spent her days wandering around the house in some kind of underwear, smoking innumerable cigarettes, playing and replaying an old tenor record of "Reviens Cherie," peering moodily at the mist and ruins across the Yangtse. If she really was a spy for Dr. Chu, she was the laziest one ever to wear fake pearls and a black satin dress, which she could do beautifully whenever she got around to it. There was a Chungking legend that when her boss asked her to write a report explaining why foreigners could be anti-Kuomintang, she had lazily farmed it out to those of her friends who she thought could do it best: Anna Wang, Agnes Smedley, and a few others of the self-declared left. The report was a huge success for all concerned.

Up and down the South Bank on either side of this oil-company house, in the moldering, ornate treaty-port buildings perched on little hills that rose from the squalid huts of the foreshore, the other lost outlanders — desperately bored — slandered, caressed, cozened, stroked, or struck each other. I think the foreigners who knew Chungking only in the later years of the Pacific war, when several thousand of them were there, when China was one of the "Big Four" and Generals and Admirals, members of Congress and Parliament, special envoys and investigators, were flying in and out, would be shocked to know how narrow, freakish, and negligible was the 1940 prototype of their community. They might also be unflattered to see how smoothly their community had grown out of the earlier one. (In 1940: "Yup, that's our kitchen-coolie, 'Cow-Flop' we call him. Got it from his real name, Kao Fu-la or some damn thing." In 1943: "Out of ignorance or arrogance, one of the ancient members of that British Parliamentary Mission has been referring to Madame Chiang as 'Mrs. Shek.' " In 1945: "I wonder how serious Patrick Hurley is in his talks with the Communists; he's begun to speak of their leader, Mao Tsetung, as 'Moose Dung.' ")

Back in 1940, discounting the Soviet Russians, the missionaries, the gunboat sailors, and others who did not mix, there were only about two hundred men and ten to twenty women in the Chungking foreign colony. They were probably the most ioslated foreign group of that size anywhere in the world. Except for the airline to Hong Kong, Chungking was as inaccessible as any Tibetan Shangri-La. But instead of the eternal life and material comforts of Shangri-La, these exiles bottled up in their Szechuanese valley faced the possibility of death by bombs and the constant discomforts of the blockade.

Against the Chinese city they lived on but not in, they even looked odd, and I vividly remember my first Sunday walk along the South Bank. I had been wandering among Chinese crowds who — no matter what they were carrying or doing — were of somewhat uniform stature, usually dressed in blue, black, or gray, with smooth old-ivory faces. Suddenly I came upon a party of foreigners of assorted heights and widths, taking their Sunday walk in Western sportswear. They were like a traveling circus, dressed for the ring. Their faces and noses were of different sizes and shapes, various shades of red and white, and some had patches of hair among their features. Their clothes were of contrasting textures and piebald colors: striped, checked, and speckled in brown, red, yellow, green, white. They were followed by the dogs of their nationalities — dachshunds, setters, Scotties, a poodle. As they passed, there was offended barking from the local Chungking dogs which were all of the same general size, color, and vaguely chow-like shape.

And as I soon found, when the foreigners gathered at the Club, the American Navy Canteen, and the other ritual places where food and liquor were sacrificed, their gossip documented their appearance:

... "Her chair-coolies want to quit, because she talks to herself so much when they carry her. They can't understand what she says, of course, but it makes them uneasy ... "

... "Each week he decides some other local food tastes the way that vile smoke from the coolie restaurant smells, and refuses to eat it. First it was the rice, then the greens, and now he complains about the meat. He lives on whisky and canned goods from Hong Kong, but his supply is almost finished ... "

... "You must mean that willowy State Department clerk who was so proud of his flower arrangements. He's gone. The air raids got on his nerves and he began having a looseness every time the sirens blew. Later he had trouble with his bowels whenever anyone talked about raids, and that finished him in Chungking. He's been transferred to the Embassy in Tokyo ... "

The European war was certainly a serious problem for the Chungking foreigners whose nations were then in it, and for many it must have been a source of real concern as well as nervous crotchets. They were in a bad place for showing it, though. Just by being foreigners in China, the enemies belonged to an economic aristocracy more distinct from its Chinese surrounding than any of its members could be from each other. In Shanghai, on my way to Hong Kong, I had my first taste of the travesties this could produce, for there had occurred the great Battle of the Hotels. German guests were forced to move out of the luxury hotels controlled by British interests, and had moved into the fashionable Chinese- and Japanese-owned hotels in such numbers that they could arrange for the eviction of British guests. The

warriors on both sides had moved from one comfortable hotel to another through streets where thousands of destitute Chinese war-
refugees camped on the sidewalks. It was the same in Chungking, on
a smaller scale. A battle would be fought with icy stares between
groups of German-Italian and British-French guests clustering at
opposite sides of a neutral American cocktail party, near the windows
opening on a panorama of Chinese poverty and ruin.

Only occasionally did the skirmishes give more open outlet to their
implicit fantasy. During one South Bank evening, a young American
correspondent criticizing the surrender of King Leopold of Belgium,
was overheard by a member of the Belgian Embassy staff, a dramatic
junior nobleman who had already startled the other Chungking diplo-
mats by visiting them in their offices, showing a pistol, and challeng-
ing: "Now! Have you anything to say against my Keeng?" He
darted to this offending journalist and dashed his glass on the floor
with a manner which would have done credit to a full-length cape.
"You know what thees means in my country?" he cried.

"Nope," said the American.

The Belgian scurried off for another glass, and smashed that too.
He was starting off for a third when his host collared him and tried to
explain that you couldn't duel with Americans; they didn't even know
when they were challenged. Besides, these were good glasses, irreplaceable ones brought up from Shanghai before the blockade. That
seemed to settle the problem of further challenges.

Beyond personal anecdotes, the débris of the summer bombings,
there was little talk of the Chinese war on the foreign South Bank.
Nobody paid much attention to the *National Herald*, the government-
sponsored English newspaper printed over in the city; except for
rumors, there were few other ways to get news except by waiting until
it had been sent to Europe or America, printed in magazines and
papers there, then mailed back to China. By that time it was stale, and
when the imported journals did arrive with words about China's indomitable resistance, the South Bank reaction was usually amused
condescension.

And the longer the bombing weather receded into the past, the more
did the foreign stories concern a humbler folklore which underlay
the legends of the planes as the homely stories of gnomes and elfs,
fauns and nymphs, underlie the terrible ones of flying monsters,
dragons, gorgons, and minotaurs. This was the lore of the blockade,

of the good, accustomed, foreign things to own, drink, wear, or eat, so hard to buy and keep in Chungking. South Bank gatherings exhaustively discussed the best way to safeguard the precious things during raids — some agreed with the squirrels who hid their nuts all over the grove, some with the bears who kept their supplies in one place, going into their caves with their winter's food in their stomachs. By December, more than half the talk in the foreign compartment of Chungking was about the possessed things: where they were or weren't, who was buying or selling or enjoying them.

Of course it was still only a folklore in the making:

. . . "Betty has finally bought that blue dress from Rusty; the one Rusty got from Mrs. Ford, who had it from Madame Da Costa, who got it from Edith, who brought it up from Hankow three years ago. I'm going to get it from Betty when she is tired of it . . . "

. . . "The French say they have found a way to get fresh butter by air from the Methodist cows in Chengtu . . . "

But the lore already had its shrines, its rites, and its heroes. Sometimes enthroned behind the bar at the Club were packages of American or English cigarettes with the owner's names pasted on them the way private bottles of liquor used to be labelled before the blockade. Once or twice a week the owners would reverently drop in for a smoke; for the rest of the week, the packages were worshiped by the cigaretteless drinkers. A ritual gesture which developed out of this shortage was the furtive swoop with which a cigarette owner would pull one for himself out of the package in his pocket, without showing the package. In the evenings in houses which had radios, other devotees crouched in silent circles, nearly thrusting their heads into the box to hear the rich music which could substitute a world of smooth pavements and well-stocked shops for the muddy streets, dim lights, cracked doors, and frayed upholstery around them.

The first hero of the lore was a man who had flown in from Hong Kong on one of the hottest days of the summer, in a state near collapse. He had weighed in wearing half a dozen sets of underwear, three pajamas, two winter suits, and an overcoat stuffed with socks and handkerchiefs. A woman who left Chungking after selling or giving so much to friends that she flew away without brassière or girdle was also venerated. So was the jovial American ex-Marine who had made more than enough money for retirement but still lived in Chungking, manufacturing ice, gin, dill pickles, marmalade, and shaving lotion. So was the Greek dentist who distilled vodka and promised to make beer as soon as he could get a bottle capper smuggled in from the coast.

If the war and the blockade had gone on many more years, this talk might have resulted in a real folklore, with supernatural trimmings. One time when I returned to Chungking toward the end of the Pacific war, some recently arrived foreigners told me a legend that had developed from a small incident — by no means mysterious or improper — I had known of in 1940.

According to the 1945 tale, an American girl from the Press Hostel had been invited by a friend to celebrate her twenty-second birthday with lunch at the one little foreign restaurant on the South Bank. The pair fell in with French sailors who had brandy from Indo-China and stayed until after dark, when they had to run back up the foreshore to catch the last ferry to the city. The young lady missed her footing and rolled so rapidly down the sandy bank that her escort only just managed to keep her out of the river. Then the happy girl decided she liked rolling on the beach, and threw herself down again and again. They missed the ferry. Sedan chairs were hailed to take them to one of the treaty-port houses where they had friends, and in her chair the birthday girl dozed off. She could not be wakened when

they arrived, but the younger officers from the American gunboat and several Embassy clerks were dining there, and they were eager to help put her to bed. For the lunch she had been wearing one of her birthday presents, a fine green wool sweater which had been brought from Hong Kong less than two years before and had had only four previous owners. Next morning when she was dimly trying to remember if she had lost anything besides face, she found the sweater was gone. Instead there was one strange sock, of the same green wool, tangled in the sheets at the foot of her bed.

Life was foolish indeed on the South Bank in those days, but on the levels where I circulated, the trivia was at least harmless. Unfortunately, trifling wasn't limited to those levels. The low quality of the relations America and the other Western nations had with China often gave its flavor to South Bank life. One of the ranking naval officers connected with the American Embassy, for example, was a man who didn't mind declaring in very mixed gatherings, that he couldn't stand "anyone with a drop of non-white blood in his veins, or anyone who doesn't speak English with an American accent."

The Embassy itself was sequestered by prejudices or indifference. I remember one Navy Canteen party when a junior Embassy staff member accused an American correspondent of being a Communist. When the correspondent asked where he had got such an idea, the fledgling diplomat laughed and said: "Up at the Nunnery." That was what the younger State Department men called the house where Ambassador Johnson lived in seclusion with a few older members of his staff. This correspondent was the only one with a major reputation to come to Chungking that winter and stay long enough to find out what was going on; the State Department belief in his communism had undoubtedly come from his effort to learn both sides of the developing New 4th Army Incident. Later in the winter, when the Incident came to a head, this same correspondent was called over to the South Bank to brief the Ambassador on it. Apparently Johnson had ignored the subject until it broke in the world press, and he was queried from Washington. The correspondent found him uncertain or ignorant of background facts which had been known in Chungking for months.

I had my first inkling of the higher nonsense on an afternoon in early winter, when I crossed the Yangtse from the South Bank to Wang Lung Men, Chungking's main river-gate. Here the old city wall and the motor road ran along the top of a cliff, and to reach the city from the ferry, you had to climb up a crazy flight of several hundred crooked, filthy stone steps, winding among hovels of bamboo and matting like those below the bus station for Sapingba, on the other side of the Chungking peninsula. These cliffs outside the walls were the worst place in the city to live, perilously hung over the river and always drenched with refuse, and here the very poorest — coolies and boat trackers and refugees — had built their huts.

That afternoon as the ferry docked at Wang Lung Men, there was running and shouting on the beach and at first the passengers refused to get out, fearing a mad dog or an out-of-season air raid.

When they had been reassured enough to pour up the gangplank, I saw something I had never witnessed during the weeks of impersonal bombing: anger and despair, openly expressed. Fifteen or twenty pauper women were standing on a ledge of the cliff, weeping and cursing, throwing dirt and rocks down on an unfinished hut on the beach. Another group of distraught women charged down the steps with bamboo staves and began to thrash the hut and pry at its timbers. Hundreds of badly dressed men, women, and children watched from the houses on the cliff, howling approval in a deep, menacing tone.

There was laughter as a party of police double-timed down the steps, then boos and bloodcurdling shrieks as they attacked the women, hauling them out of the hut, striking and kicking them if they resisted. Several women threw themselves on the ground and were dragged up the dirty beach, lunging and flopping like fish. Their smaller children ran down from the houses and followed with terrified wails. The noise from the cliffs deepened to a full-throated roar as the women were beaten off toward the police station.

I later learned the disturbance had been caused by an American Red Cross donation of ten thousand dollars sent for relief of bomb victims. Since the Red Cross had no agent in Chungking, the money was supposed to be handled by a missionary committee. As most of the committee were away at the time, it had been sent to the Ambassador, to use as he saw fit. Johnson was a kindly man whose fondness for China was well known, but Chungking seemed to have been China in more concentrated and unpleasant form than he could or would cope with. Peking with its mild weather, fine houses, and incomparable servants had been his milieu, and no doubt Chungking with its ugliness, inconvenience, and suffering was as distressing as it was repulsive to the old gentleman. In any case he evidently preferred to see as little of it as possible. He had become pleased with the Kuomintang in the pre-war years on the coast and appeared to think he need not learn how it might be changing. When he received the money from the Red Cross he must have realized that he was too far out of touch with conditions in the capital to allocate it himself. He sent it on to his friend, K. C. Wu, Mayor of Chungking.

Wu was a member of the central group around the Generalissimo. American-educated, he was a shrewd, efficient-seeming man by Western standards. Among the Kuomintang leaders, he was one of the most glib on the subject of democracy, and with his excellent English and easy American manners, had held a string of government jobs where he met and convinced foreigners that Chiang and his associates where the right trustees for the welfare of the Chinese people.

With prices and exchange as they were then, ten thousand American dollars would have built unassuming shelter for several hundred needy bomb victims. Mayor Wu, however, must have decided this would not be impressive enough. His office announced that as American generosity had been so splendid, its memorial should be permanent. A "Model Refugee Village" would be erected at Wang Lung Men, and as a setting for it, the pestiferous old steps would be rebuilt. The publicity about the "village" made no mention that this would give the city a face-lifting at the gate most used by South Bank commuters and other foreigners, among them dignitaries like Ambassador Johnson, who must have had qualms about Kuomintang democracy at sight of the open wretchedness on the old steps.

The plans called for a grandiose flight of stone stairs and terraces, not only near the "Model Village" but all the way from the river to the motor road. Nearly half the squatters on the Wang Lung Men cliffs, many of them bomb victims themselves, had to be evicted. The women I had seen attacking the hut that afternoon were the mothers of dispossessed families. The hut was a barracks for the workmen who had come to tear down their homes and start work on the steps.

When the women had been removed, the work began. It was finished several months later. The steps were indeed handsome, garnished with ten flimsy houses which could have cost hardly a fraction of what the stonework did. The "Village" was opened with a ceremony at which our Ambassador and Mayor Wu made speeches about Sino-American friendship, and I fear some of the wretches who lost their homes to American generosity were still skulking around the neighborhood and may have listened. "Model Refugees," Kuomintang-approved, were installed in the ten houses at first, but later the buildings were turned over to municipal gendarmes.

At the time I was shocked by the case of the Red Cross steps, but thought it an unlucky accident of the moment, the place, and the people involved. Since then, it has come to seem a typical, or even symbolic, incident in the relations between the Chinese and American peoples.

Most Americans at home, deep in our national compartment, seem to believe that the early history of Sino-American intercourse has run somewhat as follows:

"America has always had a benevolent and big-brotherly interest in China. In the nineteenth century, when the other Western nations were trying to split China into colonies, we Americans established the "Open Door Policy," which guaranteed China would never be dominated by a foreign power. While other nations used force to get unequal treaties and treaty-port concessions from China, we Americans refrained. Instead, American missionaries, relief-workers, doctors, and educators went to China to aid the country toward a decent modern way of life. American businessmen helped establish the framework for modern economic development. Many promising Chinese students came to America and returned to become their country's leaders, full of American "know-how" and democratic ideals. As China progressed toward democratic statehood, America supplied sympathy and aid."

The sincerity of this American belief cannot be questioned. The American money which helped build the Red Cross steps, for instance, was a token of the unselfish good intentions toward China which have existed in America. But the idealistic American belief does not take into account that in international relations, far more than personal ones, good intentions may not be enough. Immense difficulties face any people, shut away in their national compartment, when they take action affecting another people, invisible behind the walls of their own enclosure. The contact between the compartments is in the hands of relatively few official and private organizations and individuals. Sometimes they are not representative of their country, and warp the contact to their own ends. Sometimes they unconsciously warp it because of traditions and prejudices they share with the rest of their country. The mechanics of international relations make it fatally easy for good intentions to be corrupted or miscarried in their application.

The Chinese in China naturally cannot judge us by what we think we are or think we are doing. They must judge us by what we seem to be doing or actually do in China. From the Chinese national compartment, the Sino-American relationship looks less idealistic. In 1940, a Chinese might analyze it as follows:

"While you Americans have never yet used violence like some other nations, you have not lagged in advancing your own interests at the expense of the Chinese. Your "Open-Door Policy" was not to help China; it was a warning that America would not allow any other nation to exclude it from the exploitation of China by making this country a one-nation colony. In demanding that all nations have equal rights in China, your "Open-Door Policy" also ensured that America would profit by any advantages obtained by other nations. You Americans insisted on claiming a "most favored nation" status which gave you all benefits of the unequal treaties forced upon China by more aggressive countries.

"American business in China has helped destroy the static balance of our old economy. American "know-how" among Chinese has been used to maintain and increase inherited private advantages more than to improve public welfare.

"In foreign policy, instead of aiding China's progress toward democratic statehood, America has appeared more anxious to preserve the status quo. In the nineteenth century, America indirectly aided the other Western powers in bolstering the Manchu Empire against the Taiping rebellion. During Sun Yat-sen's revolution against the Manchus in 1911, America was noncommittal. America's coolness toward his plans was one reason why Dr. Sun began to pattern our revolution more on the Russian one, and asked for Soviet advisers.

"Before 1927, while the revolution led by the coalition Kuomintang was struggling to gain control of the country, America recognized its opposition, the northern warlords. After the Shanghai coup, when Chiang Kai-shek halted the revolution, but proved he would establish a status quo favorable to the Western nations, America supported him until the Japanese drove him out of the coastal areas of America's greatest interest. Then America supported the Japanese — not politically or morally, of course, since that would have harmed America's international face, but with the trade and military supplies essential to Japan's invasion. By this record, America's chief interest in China has been as a market."

I would say this comes closer to the truth than does the idealistic American view. Even if it is the truth, there is nothing too blameworthy in the American rôle by the accepted standards of national conduct. It has been an American tradition that we are not our brother's keeper; if a peaceful and friendly China was not also a free and justly governed one, that was a problem for the Chinese, not for us. As a peaceable commercial nation we disliked to have the status quo tampered with, because uncertain times were risky for American nationals and bad for business.

If American trade helped upset the Chinese economy, that was also a problem for the Chinese, not for us. Businessmen could not be ex-

pected to stay out of a market because they might ruin their com-
petitors. If American education and mission effort were exploited by
China's traditional ruling minority, there was not much the Americans
could do about it. They hadn't come to China to change the country
themselves; they could only supply the Chinese with the means of
changing it. They tried to broaden their work to include the under-
privileged through scholarships and charity. For all its complaisance
towards bad government in China, America at least saved the Chinese
from the final victimization of formal colonial status.

I think that if any blame attaches to this chapter in past history it
belongs to those Americans who have tried to encourage a national
delusion that our rôle in China has been exceptionally noble instead of
a normal one. In the years after 1940, we interfered most seriously in
Chinese affairs, and the result was failure for us and great suffering
for many Chinese. But there are Americans who still maintain we can
easily wipe out this recent mistake, and win China as a friend again,
just because so many Chinese once regarded us as benevolent big
brothers. It seems wiser to recognize that even in the past, America's
character as a rich, strong, and consequently indifferent country, and
China's as a poor, weak, and hence sensitive one, made much of our
behavior in China seem to fall short of benevolence. At least it can
appear that way to Chinese.

Two other incidents during my first stay in Chungking showed
how our relations with China apparently had to work. One was a
tea party given by the "Sino-American Institute of Cultural Relations,"
on the November day when Roosevelt was elected to his third term.

On the Chinese side the "Institute" was sponsored by H. H. Kung,
currently the head of the civil government; in Chungking, that made
it official. On the American side it was semi-official since our Ambassador was one of its patrons; after Pearl Harbor the State Department was to make it official by a grant of funds. In 1940, its Chinese members included the most prominent American-returned students, the most successful men with the "know-how," in and out of
the government. Its American members included all the Chungking
American colony except for a few of the most hard-bitten old treaty-
porters.

As Russia was once more the Kuomintang's most active foreign
backer in 1940, the Communist line was pro-Kuomintang, but in later
years the kind of Americans and Chinese who collected at that after-

noon tea were to be described in Communist statements as "imperialist beasts and their running dogs." In the cartoon style of those later years, it should have been an interesting affair, with fat men in silk hats chasing luscious kidnaped peasant girls up and down stairs. But we Americans and our protégées seem to have a genius for attaching a moral tone, jolly but refined, to whatever we do. The party was deadly dull.

Its setting did suggest what it might have been, for it was held in Chialing House, a semi-official hotel hung like a swallow's nest on the cliffs of the luxury suburb overlooking the Chialing River. By the standards of unblockaded capitals, Chialing House was unremarkable — a rather naked barracks of a hotel, sparsely trimmed with the red lacquer columns and chunky furniture of the Shanghai-moderne style — but with its stepped-up lights, and cleanly repaired walls, rarities elsewhere in the city, it floated over ruined, fog-drenched Chungking like a hallucination as detached as the roof garden where I had feasted with the general in charge of derelict Tam Shui Ko, down in the West River delta.

The Chinese guests, too, were creatures apart from the shabby, shivering multitudes who climbed up and down the muddy Chungking streets. Their standard of dress was the highest I had seen anywhere in the city. Most of the men wore well-tailored Western business suits while the women — extensively painted and powdered — wore Chinese gowns of silk, velvet, or lamé. There were only a few men or women whose modest dress showed them to be in teaching or some other low-salaried work. Hardly any wore uniforms. Many were bureaucrats and others were bankers, especially from the two great state banks headed by the American-educated H. H. Kung and T. V. Soong. Their tea-party chatter inclined to such statements as, "We Chinese have been fighting for democracy longer than any other nation," or "We Chinese are the best guerrilla fighters in the world." This made for stiltedness and gales of uneasy laughter.

The formal entertainment started with the seating on thrones, on a dais, of Ambassador Johnson and H. H. Kung, twin Buddhas in double-breasted blue suits. That Johnson had made one of his rare trips to the city to honor the "Institute" made the meeting more official. A handsome Chinese girl appeared on the dais, and after adjustment of her furs, her gloves, her purse, sat at a piano and rewarded the audience with some culture which was neither very Chinese nor American — tinkly numbers from *Fifty Famous Favorites, or Piano Pieces the Whole World is Playing.* When she finished, and covered her giggles with both hands, Johnson and Kung made speeches about the traditional friendship of the American and Chinese democracies, and the rest of the afternoon was turned over to J. L. Huang, "Colonel" or "Fatty" Huang as he humorously liked to be called. He was an ex-YMCA secretary whom Madame Chiang had installed as head of the New Life Movement, and he was the busiest of the palace jesters.

The audience knew what a card he was thought in high places, for there was polite laughter, courteously suppressed, as he mounted the dais and made the plain statement that he would auction off a coat donated by Madame Chiang, to raise money for her "warphanages." It was a garish white fur with a gold fabric lining and somebody behind me whispered that in view of Madame Chiang's self-indulgence and excellent taste in clothes, it must have reached her hands as an unwanted gift. The "Colonel" livened the bidding with many jokes and capers he had perfected before YMCA audiences; he had lots of fun putting on the coat and pretending he was a lady.

As it was Election Day in America, the big event of the afternoon was an "Election Race" between a pasteboard elephant for Willkie and a pasteboard donkey for Roosevelt. These symbols were hung on parallel strings stretching down the hall and marked off by bows of ribbon. The "Colonel" herded two embarrassed young men from the American Embassy up to the dais and appointed one a Republican, one a Democrat. They were given dice, and the pasteboard animals were advanced along the marked strings by their luck with numbers. Through Dr. Kung, the "Institute" had tried to get Central News to suppress the election returns until the time of the party. The real

The wall-slogan reads: THIS WILL NEVER
                      BE FORGOTTEN!

results were to be announced at the end of "Election Race," when they would come as a double surprise. Though Central News had agreed, the information that Roosevelt was re-elected with a substantial margin had leaked out early in the day; it was known among the guests at Chialing House. As the "Colonel" skipped and whirled and shouted, they sat in a politely sodden silence, one eye on the waiters who were bringing in the tea and cakes.

Willkie's elephant won by more than half the length of the room.

Later in the winter I met an American-returned student who did not attend tea parties of the "Sino-American Institute of Cultural Relations": Professor Ma Yin-chu of Chungking University, a graduate of Yale in the class of 1910. He was an old Kuomintang member — even in the days of his later troubles, he was never accused of being a Communist — and was considered Kuomintang China's leading economist. He had tutored the Generalissimo in economics in the early years following the Shanghai coup.

He was currently attracting attention with articles and speeches fearlessly criticizing the economic policies of the Kuomintang, exposing corruption and profiteering in high places. It was rumored he would soon be arrested, so with a friend from the Press Hostel I went to call on him. We found him a dignified, quiet-spoken man with gray hair, very cordial to the only foreign visitors who had come near him since his notoriety. We asked him to speak frankly, promising neither to publish nor to quote his remarks. Blinking as if he were going to cry, he asked us to do both. Inequalities had become so extreme, he

Two years earlier, the wall-slogan behind the advertisements had read: THIS WILL NEVER BE FORGOTTEN!

said, and the distress so great, it was time for someone to speak out. He was an old man, and no longer cared what happened to him. He thought it a patriotic duty to speak the truth for the public.

He talked for nearly an hour, with the intense concentration and emotional manner of an honest and deeply convinced man. He could not regard the Generalissimo as a national hero as long as he allowed the Kungs and Soongs to be the chief profiteers on his country's misfortunes. The burden on the poor was becoming unbearable. He detailed his plans for a "capital levy" which would place the heaviest burden of the war on those with the most money. The Generalissimo was the only man who could give the orders to carry out the levy. If he failed to, the resulting misery would be his personal responsibility.

Toward the end of our interview, some students came in dragging a man in civil uniform without insignia, and said they found him listening at the door of Professor Ma's office. He had told them he came with the two foreigners but he was a stranger to us, so the students escorted him out of the building. He was almost certainly a police spy but Professor Ma finished the interview with no change in his calm manner or severe views.

A few weeks later, after I had moved out to Chungking University to stay with a Chinese friend who was teaching there, and had a good chance to hear what was happening, a party of gendarmes called on Ma Yin-chu while he was conducting a class.

"The Generalissimo wants to see you," said their captain. This was the standard procedure for important political arrests. Professor Ma pointed out that it might cause student unrest if he were taken from his classroom, so the gendarmes agreed to wait for him at his home and arrest him during recess. They took him away in an automobile, refusing to tell his family where or why he was going, or when he would come back.

Professor Ma was popular among his students, and they organized a mass meeting of protest to be held in the school auditorium. Like all Kuomintang colleges, however, this one had a branch of the San Min Chu Yi Youth Corps, junior auxiliary of the Kuomintang Party. Its members spied out the plans for the meeting and told them to the University president, a conservative man. On the morning of the meeting the students gathered to find the president already seated on the platform of the auditorium. By the protocol of paternalist teacher-student relationships, they were defeated and had to listen to him instead of making their own protests. He told them not to worry;

Ma Yin-chu was perfectly safe. They must forget Ma's ideas, he said, for Ma himself had decided he was mistaken and regretted having misled his students.

As it proved, the president had gone out on a limb. The students were not satisfied, and while the Youth Corps was able to sabotage further attempts at a mass demonstration, the campus remained disturbed and a few days later Professor Ma was brought back with a guard of gendarmes. A meeting of all students was called. Apparently Ma had agreed to tell them that whatever they thought of national affairs, they must now get back to their studies.

But perhaps the professor had reckoned without his own integrity. The captain of gendarmes made an introductory speech for him, emphasizing that in wartime a unified nation and one leader were essential. He said Professor Ma had been talking illegally. If he had complaints, he should have told them to the Generalissimo, not the public.

Professor Ma angrily leaped to his feet.

"Why should I tell the Generalissimo things he already knows?" he shouted. "It's the public that needs to be told! And why should there be any question of a man's talking illegally or not, when so many who are acting criminally go unpunished? . . . "

"That's enough!" thundered the captain of gendarmes. The meeting was dissolved. After posing for a group photograph with his students, at their insistent request, Professor Ma was taken off again to his unknown place of detention. He was held incommunicado, without trial and without charge, for four years, then released only to go into "retirement," under orders not to speak or write for the public.

Taken together, I think the "Institute" tea party and the case of Professor Ma show the difficulties which confront Americans in getting the kind of foreign policy we may want, since policy is influenced not only by the decisions made on a national level, but by all the smaller contacts between Americans and the nationals of other countries.

Despite his American education, H. H. Kung represented the rottenest elements of Kuomintang rule. His war profiteering, the corruption of his banks, his political empire of dependent "men" — all this was generally known, and in those years of his eminence Kung was the most unpopular man in China. He was not feared, like the men who ran the secret police, but plainly despised.

Naturally, Kung would not sponsor the "Institute" and its silly parties because he thought they were cultural or because he loved Americans. He wanted the face he could get from association with Americans, with its implications of American support, for the help it gave him in internal politics. The "Institute" parties were well publicized in the newspapers he controlled.

Obviously, it was not to the American interest to support Kung, but by American tradition our Ambassador could hardly decline to be associated with his "Institute" when Kung was civil head of the government and brother-in-law of the great man himself. Refusing a Kung invitation was the kind of thing an American Ambassador just did not do.

Professor Ma, on the other hand, embodied the point of view most of us believe we stand for. His "capital levy" was similar to the wartime taxes we adopted after Pearl Harbor. If we had supported him when his danger was rumored, he might not have been arrested, and the cause of free speech and American-style democracy would have been that much advanced. Since Professor Ma was so distinguished an American-returned student, it would have been easy to make a gesture; if Ambassador Johnson had invited him to lunch along with some government officials, it would probably have been enough of a hint. But in his isolation on the South Bank, I doubt if our Ambassador heard about Ma's trouble until after the arrest, if then, and he certainly took no action about it. It would have been gauche.

During the later years I was in China, the American government was to interfere increasingly in Chinese affairs. Except for a brief period preceding the Stilwell Incident, and later during Marshall's negotiations, we not only gave unqualified military and economic support to the Kuomintang, but in our propaganda, our social relations, and the other minor aspects of international contact we consistently threw the weight of our prestige behind the central group dominating the Kuomintang. Except for a brief period while Marshall was negotiating in 1946, we ignored and thereby damaged the liberal opposition. Even then, after the Kuomintang had become crucially dependent on American support, the American government made no comment when a liberal American-educated professor, Wen I-to, was assassinated by Kuomintang secret police. Later, America silently watched while the Kuomintang dissolved, as an alleged Communist-Front organization, the liberal Democratic League. Although our envoys had been convinced enough of the League's non-communism to use its members as go-betweens in the Kuomintang-Communist negotiations, we took no action to save it.

When Marshall returned from China in early 1947, he made a statement criticizing both the Communists and the Kuomintang, recommending more power be given to the middle-of-the-road liberals. Later official statements repeated that America wished to help the liberals, and it became a part of our national delusion that we had indeed been helping Chinese liberals.

The young teacher I went to stay with at Chungking University at the time of Professor Ma's abduction was one of the first Chinese I knew as someone more than a figure in a bizarre pantomime of the streets. He was a liberal, rather a courageous one to make foreign friends when he was not "authorized," but at first I found it hard to make much sense out of him, for he seemed determined to lead his own life in as much of the pantomime style as possible. He was a fairly well-known literary figure in Chungking, having published a novel in Esperanto while in college, and was currently translating English and American short stories into Chinese, offering them to the public under his pen name, "Horse's Ear." He dressed in garish Western tweeds from Hong Kong but in his leisure in his attic at the University, sketchily divided into rooms by walls he had pasted together from reeds and paper, he cultivated a rather austere form of "Pure Discourse," arranging and rearranging his collection of odd-shaped pebbles, inventing calligraphic poems and puns.

He had a strong taste for evasion and I sometimes thought he had studied English for the same reason he learned Esperanto: so few people he knew could speak it to him. I suspect his dealings with a crass English-speaker like myself were sometimes a trial to him for I hardly ever got a flat "yes" or "no" out of him. Later he told me something of his background and it explained quite a bit.

He came from a conservative clan of rural landlords in central China, but in 1926 his two older brothers, young men at the time, had caught the political fever from the northward march of the coalition Kuomintang and went to Hankow where they took part in the revolutionary government. After Chiang's Shanghai coup, when the hunting of liberals and leftists began, both were on the black-list but managed to escape. One went to Shanghai where he became a successful compradore and merchant, obsessed with the idea of living in completely Western style; he was particularly fanatic about his collections

of fancy Swiss clocks. When the Japanese took Shanghai, he contentedly stayed on, doing business as usual. The other brother returned
to the family village in Hupeh and buried himself in the study of
Taoism. His solitary ways made the peasants think he was a
sorcerer, and sometimes he amused himself by frightening them with
tales of tiny white man-shaped roots, or root-shaped men, whom he
claimed to have seen walking about in the woods, stark naked except
for straw hats and straw fans. When the Japanese occupied the village,
he was content to stay on too.

During that first stay in Chungking, I met only one other Chinese
whom I later knew well. His life had been just as plainly tipped off
balance by the clash of revolution and reaction in modern China. He
was a young man from a wealthy family on the coast; originally it was
a great rural landlord family, owning many thousand acres of riceland,
but two generations ago it had moved to one of the treaty-ports and
invested in real estate, a flour mill, and a cotton factory. The men of
the family had long been politically active, as governors and ministers
under the Manchu Empire.

In the old manner my friend was brought up by a wet-nurse, an
amah who had a son just his own age. The two boys lived together
as brothers until they were nearly twelve, when my friend was sent off
to school and the amah's son was put to work in a factory belonging
to my friend's father. A year or two later, the boy in the factory
was badly hurt in an industrial accident, the cruel kind which were
always happening in mills where the machines were valued more than
their operators. The factory owner refused to hear his son's arguments
that he be held responsible. That fixed his son's political direction.

He had just graduated from college when the Japanese invaded,
and knowing he was already on the Japanese black-list because of his
part in the anti-Japanese student movement, he went in from the coast
ahead of the invasion. For two years he worked at the front, in the
Political Department of one of the Kuomintang armies; the government then tolerated and sometimes encouraged liberal political work to
promote soldier-peasant co-operation.

When the United Front weakened, however, the Kuomintang
stopped such work as a dangerous leftist tendency. In my friend's
army group, several men were arrested as Communists. He himself
was accused and it was only through a lucky warning that he was able
to leave in time to get safely to Chungking. People who had been
threatened with political arrest in the provinces could usually live

safely and openly in Chungking, if they could get there. Too many repressive arrests in Chungking might be noticed by foreigners and the Kuomintang wanted to avoid that.

When he reached Chungking, my friend managed to have some of his family money remitted from occupied territory. He went into business, apparently as a speculator, and took to drinking and gambling. In later years when I knew him better, after he had got back into the war, he told me that this earlier reaction had been entirely emotional and often surprised and shocked him while it was taking place.

"But at least I had made my political stand clear," he would say bitterly. "I was acting like a regular Kuomintang man."

After I came to know more non-party Chinese liberals, it seemed as if their unhappy compartment of life were like a crazy-house at an amusement park, built on a slant with the floors tipping up and the walls leaning over. No windows opened out of such a house, and when you had been in one for a while, your eyes could convince your mind that since the floor was still at right angles to the walls, the floor must be horizontal and the walls vertical; you began to believe that your companions were staggering over at a ridiculous angle, that dropped objects could fall sidewise, and water could run uphill.

I don't think anyone who has not seen it can imagine how corrupting life can be under a tyranny which is not only reactionary but inefficient. The leftist press in America used to make much of the fact that the Kuomintang ran a police state, but I have never seen it explained that the techniques of Kuomintang rule, which ensured that even the political police should be corrupt and weak, could destroy morale more insidiously than the regimentation of a real fascist state.

During the Japanese war, there were two major secret police forces in Kuomintang China. Though their functions sometimes overlapped, the larger one — General Tai Li's — was under the Supreme Military Council and handled military security, including anti-Japanese and anti-Communist espionage at the front and in occupied territory. The Kuomintang Party police, controlled by the two Chen brothers, concentrated on liberals, leftists, and other with "dangerous thoughts" in the rear areas of unoccupied China.

The brothers Chen Li-fu and Chen Kuo-fu, incidentally, can be considered the key figures in the central group around the Generalissimo. They were old family friends of his, for their uncle, Chen Chi-mei, a political power in Shanghai in the twenties, had helped Chiang in the first stages of his career. Later the Chens' political group — the CC Clique — became the Generalissimo's favored tool for dividing and ruling all others. The CC Clique was reputed the most reactionary in the Kuomintang, also the one most given to neo-Confucianist mysticism and perhaps to profiteering. Chen Li-fu, the more prominent brother, was partly educated in America and later became a Buchmanite.

Among the lesser secret police organizations Dr. Chu Chia-hwa's was probably the most active. It took its authority from the Kuomintang Party, and while it was run by rivals of the CC Clique, it did much the same kind of work. The still smaller espionage networks were innumerable; almost every important official and general had some kind of intelligence system of his own; so did the provincial governments.

By 1940, however, even the major police forces were believed to be succumbing to the country's illnesses. Tai Li's agents were reported to have used their position at the front to enter the smuggling business. The Chen brothers' and Chu Chia-hwa's agencies were said to be clogged with inefficient "men," appointed because of their loyalty to their masters, not their aptitude for police work. In the smaller espionage nets, private profit and power were the chief aims. All this fitted congenially into the general Kuomintang pattern, for if any police organization had been efficient it would also have become uncomfortably strong, and would have to be harried, divided, and reduced to preserve the national balance of weakness.

Naturally it was hard for any foreigner to know for sure what was taking place inside a secret organization, but the police had unlimited powers of arrest and punishment — despite the civil rights the Kuomintang had committed to paper — and from what could be seen of their work, the rumors of their decay were correct. Obviously, most police were distracted by other interests, only now and then saving face by unwarranted and capricious arrests. Real Japanese and Communist agents could travel about Kuomintang China with relative safety, while the political concentration camps were commonly filled with innocent small fry; middle-school students whose childish curiosity had led them to read Marx, petty government workers denounced for personal reasons, and so forth. This was to become plainer during the Pacific war, when American support encouraged the Kuomintang to greater relaxation. In South China I saw positive proof — locally printed pamphlets and manifestos — that a Communist underground existed there. Some liberal Chinese friends of mine who spent time in Kuomintang concentration camps in those years, reported that most of their fellow prisoners had been marginal cases, amateur leftists at the worst. Many were children.

While this idiotic variety of police control was born of laziness and opportunism, it was more effective than might be supposed. Except for a few strong-minded men like Professor Ma Yin-chu, most of the Chinese I knew who tried to lead political lives of their own, outside the Kuomintang and Communist Parties, were sooner or later tipped, warped, or otherwise rendered impotent by the haphazard repression. There were signs in public places saying, "Don't Talk Politics," but everyone knew it was reasonably safe to be critical of the government in public. Anybody who wished to talk to the Communist representatives in Chungking would probably be untouched if he observed a few precautions; on the other hand, if the police did turn their attention to him, he could be imprisoned for sentiments he had expressed years earlier, or those which had been misunderstood by their hearers. Always, when they did act, the police could act brutally, without any pretense of legality. This frightened many men out of politics, driving them off into wizardry, profiteering, mah-jong, calligraphy, and the various forms of "Pure Discourse." Others became devious and conspiratorial, talking so much they could not act. Within themselves, they were divided and ruled.

I don't know how much longer I might have stayed in the Chung-king fog if it hadn't been for the arrival of Rewi Alley, the New Zealander who in these years was attracting much attention as one of the founders of the Chinese Industrial Co-operatives, or CIC, an experiment in decentralized, mildly socialized industry. As he had with every other foreigner who showed signs of writing, he suggested I travel with him on his next field trip. This time he was going to Paochi in southern Shensi, the largest Co-op center, several hundred miles up the northwest road toward Russia.

In reading history, I had been bored by the way the record usually stuck to the big events in the big cities. Particularly when revolution was in the air, as in modern China, it seemed more interesting to know what was going on in the less spectacular, more typical, smaller places. Reading about the French Revolution, I had wondered what life was like in Tours or Dijon between 1789 and 1793. I speculated about

Hartford and Savannah in 1776, Omsk and Odessa in 1919. After some
time in Chungking, one of my main aims was to find what was happening in villages and small towns as far from the capital as possible.
Rewi's invitation seemed the best way of getting away again, since
the Kuomintang Ministry of Information had shown no interest in
aiding such a departure. When Rewi left for Chengtu in late December I managed to get a visa and arranged to follow in January, on
the Co-op truck which would take him from Chengtu to Paochi.

   Those last cold weeks in Chungking had a tinge of complete dream
or nightmare. The winter fog was so thick that twilight and noon
were the same color. The streets, inches deep in liquid mud, were
jammed with the full wartime population; every door and window
seemed to bulge with people. The noise of shouting and thumping and
chanting which eddied around the cliffs was deepened by the dim,
billowing songs and slogans shouted at the meetings and parades
arranged for the season. Christmas was a Kuomintang holiday, the
anniversary of the Generalissimo's release from his Sian captivity in
1936. New Year's Day was a holiday for the same reason as in Western
countries. Though the Kuomintang in its more successful years on
the coast had forbidden all observance of the old Chinese New Year,
which came several weeks later, it now allowed the old customs at the
time of the new New Year, to offset war-weariness.

   My impression of those last days in Chungking was one of people
bound on journeys whose end they did not know, possibly because I

was planning such a trip myself. The great holiday parades were compulsory affairs, with every Pao and Chia ordered to supply marchers. In the apathy of people who had not the slightest idea what they were doing, the celebrants would shamble along, raising their fists and shouting the slogans only when they were told to. Those on the sidewalks noticed the parades only when something amusing came along: a fanciful cannon or tank or airplane of bamboo and painted paper, in the style of the traditional funerary figures. Up at Chialing House on New Year's Eve, the American Embassy staff and other select foreigners invited by H. H. Kung followed "Fatty" Huang as mechanically as the paraders, singing "For He's a Jolly Good Fellow" in reference to Dr. Kung.

On a drizzly afternoon shortly after the New Year I saw the Generalissimo for the first time, as he was speeding through the city to address a mass meeting of soldiers waiting in the mud of the commercial airfield in the Yangtse. As always, he traveled in one of a cavalcade of big black cars, the others packed with attendants and guards. His own car had dark blue curtains drawn over the back windows — to hide the sheet metal, I was told — and he was dimly visible as a rigid figure in the center of the back seat. When the first car of his suite came speeding through the traffic, the people walking and loitering in the road hurried to the sidewalks. While the limousine of their leader passed, bouncing smoothly over the uneven pavement like a great black panther, they took their umbrellas from over their heads and held them against their ankles, to protect themselves from the sheets of filth fanning out from the wheels.

PART II
The Edge of the Shadow

7 · Road to the North

ALMOST ANYWHERE in America, an auto trip between two places as close together as Chungking and Paochi would take no more than a day of unhurried driving over a choice of paved highways. Chungking is near the latitude of New Orleans. Paochi, some three hundred and fifty crow-miles north, is near the latitude of Memphis, Tennessee. Many Americans think nothing of covering such a distance for a holiday with friends or a weekend in a big city.

It took the CIC truck I rode one week to get from Chungking to Paochi. Apart from its own debility, it was greatly slowed by the road, a narrow dirt track which wound tortuously over the hills and mountains. This was the only auto highway between the wartime capital and all its northern provinces and fronts, but many grades were so steep that the engine could not take them without resting. Some corners were so sharp that a truck could not get around them without backing and filling. Since the whole route was indirect, with a two-hundred-mile western detour through Chengtu, the road-miles must have totalled nearly a thousand.

The trip also seemed longer because the difference of climate between Chungking and Paochi was as great as if the cities were separated by a thousand straight miles. In its last stretch before Paochi, the road zigzagged over the Tsinling Mountains, the easternmost spur of the Tibetan massif. This formed the northern rim of the Szechuan basin, and was also the watershed between the Yangtse and Yellow River valleys. The five- and six-thousand-foot mountains made a distinct boundary between the South and the North. Near Chungking, where the moist air never brought frost, palms and orange trees flourished in the rich valleys, and monkeys and civet cats lived in the shrubbery of the wilder hills. At Paochi, where arctic winds from Siberia sometimes drove the temperature down near zero, the few trees on the semi-desert land of Shensi Province were typical of the upper temperate zone — firs, willows, oaks, alders. Wolves howled among the bare hills at night.

Before dawn on the dismal January morning when I left Chungking, I mounted the Co-op truck with two dozen CIC passengers. As we clanked out through the miles of air-raid suburbs — the drifts of mud-and-bamboo offices, dormitories, shops, where so much of the life of the capital dispersed during the summers — we beat and twisted our luggage into rows of nests or fox holes where we could sit in some shelter from the cold wind.

In the hole next to mine crouched an old gentleman dressed with the carefully picturesque squalor some Chinese intellectuals affected. I don't think he had a single button in all his ragged layers of jackets, coats, and hoods, preferring to fasten up with pins and twigs and colored twine. He clutched a gnarly wooden cane which was also a flute. He had been pointed out to me as a son of one of the wealthiest compradore families in Shanghai, and he spent the day's ride telling me of the thirty years he had passed at colleges in Europe, studying whenever, wherever, and whatever he pleased. He knew a little about everything from Racine to beekeeping, and when he found I was going all the way to Paochi, he urged me to come on a pilgrimage to Hua Shan, the sacred mountain of the North, promising we could ride like poets on milk-white jennets with scarlet saddles.

We shared a room at a roadside inn that night, and when I woke at dawn, I discovered him fully dressed and packed, trimming his

eyebrows by candlelight with Japanese nail scissors of intricate design. As he walked out, he remarked that our truck would leave within five minutes. By great scrambling I was just able to get myself on top of it, where I found the vagabond scholar deep in a fine nest, so wrapped in checkered towels that only the tip of his wrinkled nose showed. He drew one cloth aside and started this day's conversation by deploring the ideas about China that prevail abroad, and suggested that books on Chinese history should be donated to every library in Europe and America. Naturally I agreed, but even after we had given the books he was not satisfied. He thought they should be displayed in a way to show they were about China, and as the truck careened through the mists and flooded rice paddies, he pondered.

"I've thought of just the thing!" he cried at last. "They should be kept in pink bookcases shaped like Chinese pagodas!"

The truck flashed through a pine grove and raced uphill past the graceful, hooked, pink and white tower which had given him the idea. Even before breakfast on a damply chilly morning, such fancies seemed a pleasant change from the interminable political talk of Chungking, but on the third day of the trip, when Rewi Alley got on the truck at Chengtu, I learned the old gentleman's eccentricity was political.

In the early days of the Kuomintang, Rewi said, the vagabond scholar had been an active Party member. That had been before the Shanghai coup, when the northern warlords and foreign powers thought the Kuomintang a radical movement and their police hounded, imprisoned, and sometimes executed its members. At risk of his freedom and sometimes of his life, the old gentleman had done Kuomintang underground work until Chiang founded the Nanking government; then there was no more use for him. With no aptitude for political horse-trading, he had been one of the first to find himself outside the decreasing circle of privilege.

When the Japanese invasion began, he could get no government job for the patriotic work he wanted. After months of privately helping wounded soldiers escape to the interior, he came inland and puttered about with odd jobs in public organizations like the CIC and the Red Cross. Often he lived humbly at army hospitals as a volunteer orderly, boiling clean drinking water for the wounded, writing letters for the illiterate. But the farther the world he had helped create receded from him, the more preoccupied he became with his flute-cane, his legends, the color of clouds, and the shape of insects' wings.

In his own way, Rewi seemed quite as unusual as the old gentleman. He was not a large man, but built on such rugged lines with wide shoulders and a strongly aquiline face, that he gave an effect of size, particularly when he was sitting down. As he hunched on top of that truck, with his chunky blanket-wrapped torso emerging above a welter of boxes, bedrolls, and lesser bodies, with his prow of a face turned into the wind, he looked like a seer, although a beardless and red-headed one.

He was not interested in talking about his life before he came to China, and I learned little of it, except that he had been born and brought up in New Zealand, and was named after a Maori chieftain his father admired. He had been wounded before he was twenty in the First World War. He wandered to Shanghai a few years later and went to work for the Municipal Council which governed the international treaty-port section of the city. Settling in the Council's Industrial Department, he worked up to the post of Chief Factory Inspector. He was supposed to make sure that no factories had fire hazards or unsanitary conditions which threatened the community outside, but he could not learn such things without seeing the semi-slaves who worked the machines inside. Because of his job, he found little pleasure in the country-club, night-club life common for Shanghai's foreigners. He never married, but instead of investing in house-boats and racing ponies like the more fashionable bachelors, he adopted and educated two Chinese boys, famine orphans, and spent his spare money on charities and an enormous library on all possible subjects, particularly labor and the economic problems of China. He spent his vacations traveling in the interior, sometimes in volunteer relief work.

Shortly after the Japanese took Shanghai, both his adopted sons went off to the war, leaving him alone and lost in his comfortable house. When the CIC idea was first broached, by Edgar Snow and his wife, and a few other foreigners and some Chinese, Rewi seized on it. He gave up his job and abandoned his library and other possessions. He took most of his savings as a contribution to CIC capital, if the movement should be founded, and in the spring of 1938 followed his sons inland to Hankow. In the hectic, grasping-at-straws atmosphere of the temporary capital, the British Ambassador, Clark-Kerr, helped him to secure recognition from the Kuomintang, then at the modest height of its United Front tolerance, and the government allowed the CIC a yearly grant for its plans to replace industries lost in the war. Additional funds came from volunteer committees in America, England, Hong Kong, and other parts of the British Empire.

I think Rewi would be the first to belittle his own place as a single individual, and a foreigner, in a project like the Co-ops, which could only succeed as a mass movement among Chinese. Still, he was recognized as the most active force in getting the CIC started and later devoted more effort to it than any other foreigner, more than all but a handful of Chinese.

For the first four or five years of its existence, he was traveling field secretary and general trouble-shooter. Except for brief annual trips to Hong Kong and once to Singapore to raise funds, most of his time was spent on the crude roads of western China, with stops ranging from some minutes to some weeks where there were Co-ops. From what I saw of him during the time I was with him, more than any other foreigner I knew he had made his life a Chinese one, and in the main stream of the country's activity instead of the scholarly or artistic backwaters where most other expatriates collected. Unlike foreign businessmen and many religious missionaries, he did not feel he had to insulate himself with Western-style habits and comforts; his unfailing supply of coffee, sent from well-wishers abroad, was his only concession to his former tastes. Living with his Chinese colleagues on equal terms, he had turned the fact of being a foreigner into an advantage, providing that slight exotic difference which often made troubled CIC people more willing to speak frankly to him than to those of their own race.

Before I left Chungking, I had heard that he was in difficulties because of the inexorable trend of Kuomintang politics. A clique of American missionaries friendly with H. H. Kung and other conservative figures were apparently running a campaign of gossip and intrigue to oust him and his liberal associates from the Co-ops, and take them over. This would be pleasant for the missionaries because of the CIC's prestige and money-raising ability abroad, and agreeable to Kuomintang elements who were uneasy about the Co-ops as a danger to the economic status quo. The missionaries would treat the CIC as a relief organization, a paternalist outfit turning money from abroad into food, clothing, and supervised work for the poor, while Rewi and the committees which backed him believed the foreign money should be used for social and educational work — particularly technical training — which might change the CIC from an inert group of amateurish small industries, swallowing relief funds, into a movement toward independent prosperity. His critics were ingeniously calling him a "new imperialist." By promoting reforms which had not been started by the Kuomintang, they reasoned, he showed as much arrogance as the commercial adventures of the nineteenth century.

I never did figure out how these critics justified their own presence in China, as missionaries of a religion which had not been invented by the Kuomintang, but I am afraid they were right about Rewi. He was an "imperialist" by their definition. There were two examples on our trip north.

In one valley he halted the truck while it was passing a line of weary soldiers on the march. A petty officer was using his gun butt to beat an emaciated soldier, too sick and weak to keep up with the rest. Rewi leaped to the road, swung the officer away, and cursed him in such explosive and explicit Chinese that I am sure he beat no more soldiers that day.

Farther on, in a village where the truck stopped for water, Rewi got into conversation with a party of young conscripts resting beside the road. They were roped together like slaves, as conscripts nearly always were in Kuomintang China. One boy, hardly more than thirteen or fourteen, had been able to work his arms out of his shackles and implored for help in getting away; the armed conscript guards were in a tea shop on the other side of the road, partly out of sight. Rewi was sitting on the edge of the truck near the conscripts and as we started up again, he dangled one leg over the side and called to the boy. The child leaped up and clung to the leg, his feet braced against the side, until we were clear of the village. Then he dropped off into the fields where he had a fair chance of escaping safely home.

On the first day out of Chengtu, we traveled through cloud-covered, dully verdant country where the rice fields had been flooded but not yet planted, and half the landscape was water. The distant gray hills were aligned like rows of sleeping animals. By the road, hive-shaped sugar mills sent up twin columns of smoke and steam, one black, the other pure white. At the approach of the truck, silvery herons would fly up from the funeral groves among the empty sugar fields, taking to the air with long skipping motions of legs and wings.

Next morning, the sky was faintly blue and between their bleached banks the streams flashed a clear obsidian green, roaring as they tumbled the round white rocks down their winding beds. There was frost on the hilltops but in the sunlight of the sheltered valleys, the palms and other evergreens glistened with subtropical luxuriance. When the road broke over a summit, the whole world fell away in a sea of striped green and rust-colored hills, except in the north where dark blue mountains hulked across the horizon like a line of great indistinct boxes. Siberian cranes wheeled overhead, and Muscovy ducks with black and white wings rocked their bottoms in the rushing rivers. A double row of ancient cypresses stood beside the motor road, shading the remains of the ancient stone highway from Chengtu to Sian, along which the armies of so many dynasties had campaigned with their bannered spears. On some crests, great red and yellow temples decayed among their black pines, the same shrines which had been battled over in fact and legend since the period of the Three Kingdoms, two thousand years before.

As we approached Kwangyuen at the end of the second day's travel from Chengtu, North China began to appear. This town was built on the north bank of the Chialing River and as the truck came up to the southern shore, a party of farmers were plowing the flooded ricefields beside the road. They used water-buffalo, the work animal common from here south to Indo-China, and in the last light of the watery afternoon sun, the rice shoots in the seedling beds glistened as pure and summery a shade of emerald as could be found anywhere in all the green rice-growing half of the country which lay behind. Beyond the fields the wide Chialing River circled east and south toward Chungking, filled with the junks and sampans which carried so much of the traffic of the southern, river-laced half of the country. But its northern bank was covered with camels, the ships of the dry North, and crowds of men in the fur hats of the North and men in the turbans of the South were carrying goods from camels to the ships, from the ships to the camels: wheat, hides, wool, from the North for the South; rice, salt, spices from the South for the North. Above the caravans the huddled roofs of Kwangyuen had a gray, northern look. Beyond them, on the bare, red-streaked foothills of the Tsinling Range, dark clouds had settled and seemed ready for snow.

All the way up to Kwangyuen, the whole magnificent landscape had been enormously populated: I don't think our truck broke down once outside the sound of human voices. Everywhere in the water of the ricefields and on the islands made by the groves and villages, men, women, and children were intently busy. The strangeness of so much they were doing, and the unfamiliar rhythms with which they did it, gave them the air of dancers or mimes moving before their backdrop of beautiful hills and valleys. On one slope, a bound-footed woman climbed with a fantastic, towering burden of leaves on her back, her face expressionless as her tiny feet trotted and pecked in a private little jig. Three children in a thicket, tramping gravely in a circle and holding sticks which revolved one stone upon another, looked like figures in a ceremony. The carrier coolies on the road waltzed along with the rhythm of their stride keyed by the supple undulations of their carrying poles. The clusters of men tamping the highway by flinging a carved stone aloft with ropes seemed to be performing rather than laboring.

Nevertheless, this journey finally stripped me of all feeling that the figures in the Chinese countryside were somehow in a ballet for the pleasure of Western travelers. Nobody could have kept such a notion while traveling with Rewi. Although his own work was industrial, he saw that the troubles of the peasants underlay all other problems in China. His years of CIC work in small towns and villages had given him an intimate knowledge of them. From his sardonic comments on all we passed, I learned more of what lay behind the appearances than I could have found out in months by myself.

The coolies with the light swinging steps were carrying earth and were guarded by soldiers. They were conscripted road workers and the earth was precious top soil confiscated from their own fields as fill. It would be unprecedented if they were being paid enough for their labor or their earth. The children in the thicket were grinding rice flour for pastries, the fine kind sold in town, not eaten in the country; from their ragged clothes, it was doubtful if they had ever been allowed to eat the sweetmeats they manufactured. The bound-footed woman on the slope was faltering under a burden beyond her strength. In the villages, the picturesque colored papers on the houses, the fresh incense and tapers for the approaching Chinese New Year

— still observed at its traditional time outside Chungking — were pathetic signs of superstition, an expensive and hopeless way of coping with uncomprehended troubles. The bold mottoes painted on the public buildings — which I assumed were war slogans — more often advised local obedience than national resistance: OBEY THE LEADER AND RECONSTRUCT THE COUNTRY, OBEY THE LEADER AND OBSERVE THE THREE PEOPLE'S PRINCIPLES.

The strange costumes and attitudes of the folk by the road soon became less noticeable than their limbs knotted in ugly lumps by years of overexertion, their wrists and ankles thickened with malnutrition, their hair dull and their eyes glistening with disease. Even the splendor of the landscape was tainted by human misery: the peculiar trees, like powder puffs on sticks, looked that way because generations of farmers hunting every possible stick of firewood had torn off all the lower branches as they grew. By the old stone highway, the imperial cypresses bore pink scars where bark and limbs had been freshly ripped away by the shivering. The spirit of this remote and exotic part of the world was less expressed by the golden pheasants we sometimes saw stepping fancifully about in the underbrush than by the dead, abandoned soldier we passed in a stream, facing the sky with unserene face as the cold water eddied around his waist and shoulders.

On the third day out of Chengtu, beyond Kwangyuen, the truck had one of its breakdowns in a gorge of the Chialing, where the road was cut high into a cliff, and the valley walls plunged straight into the river in a tumble of white boulders. The river was deep and

quiet here, so clear that the rocks on its bottom were almost as distinct as those on its shores. Floating down its unrippled surface, the junks and sampans below the road seemed to be sliding through the air on a thin sheet of green glass. Just up the valley, on the opposite side, stood the remains of a pavilion where legend claimed that Su Tung-po and other great dead poets had come for inspiration. On the same side as the road, a modern ruin of a shack hung on a ledge, and while the chauffeur poked into the engine with a twig, we passengers walked ahead to see if we could buy tea or boiled water.

The woodcutter and wife who lived in the shack had nothing but cold river-water to sell; they never afforded themselves hot water, they said, except on New Year's day and the other great holidays, and even then could not pay for tea leaves. Rewi lingered to talk with them after the other passengers had gone disgustedly back to the truck. The woodcutter — actually a bush and straw cutter since most of the real trees on these mountains were already gone — said he farmed a tiny patch of inherited land farther up the slope, but it was only by selling fuel that he was able to live from day to day. He seldom had any money at night; he and his wife could not eat in the mornings until he had sold enough fuel in town to buy porridge. His taxes came to three dollars a year, but he could only meet them if he planted beans and corn illegally, in hidden crannies of the mountains which did not belong to him. Times had been a little better, he said, when his three sons were alive, but they had all died long ago, of "sickness." He said more than twice that it was bitter to be old with no sons. He had never heard of Su Tung-po, indeed he didn't know what a poet was.

All the rest of that day we traveled through higher hills, rocky and mostly denuded of trees, and as the cultivated valleys dwindled, Rewi pointed out how the grave mounds were always located in the good level farmland. Even in the open country they broke up the fields; near the town and large villages, acres of the richest land were planted with the dead instead of food for the living.

Graves were believed to block off nearly one tenth of the best land in China, Rewi said; then he stared moodily at the mounds we were passing, the newer ones feebly decorated with sticks of punk and strips of colored paper. At length he snapped with grim pleasantry that if *he* were the modern emperor, he would round up every priest and wizard and geomancer who selected grave sites, and warn them they would have their heads chopped off if they didn't make people bury their dead in the hills and plant trees at the corners of the graves. That might solve the deforestation problem too, he added savagely.

The fourth day out of Chengtu, we drove into Shensi Province and crossed the Tsinling Mountains. On the southern side of the range it was bitterly cold; the clouds pressed in with snow flurries and little drifts began to form in the crevices where the northernmost palms sheltered, their fringed leaves incongruously laced with white. One of the high, icy winds from north of the weather barrier must have tangled with a wet cloudbank strayed up from the south. At the summit, in wild country covered with thickets, Rewi was reminded how full and ravenous this empty-looking land really was. On an earlier trip, he noticed a bus which had broken down and been temporarily abandoned. The mountain peasants had already torn up its engine and stolen the parts to sell. He didn't think they could make off with the chassis so he sent a CIC truck back to salvage that, but before it got there, the chassis was gone too.

Beyond the pass the clouds thinned away, and our truck coasted briskly down the northern slopes. This country was wintry in that it was leafless, but its colors as well as its weather made a cheerful contrast to the cloudy, morosely green, ravines farther south.

Under a cobalt sky, the bare loess clay hills of the North stretched away in tawny orange billows tinged with red, purple, and yellow. Along the white sands at the bottom of the arid valleys, lines of poplars stood like silvery feathers. At longer intervals, there were larger trees, their gnarled black branches hooked like the claws of a dragon. In the center of the vivid sky, without a trace of mist or cloud to obscure it, burned the great fat sun which had hardly touched Chungking since November. Its strong light glittered on the sandy earth, creating real warmth in the windless hollows. Up the road from Paochi came a caravan of wooden carts with rubber-tired auto wheels taken from cars abandoned in the "Roadless Areas" or those broken down because of the Japanese blockade on auto parts. They were hauling furs and crude oil to the South. As the drivers urged their horses and mules up the slope, the staccato cracking of their long whips was just the right music for this ruddy, vibrant landscape.

Rewi remarked on the brakes the carts used — heavy wooden beams pressed on the outer surface of the tires. They had been invented an unknown number of centuries ago, he said, for wooden wheels with iron tires. He pointed out how they were ruining these rubber ones, expensive and irreplaceable now. With some discouragement he said this was typical of a problem he was always meeting in the Co-ops. He would introduce a new Western method or device, and would later find that an ancient habit or technique he never dreamed of warning against had been tacked on, cutting into the improvement. He looked gloomy for a while, but the next time the truck broke down, he took out a pencil and paper and whistled as he began designing a wooden brake which would press on the inner metal rim of a cart's auto wheels.

Much later in the war, when foreign correspondents were allowed to fly from Chungking to Yenan, the Chinese Communist capital in northern Shensi, and returned with favorable reports, Kuomintang spokesmen suggested that the innocent foreigners had been carried away by eternal differences of geography and weather and population: that these inexperienced observers had come to the political conclusions because of such non-political facts as the clear desert climate of Yenan which made the poorest look rosy, and the fogs of Chungking which made even the Generalissimo pale. I never got to Yenan, but remember that in traveling that first time out from the miasmas of Szechuan, into the sunlit stretches of the North, I grew my most flourishing crop of illusions about Kuomintang China.

Down the long hill from the Tsinling Pass, everything looked fine in the sun; Rewi seemed pleased to get back to the north too, and kept his acid comments to himself. The farmhouses were a bit more ruined than those on the Szechuan side, but the people were taller and thicker and browner, and they grinned and waved at the truck. The village streets had been cleanly swept for the old New Year holiday period and many families in their annual new suits of blue padded cotton were wandering around, bowing to each other and shooting off firecrackers. In Shuangshihpu — "Twin Rock Village" — the first big settlement, there were freshly whitewashed buildings and busy new shops and stores. Over the roofs, the scarlet and blue Kuomintang flags looked bright, and behind a high wall a chorus of young men — pupils in a private school for officers' children, I later learned — were singing "San Min Chu Yi," the Kuomintang anthem, with skill and enthusiasm.

All the way from Chengtu, Rewi had filled my ear with talk about his Co-ops. They sounded millennial, but at Shuangshihpu appeared the first faint cloud on the prospect. He and I had been planning to stop off here, because the year before he had sent a few hundred dollars of his remaining savings to the Shuangshihpu CIC, and had asked that a house be built for him; he had no other home in any country and all he wanted in this Co-op center he often passed through was a one-room shack with an open fireplace. On the road from Chengtu he had boasted he was a householder with a hearth, while all I needed to be a professional tramp was a cane I could flute through. But at Shuangshihpu we spent two polite hours in the CIC hostel while, with much uneasy laughter, it was gradually revealed that his house was not yet built. The local CIC people had decided a one-room house hardly suited the dignity of their foreign friend and had used official Co-op funds to build a house of six large rooms. Then they felt one man could not use so much space and divided most of it into quarters for themselves. Next they realized Mr. Alley would not like living in a crowd and planned to build another house for him. That would take more time, and as Alley's money had already gone into the six-room house, it would take more funds. Rewi would have no hearth this trip, but for a man of his sanguine temper this was a small inconvenience. With many smiles on both sides, we took our leave and remounted the truck to go on to Paochi, over the last range.

This city at the foot of the Tsinling Mountains, near the head of a corridor of fairly flat country which led from the western uplands out to the Yellow River and on to the great plains of the northern coast, seemed at first to be the fabled wartime China at its best. Though the Lunghai Railway was being extended into the mountains farther west, with rails and ties salvaged from the "Roadless Areas," Paochi was still the inland terminus of the Kuomintang's one remaining line in North China. The locomotives chuffing in the yards, whistling and sending up columns of steam, were the first heartening sign to the traveler that he had emerged from isolated Szechuan, into a separate world of more normal trade and industry and war.

At the western end of the narrow city, strung out between the ice-choked Wei River and a high loess clay bluff, stood the pre-war town, a county capital with medieval walls and a few crumbling temples and yamens, where some ten thousand native Paochi people lived in sleepy squalor. Stretching east of the railway station, lay the grid of modern streets lined with new shops and homes and factories where the prosperous refugee population of seventy or eighty thousand had settled. The main street here was more citified than anything in Chungking, with wide graveled traffic lanes, brick sidewalks, newly planted trees, and buildings lacking that Chungking look of having been hurriedly pasted together from mud, laths, and paper. There were even large panes of glass in the windows of these rarely bombed stores and banks. Our truck came in at dusk and the lavish electric lights, burning full strength, were dazzling after the feeble, half-power glow of the capital.

But Paochi was admirable for more than its physical amenities, which would have been surpassed in a smaller American town. The refugee city had been built during a few months of great stress, just before and after the fall of Hankow. In the summer of 1938, this had been the farthest western point which could be reached directly by rail from the doomed temporary capital. Thousands of families, and whole

factories, schools, and government bureaus had made the trip. When
Hankow fell in October, the plain around old Paochi and its railway
station was a sea of people, animals, tents, huts, crated merchandise
and machinery. As the winter winds blew down over the bluff and
it could be hoped that the Japanese were through with their conquests
for that year, the building began.

When Rewi and his Chinese and foreign associates founded the CIC
at Hankow, they had realized that geography and war would make
Paochi important and used their first funds — a loan of five million
Kuomintang dollars from the government — for developing the Paochi
area. They sent organizers up from Hankow before the mass evacuation began, and by lobbying with T. V. Soong, H. H. Kung, and
Madame Chiang, all favorably disposed to the CIC in those days of

emergency, they got a young and progressive official, friendly to the
CIC, appointed Magistrate of the county. The first Industrial Co-op
in China was soon organized in Paochi, and dozens more were set up
in the next few months, as the refugees poured in and many grew
destitute.

The new magistrate, busy laying out the wide streets and other
unique features of his county seat, was willing and able to protect the
CIC from the few politicians and manufacturers who saw it as a radical movement. Perhaps more important, private interests were holding back until they were sure what the Japanese would do next; meanwhile they were willing to leave business risks to anyone foolish
enough to take them. By the time I went to Paochi, there were over
seventy Co-ops in its neighborhood, employing about five thousand
workmen. They made wool and cotton yarn and cloth, leather and
leather goods including shoes; rope, soap, charcoal, and many other
commodities. There were carpenters' and blacksmiths' Co-ops, a printers' Co-op, a transport Co-op. The Paochi CIC Federation had a marketing department for wholesale disposal of goods, plus three retail
stores on the Paochi main street. It supported a primary school for
the children of members, a series of night classes for adults, and a small
hospital. It ran a bank, and a consumers' Co-op where members could
buy non-CIC goods at wholesale prices.

On the truck from Chengtu, I had learned that the CIC plan was
simple in words. When the organizers from Central CIC Headquarters came into a locality, they made a survey to find where the war
had created unemployment, where a market was not being filled, or a
supply of raw materials not used. Then they set up small industries
to fill the gaps, raising as much of the capital as they could among the
workmen themselves, supplementing it with loans from the CIC Headquarters and, whenever possible, from the local or state banks. As
soon as there were enough Co-ops to justify it, a Federation would
be organized to run the wholesale marketing and other services. To
some extent, the Federations were financed with the annual grant from
the government; to a slightly larger extent, they depended on the relief
funds from abroad. For the rest, the CIC was self-supporting.

Each Co-op had to have at least seven members and every member
had to own at least one share of his Co-op's stock. Only the workman
in a Co-op could own its stock. None could own more than one
fourth of the total. Wages and working hours were settled by vote

in a general meeting, with every member casting an equal vote, no matter how little stock he owned. Daily work was carried on under an elected foreman, and frequent "Examine-Discuss" meetings were held to consider plans and problems. Members, or a foreman, accused of shirking, dishonesty, or other "un-co-operative conduct" could be expelled by a majority vote. If it were more practical for the members to live together in their place of business, as it usually was, a kitchen and dormitory were run by an elected committee, with or without paid help.

Profits could be divided at the end of the year in any way a Co-op voted, but the organizers tried to persuade the members to put one fifth back into their business. They advised them to set aside one tenth for medical attention and better living conditions in the Co-op, and asked them to pay another tenth to the local Federation for its services. The rest was divided among the members.

I was impressed with the Co-ops right from the first evening in Paochi, when we were put up at the CIC Regional Headquarters, in the house of Lu Kwang-mien, Director for the Northwest. The compound was at the far end of the old walled town and to step from the littered street with its tawdry shop fronts, into an enclosure of plain whitewashed walls, neatly swept courts, and simple sensible furnishings, was as surprising as entering a foreign mission or treaty-port compound with its elaborate imported furniture — more so, because nothing here was imported, not even the determination which had made the change.

It was the same next day, when I followed Rewi on his inspection of half a dozen Co-ops. The members must have tidied up because he was expected, but it couldn't all have been done for him. Wherever they were — in a line of caves, an abandoned temple, a collection of mat sheds — the Co-ops were marked off from the slatternly places of the local people and the pauper refugees, and the fancy ones of the rich refugees, by a busy, modest air of industry, care, direction, proceedings propriety: it was hard to define, though it was as distinctive and ubiquitous as the CIC emblem which Rewi had invented by combining the YMCA triangle and the Chinese characters for "Gung Ho" — "Work Together."

Most Co-op machines were homemade wooden ones or salvaged metal ones, some reclaimed with wooden parts, and polished and oiled as if they were the newest imported equipment. The workrooms and living quarters were swept and whitewashed, and the older structures had been modified for more light and air. There were slogans and graphs posted by the organizers, cheerful pictures and decorations hung by the members. In the dormitories each bed was flanked by a careful arrangement of toilet articles — personal dirt was a form of "un-co-operative conduct" which could be criticized in the "Examine-Discuss" meetings. Dressed in simple cotton uniforms, the members themselves were the best proof that something new was going on here. Smiling, confident, a little proud in a shy way, they were plainly constructing a compartment of life very different from the poverty-struck landscape between Chungking and Paochi. In the Co-op stores, the piles of slightly homemade-looking, but sturdy and well-made, goods spoke better of the movement than could Rewi, his organizers, or their graphs.

My enthusiasm for the CIC reached its peak on the second or third night after we reached Paochi, when the whole Federation collected for a mass meeting to welcome Rewi. This assembly was held in the auditorium of the Northwest Headquarters, a hall of what had once been a great landlord's house. The dark old carved ceiling had been whitewashed and on the walls were murals of idealized factories. The program began with short speeches by Lu Kwang-mien and some of the organizers, but Rewi was the main feature. From the laughter which preceded the stories he told to open his talk, it seemed that most of the audience had heard and liked his speech every time he came to Paochi. I knew their reaction was just what he wanted; he had told me the easiest way to get along with people who were suspicious of foreigners was to make the state of being a foreigner seem ridiculous. Much as some cripples or odd-size people try to turn away condescension by light mention of their handicap, he told his audience of silly fixes he had got into because of his great nose and red hair. When he had them well with him, he went on into the ideas about the CIC which I had been hearing since Chengtu. They followed something like this:

You could see the nature of China's past industrialization in any one of the hundreds of thousands of country markets where the trade was in cloth, shoes, and household and farm equipment for the peasants. Most of these goods came from old-fashioned handicraft shops, whose stock was of types developed centuries ago and still made in the laborious old ways. Few were manufactured by modern industrial methods. Since machine-made goods required a larger investment by the manufacturer, they had to be more expensive than handmade goods, at least in the beginning. There was little demand for them. The peasants could not afford anything but the cheapest. The press of overpopulation and poverty made hand labor terribly cheap.

The larger country towns had a certain number of stores which sold simple and useful manufactured goods, particularly cloth, even in the years when such things had to be smuggled from enemy territory. These goods were of the same general quality and price as those used by the farmers and workmen — the majority of the people — in any Western country. But in the interior of China they could be enjoyed only by the middle and upper class, a tiny minority. Furthermore, a great number of the manufactured goods sold in any provincial town were outright luxuries or useless novelties — fancy mirrors and thermos bottles, drinking glasses with Mickey Mouse etched on them, boudoir lamps in skyscraper style, trick clocks in the shape of boats or cottages, and many gadgets for smoking or painting the face. In a way, all stores selling manufactured articles were toy shops for the few well-to-do Chinese, who often bought Western-style goods as much for amusement or prestige as for use.

As these stores suggested, modern industry had so far touched only the surface of China, around its outer edges. It had helped unbalance the old rural economy but had not produced a new industrial economy. Nine out of every ten modern factories were in Shanghai and the rest were in a handful of other coastal or river cities. Taken together, they represented less industrial power than a small Western country like Belgium had.

China could not start an industrial revolution like that of the West until more Chinese could afford to use manufactured goods in their daily lives. That was why Industrial Co-operatives were a sensible solution. With the workmen co-owners of their small industries, sharing their profits, they increased their own purchasing power as their business grew. The CIC created its own market as it expanded. The Co-ops manufactured serviceable goods of the sort ordinary people needed, at prices they could afford. Since the Co-ops started as very small industries, often using handicraft methods at first, they had no great overhead forcing them to charge high prices.

CIC could also attack China's basic problem, the poverty of the farming peasants. With the workmen their own employers, setting their own hours and tasks, part-time or part-year Co-ops could be organized in the villages, helping the farmers supplement their income during the winter and other times of idleness. At present, only a few who would like to set up as part-time weavers or blacksmiths or potters could find the money to start. If seven or more pooled their resources in a Co-op, they would almost certainly have enough.

CIC had been founded as a patriotic wartime movement, and as such it was still important. In a long war like this one, economic factors were crucial. Free China would have become a better place to live in than occupied China, if it were to win. Co-op goods and jobs could help. If CIC ended the war successfully — and there was no reason why it could not become a nation-wide net of growing industries before victory — it would influence all post-war business. Private industrialists would never again be able to employ workmen under the conditions of semi-slavery which had prevailed in the coastal factories before the war. The Co-ops could help keep coastal industry from again becoming a trinket, manufacturing trinkets on the edge of the country. They could help prevent China from returning to its old position as an open and inert market for goods from other countries.

It was in the political and social fields, however, that the CIC could be of greatest service. China was on its way toward democracy, by the declared intention of both the government and the people. Co-operative work was the best way of making the people ready for it. Co-ops could succeed only when their members had developed individual and group responsibility. Democracy could succeed only through these traits.

In China, poverty made it hard for such characteristics to grow, since they developed more smoothly among men who had some economic security. Here again, the CIC was leading the way. By improving his own livelihood through a co-operative, democratic organization, each CIC member could feel he was working for his country's future.

No matter how many times they had heard this speech before, the Paochi CIC audience, their faces upturned, now wore the expression of a family who had just been told those old books in the attic were first folios of Shakespeare. Rewi sat down to thunderous applause. Tea and peanuts and melon seeds were passed around and the rest of the evening was given over to volunteer entertainment.

This was more of the new world, or at least the new compartment. It wasn't just the clean, healthy faces and substantial, unpretentious clothes, though there were more of both in the auditorium than could be found among many times this number of people on the average Chinese street. The difference lay more in the prevailing air of self-assurance, of unworried gaiety, of family solidarity and even familiarity, which infused both the amateur performers and the audience, both the educated — technically upper class — organizers and administrators and accountants, and the workmen and their families. Obviously, this was something not only valued but new and unaccustomed. As the performers popped on and off the stage, heckled by the audience and heckling it back, the gaiety was often naïve foolishness, the confidence verged on bumptiousness, and the familiarity on riot. I had never seen anything like it in China, where Kuomintang meetings were characterized by cold impressiveness and respect. The only comparable meetings I could think of were the "social evenings" I remembered from my days as a Boy Scout Cub.

There were nearly two hours of songs and other specialties. A young organizer imitated barnyard noises, then an air-raid siren, and a charcoal-burning truck breaking down on a long hill, all very popular. A covey of little girls from the CIC kindergarten sang a gibberish Japanese song they had made up themselves; it was all "tuk-tuk-tuk" and "br-br-br" and sounded like a clock picking up speed to the point of explosion. Half a dozen bound-footed old farm women from a spinning Co-op were urged on the stage by unanimous cheers and when they finished a spell of giggling more girlish than the kindergarten performers, they gave a fine wailing rendition of a village folk song about a little shepherd who flirted with a girl from the sky. Later an engineer from the coast crooned a love song from a pre-war Shanghai movie, in the early Bing Crosby style with "buh-buh-buh-buh" at the end of each verse. He was followed by a chauffeur from the transport Co-op, a native of the Kansu border, who half chanted, half shouted a gusty Tibetan ditty about the personal life of the camel.

The floor of the auditorium gradually disappeared under drifts of peanut shells, its roof in a haze of cigarette smoke.

The party ended toward midnight, with group singing. Rising to their feet with the solemnity of Boy Scouts about to sing the "Star Spangled Banner," the men and women put the most possible volume into four or five of the moving war songs which had been widely sung in the early years of the invasion, but were now so seldom heard. Between songs there was a burst of rifle fire not far away, apparently on the loess bluff overlooking town. It was clearly audible in the warm, glary auditorium but nobody paid attention to the disturbance in the night.

"What's that?" I asked the organizer standing next to me.

"Bandits, I suppose," he laughed. "Soldiers. Deserters. The ones who escaped from their armies before they starved to death and are afraid they will be conscripted again if they go back home. There have been more of them in the mountains every year, and this winter they have been plundering right down to the edge of town."

8 · *Good Intentions*

REWI willingly admitted he had suggested I come along with him because he hoped he could rush me into writing optimistic articles about the CIC, to help raise funds abroad; the news that the Co-ops were getting along wonderfully always made foreign friends more anxious to help. But he was too honest to misrepresent the CIC and it was largely through him that my optimism about the Co-ops was soon impaired. The singers in the auditorium could ignore the rifles on the hillside, but their movement could not be made invulnerable against the society in which it grew.

I roomed with Rewi at Paochi and as soon as word spread that he had arrived, Co-op workmen, organizers, and administrators poured in to see him from dawn to bedtime. Each visitor had his special grievance or problem, and in a few days my clear, simple idea of the CIC was obscured by a tangle of troubles, intrigues, and failures. This was a vastly complex organization, tottering always on the edge of bankruptcy, hounded by political opposition, balked by ignorance and backwardness, buffeted by war and weather, and composed of fallible human creatures.

At first it was only the smaller details which did not seem promising: a ropemaking Co-op had misappropriated funds to whitewash its buildings for Rewi's visit; one shoemakers' Co-op had begun making luxury styles for the higher profits, while another had let its workmanship slip so badly that it could not compete with the private shops. The carefully inked graphs in all CIC offices and workrooms, with their upward-swooping lines for the increasing sums in capitalization, production, profits, charted not so much Co-op success as Kuomintang inflation. The numbers were bigger for each month, but in many cases the value was less.

After the first flush of arrival had worn off, I had to recognize that the CIC was not particularly influential even in Paochi, its model city.

Workmen in private Paochi industry far outnumbered those in the Co-ops, and the CIC example had not changed their working conditions. For the three retail stores selling Co-op goods on the main street, there were at least a hundred selling goods from private sources. The most successful sold smuggled goods from Japanese territory. Private merchants and manufacturers, no longer afraid of further Japanese advances, had re-entered business and were stirring up opposition to the CIC.

But I do not intend to detail all the specific Co-op difficulties I heard about in that long-past winter. Looking back from the present, they seem unimportant, the trivial misadventures of a minor organization which was later to sink steadily toward failure. When I went to Paochi in 1941 the CIC still had more than two thousand Co-ops, some of them quite large and prosperous, scattered all over China. Eight years afterwards, in the winter of 1948–49, when the Communists started their march down to the Yangtse and the Generalissimo's government disintegrated in flight, there were a number of Communist-run Co-ops in Communist territory but only about three hundred Co-ops survived in Kuomintang territory, most of them small and nearly out of business.

These later events, however, have given the CIC more meaning as a symbol. While the CIC's philosophy was democratic-socialist instead of capitalist, it must be classed with the other Western influences which tried to help China change by reform rather than revolution. Its failure is symbolic of the failure of the whole Western effort. The CIC's general difficulties may recur in some form in the other Asiatic countries which seem to be approaching a state of crisis like China's.

I began to see how deeply compromised by their surroundings the Co-ops could be on a morning when I went out with Rewi and the Regional Director, Lu Kwang-mien, to inspect a CIC "Experimental Factory" making blankets for the Kuomintang armies. This was the largest CIC production unit anywhere in China and important apart from its size, since the contract from the Supreme Military Council, for half a million blankets, was one of the few tokens of favor recently shown the CIC by the higher ranks of the Kuomintang. For political reasons, the blankets had to be finished to the Council's specifications of time and quality. Because of the inflation, they also had to be done before the cost of production exceeded the Council's price.

As CIC organization, with all its benefits, was unavoidably slow, it had been impossible for Co-ops to do the job. Instead, the wool was being twisted into yarn on a piecework basis by several thousand home laborers: farmers' wives, school children, prostitutes, even Japanese soldiers in the Paochi camp for prisoners of war. In the big factory, the wool was woven into blankets by several hundred boys — child labor, to be exact. The "Experimental Factory" was not a Co-op in any sense and was "Experimental" only in that it was run by the CIC. The boys did have better working conditions and pay than they would have had in a private sweatshop and presumably would be organized into Co-ops, with full rights and privileges, as soon as the pressure for blankets slackened, and the boys grew up a bit. Meanwhile, their blankets for the Kuomintang were vital to the future of all real Co-ops.

The factory was outside Paochi, across the Wei River. We arrived at noon, just as the boys were swarming out of the walled yard, streaming to their dormitories for lunch. There was a great tree not far from the gate, with a long rope swing, and some of the workers were acting their age, screaming with laughter as they pushed a friend up into the frosty sunlight. Then a squad of heavily armed soldiers came running down the hill behind us. The first group rushed along a prisoner, a fat, disheveled, weeping man with his arms tied together at the back of his purple sweater. Other soldiers carried a machine gun. Those with the prisoner hauled him into the nearest factory building and, from the sounds, began flogging him. The others set up their machine gun under the tree, its muzzle pointing into the factory yard. The boys still in the yard ran silently behind the factory and those outside scattered out of sight: all except the unlucky youngster in the swing, who helplessly swept up and down right over the gun. After desperate tugging at the ropes, he sprawled off and flopped away through the dust like a wounded bird.

Director Lu seemed to take all this as routine, so we followed him into the factory yard, past the gun and the building resounding with whacks and howls. In the yard behind the factory, full of frightened boys crowding in corners, we found two uneasy-looking gentlemen in civilian uniforms, with black felt hats pulled evenly down to their ear tips. Unsurprised and most polite, Lu greeted them and introduced them as the Magistrate of Paochi and the Chief of the county Kuomintang Party. They were confounded to see us. Lu called two boys to guard the horses of the Chinese visitors whom — with stifling politeness — he ushered into the factory office, leaving two mystified foreigners outside. The confusion in the yard verged on panic when a disreputable old factory stallion, motive power for a wool-carding machine, charged out of its workshop and chased the Magistrate's pretty little black mare.

After a long wait, while the soldiers took their machine gun and prisoner away and all the boys fled to their lunch, Lu reappeared with the men in black hats and smilingly helped them depart. Then he and Rewi and I walked back to Paochi, followed by a screaming woman who had appeared at the factory gate. With operatic rage she informed the whole empty landscape that Lu had no sense of propriety. It had been bad enough for her husband when Lu had him arrested and beaten, but the whole family had lost face when his elbows were tied together behind his back, like a common criminal's.

Rewi had been as ignorant as I of what we were watching, but now he began to get the story from Lu. Mr. Sun — the beaten man in the purple sweater — had been the accountant at the "Experimental Factory." He was one of four saddled on the Regional Headquarters by the Central CIC Headquarters in Chungking which, in the common manner of bureaucracies, was jealous, perhaps a little hostile, toward those in the field who were doing the actual work and getting some prestige for it.

In Paochi the four accountants had been suspected as Central Headquarters spies and perhaps saboteurs, and were carefully watched. They were found incompetent and soon two were caught cooking their accounts. They were dismissed and the watch on the other two, one of them Mr. Sun, was increased. Mr. Sun began to say that the CIC people who claimed they were trying to eliminate corruption were really Communists sabotaging their political opponents. Then he said he had found some of the children in his "Experimental Factory" were Communists too. He began to give them excessive punishments for small, and sometimes imagined, offenses: making them kneel half a day in the yard, and so on. Later he said these boys had threatened to kill him. He collected a private and illegal arsenal of pistols and hand grenades, bought from deserters.

Shortly before Rewi and I arrived in Paochi, Director Lu had announced he was going off on a trip. Mr. Sun immediately called on the Magistrate of Paochi and the Kuomintang Party Chief, declaring he had uncovered a Communist plot in the "Experimental Factory." If the officials would meet him at the factory after Lu had gone, he would point out the children who had "dangerous thoughts." But there was still a choice of geese to be cooked. The Co-op members who were watching Mr. Sun had told Director Lu of the private arsenal and the secret plan with the officials.

As in all provinces under the Kuomintang, the politics of Shensi were then in a snarl. The most important groups were the CC clique under the Chen brothers, and the Whampoa clique of army men who had studied at the Whampoa Military Academy. The civil governor was a CC "man" and had filled most of the important civilian posts with his "men." The provincial military commander – General Hu Chung-nan, in charge of the blockade line against the Communists in northern Shensi – was a Whampoa "man," as were the garrison commanders of most Shensi towns.

Director Lu, born in Manchuria, belonged to the remains of the Manchurian regional group which had run this province before the Sian Incident, when their leader, the Young Marshal, was blockading the Communists. Through personal ties, however, Lu could also consider himself enough of a "man" of the Whampoa Clique to ask favors of its other members. The Paochi Magistrate and Party Chief were CC "men." As soon as Lu heard of Mr. Sun's plot, he called on the Paochi garrison commander, a Whampoa "man" who was their rival, and arranged to have garrison soldiers arrest Sun and bring him to the "Experimental Factory" at just the time Sun was to meet the civil officials there. When Rewi and I arrived, he made sure we went with him to complete his opponents' loss of face by providing a foreign audience.

While Lu and the Magistrate and the Party Chief were closeted in

the factory office and the two horses kicked up their heels, the troublesome case of Mr. Sun had naturally not been solved and indeed was hardly discussed; both sides found it more convenient to pretend this was a social call. The later unraveling of the affair was as typical as its winding.

It developed that Mr. Sun was himself allied with the CC clique, which was currently infiltrating the Central Co-op Headquarters in Chungking. Sun's pathological state and illegal weapons were apparently less important than his powerful connections. In the Paochi military jail he made sensationally foolish charges against the CIC — "they sing Communist songs for hours" — and hysterical demands for a special plane to fly him to Chungking so he could tell all to the Generalissimo. Nevertheless, certain important people in Sian, the provincial capital, soon arranged for his unconditional release.

He went to Sian where he ran an advertisement for five days in the newspapers saying he "had been in trouble and in jail in Paochi but was now honorably discharged and would soon go to Chungking on secret business." The next time Director Lu visited Sian, Mr. Sun tried to have him roughed up by professional rowdies but by then Lu was traveling with an armed bodyguard. Sun did finally go off toward Chungking on an official truck, full of threats. The last I heard of him, months later, he had gone on a sit-down strike in Chengtu, claiming he had enough anti-Communist information to get him a special plane at least from Chengtu to Chungking. He finally accepted a "special" seat on a public plane. Nothing more was ever heard of him or his accusations after he got to Chungking.

On the surface, this incident might seem to represent a victory for the CIC. Actually, it showed that far from reforming the society around it, a limited reform movement like the CIC was itself more likely to be corrupted. That "Experimental Factory" employed child labor because of outside political and economic pressures. The craftiness with which Director Lu liquidated the incident was a quality he had had to learn from Kuomintang politics for self-preservation: the personal ambitions he had learned along with his guile were already corrupting him in 1941, tempting him to play his own balance-of-weakness game within the CIC, harmfully juggling men about in his Regional Headquarters. His ambitions were later to lead him to abandon the CIC for a high-paying, do-nothing job under the Kuomintang.

Rewi's favorite explanation of the CIC dilemma was this: "We're trying to do it at the wrong time. We are a thousand years too early for the officials and a thousand years too late for the people." With hindsight, I think he may have touched on the crux of the whole Western problem of influencing China toward reform instead of revolution.

Any kind of modern reform had to uncover Kuomintang weaknesses and provoke countermeasures, of types which would be unexpected to anyone unfamiliar with this anachronistic government. Despite all its hullabaloo about communism, I do not think the Kuomintang was particularly hostile to the CIC for the reason which might cause American hostility: the Co-ops' rivalry to private enterprise. The Kuomintang's own plans called for state monopolies which would take all important industry out of the hands of private businessmen.

Instead, it seemed the Kuomintang was fearful and suspicious because of the CIC aims which would be most commended in America: its progress toward better working conditions, its efforts in education, health, and social services. That the CIC was trying to teach workmen to secure these benefits by unity and democratic co-operation, instead of waiting for a paternalist government to award them, was a political explosive. Once the advantages of any kind of independent unity were demonstrated anywhere in Kuomintang China, a spreading demand for all types of unity might set off a chain reaction, capable of vaporizing the Kuomintang's whole carefully built house of confusions.

The Kuomintang consequently fought the CIC as it had the regional régimes, with the difference that it did not want to destroy the CIC completely. By 1941, its atttiude was plainly one of disapproval, but it seemed unwilling to liquidate the Co-ops or even to stop supporting them, apparently for fear of bad publicity abroad.

The Kuomintang controlled the CIC through the Chungking Central Headquarters, a purely bureaucratic superstructure. All top posts in the Headquarters were held by official appointees and the government was able to inject confusion by constant "reorganizations" — reshuffling of appointees — in the Headquarters Committees. During the period when I was hearing about the CIC, these seemed to come at least once a year, hindering the development of any long-range plans. Moreover, the whole administrative side of the movement was infiltrated with enough central "men" and their "men" to check any industrial prosperity or real social unity. Promising non-central men were removed by intimidation or the bribe of better-paying jobs elsewhere.

Out in the field, the Kuomintang did not usually take action unless any group of Co-ops became successful. One reason why the Paochi Co-ops were having many difficulties when I was there was that they had been expanding rapidly in the two previous years. When it later became plain that they were beginning to wither, Kuomintang pressure was relaxed. The same thing was to happen repeatedly in following years. Local Co-ops were officially ignored, sometimes even helped, until they became successful enough to represent a real reform. Then they were reduced and left to continue their unsuccessful struggles.

This was a useful technique because never in the long period of the CIC's decline could its supporters be sure that their future was hopeless. The best CIC people were idealists and optimists or they would never have joined. The gradualness with which their movement was brought to a standstill always let them hope that somewhere else, some other time, their Co-ops might really succeed. They stayed on, deflected from activity which could be more disagreeable to the Kuomintang; within themselves, they were divided and ruled.

A second means of combating the CIC was economic starvation. Though it still contributed to the CIC budget, the Kuomintang had failed to increase its allowance to keep step with the inflation and in 1941 its monthly grant, for administrative expenses, equaled only eight thousand American dollars. Of that, three thousand was for the bureaucratic Central Headquarters in Chungking.

Sometimes the Kuomintang banks still made loans to the Regional Headquarters or to individual Co-ops, at the regular commercial rates, but these were becoming harder to get. Private merchants and manufacturers who wanted to sabotage the CIC could do it best by lobbying among the bankers, with whom they still had close connections. And even when the Co-ops could get capital, they faced the handicaps of any group who wanted to manufacture rather than hoard. By the time they made their goods, the inflation would usually have raised the price of raw materials so high that they could have realized a paper profit just by selling the materials again; making the goods had been a waste of energy and money. Also, in buying materials and marketing goods, the Co-ops — like private business — were more and more at the mercy of official monopolists.

If all else failed to keep the Co-ops in their assigned place of weakness, the Kuomintang could haul out its favorite political weapon, the accusation of communism. In this backward and tyrannized part of the world, the charges could be even more far-fetched, or more nakedly opportunist, than was usual elsewhere. When, for example, the Generalissimo's nephew rode out to inspect some Co-ops near Sian and fell off his horse, breaking his collarbone, this was rumored to be a CIC-Communist plot, possibly involving a Communist-trained horse.

Opportunist anti-communism could be seen in the difficulty of the Paochi printing Co-op, after its foreman was arrested by some city officials because he had refused to give them squeeze on the printing his Co-op did for their bureau. The members of his Co-op spent a night in front of the jail where the foreman was kept, facetiously weeping in the style customary for funerals. The officials were made to look ridiculous and had to release the foreman, but to save face they arrested a couple of the wailers as Communists. Every fresh rumor or charge of communism made it harder for the CIC to get new loans and personnel.

Even more clearly than in those of its acts against the CIC which I heard about, I think the Kuomintang's general attitude toward reform, and its countermethods, were shown in the case of the earlier magistrate of Paochi, the progressive one who had helped the CIC in its pioneering period.

For more than a year he had been banished from Paochi. If he had confined himself to the surface modernization, the roads and trees which the Kuomintang always approved, he might have survived as an official. But he had tried to change the old methods of taxation and conscription. He had abolished the practice of farming out tax-collection privileges to commercial tax collectors who were even more rapacious than the regular official ones. He had stepped on too many important toes. His enemies — local landlords and more conservative officials — tried to get rid of him by bribing the farmers in a remote part of his county to plant opium, and then charging him with connivance in opium-growing. When he was able to prove the charge was plotted, officials in Sian were persuaded to offer him a better-paying, do-nothing job on the Lunghai Railway. He had been replaced in Paochi by the black-hatted Magistrate of the "Experimental Factory" incident, who abandoned even the work on the streets; when I arrived, piles of construction material, untouched for a year, littered the main avenue outside the East Gate. The increasing number of political arrests, sometimes among CIC people, showed how the energy of county officialdom had been redirected.

The second part of Rewi's summary of the CIC problem — its coming at the wrong time for the people — may be more pertinent now. Among the other Asiatic countries which appear to be moving into a state of revolutionary ferment, I know of none which has a government quite as absurd as the Kuomintang, but a number of these countries seem to show a popular unpreparedness for reform as grave as China's.

In theory, the CIC was a movement which could spread spontaneously among the workmen. In fact, it was a reform which had to be taught from above, at least in the beginning. Among the peasant workmen, decades of deepening poverty had created such superstitious timidity and conservatism — you might say such stupidity — that they suspected anything new, even when it was to their benefit. Co-op organizers in rural areas often met with hostility because the farmers thought they were government spies and feared that their questions about local conditions were research for new taxes. When the Co-ops were set up among the peasants, their work was slowed by unexpected hangovers from the huge black past of ignorance and fear. New buildings, for instance, sometimes could not be raised because workmen feared they would interfere with the geomantic auspices of their village.

In the artisan class in the towns, Co-op organization could be almost as difficult because of the tradition of extremely hard, sly, self-interest which these city-dwellers had adopted to protect themselves in China's modern dog-eat-dog era. While I was in Paochi there were a number

of typical cases. In one shoemaker's Co-op, for example, the elected foreman — an older man who once owned his own shop and had more professional skill than his colleagues — had bullied three members into leaving, reducing the number below the CIC's stipulated seven, and had then browbeat the young boys who were left into letting him run the Co-op as his own sweatshop, for personal profit.

Yet these handicaps from China's decaying past were not insuperable. They might have been diminished if not destroyed within a generation, as soon as the machinery for education and increasing prosperity were set in motion. What was needed was a group of men or women who could patiently explain and coax, inspiring interest and confidence. To be willing to undertake such public work, particularly since the CIC paid low salaries, these men and women had to have a clear understanding of the CIC's motives and place in the country's history. They had to be familiar with modern, Western ideas. They had to be educated.

Among all the hundreds of millions of Chinese, I doubt if the present generation has produced enough educated and progressive Western-style — non-Communist — citizens to fill a small city. Though the CIC was the best-known movement toward economic resistance during the Japanese invasion, it was able to attract less than a thousand. Even during the bloodiest war years the Chinese Red Cross could find only a few hundred modern doctors for the patriotic, poorly paid service which was so needed in the Kuomintang armies; almost all China's Western-trained doctors stayed in private practice and many remained in Japanese territory. During 1946, its year of greatest prestige, when General Marshall recognized it as a liberal third party and used its leaders to mediate between the Kuomintang and the Communists, the Democratic League's national membership was certainly less than twenty thousand adults, possibly less than ten thousand. In the Kuomintang, where some men of good will survived to the end, the really incorruptible and effective Western-influenced leaders have commonly been numbered on two hands, with some fingers left over.

Since it is unlikely that any members of the old ruling minority of China will again hold national power except as the "men" of the Communists, it may seem unnecessary to write about their disabilities now. I intend to do so, though, partly because of the bearing this has on the future American attitude towards China. As this book goes to press, many influential Americans still oppose recognition of the Chinese

Communists and suggest that we should support an upper-class government in exile on the island of Formosa, and an upper-class underground on the mainland. I am sure that such a course of action can end only in failure.

Furthermore, the way the real character of the former ruling minority in China differed from the American idea of it is an example of the special American anthropomorphism which is one of our gravest handicaps in foreign affairs. As a nation, we seem over-eager to attribute our own character to other countries. When we see foreigners who can speak glib American English and seem familiar with our ways, we assume that their minds work like ours. When we notice that a foreign country is buying American automobiles, airplanes, and other goods we like to believe it is becoming modernized in all ways. One of the chief reasons why the Kuomintang was able to get so much American aid was because its relations with us were handled by untypical Americanized Chinese like T. V. Soong and Madame Chiang. I don't suppose I need remind any Americans how widely it used to be assumed that because T. V. Soong could act like an American businessman in a serge suit, and the Madame had been to Wellesley, China must be full of many little replicas of them, ready and able to turn the country into an imitation America. The current notion that the Germans and Japanese are becoming democratic because they play baseball is part of the same American failing.

It was always rather improbable that a society like the American one could be established in China, because of the vast difference in the size and nature of the classes. All that we think best about America — democratic government, a relatively decent industrialization by private interests, a fairly strong tradition of Christian behavior — had to be developed painfully in Western Europe and America over the course of several centuries. The only thing which made this possible was the growth of a middle class with enough economic security for public interests and enough education to use the increasingly complex ideas and techniques of our civilization.

At present, in an average American community of, say, two hundred thousand people, about three quarters of the total — a hundred and fifty thousand — would live in a city or its satellite towns. Only about fifty thousand would live on farms. In city and country alike, almost all adults would be literate enough to read newspapers, to vote, to take an interest in public affairs if they cared to. Almost all would think of themselves as middle class and at least half of them would be middle class or better. About a quarter of the total population would have completed high school. Almost a tenth would have been to college and perhaps half of them would have graduated. In this community of two hundred thousand people, those who had been to college and, by a very rough rule of thumb, qualified as members of our top class would number ten to twenty thousand. Actually, the total of those who understood our civilization and might be leaders would be much greater.

To imagine a Kuomintang community which would be even remotely comparable, one must change the basic figures. In China at least eighty per cent of the people are peasant farmers, so if you are to think of an urban population of a hundred and fifty thousand you must first surround the city with a countryside crowded by some six hundred thousand farming people, instead of the American fifty thousand.

In this mass of peasants, the overwhelming majority would be, for all practical purposes, illiterate. The Kuomintang used to claim that about one quarter of the total population was literate, but as I saw it work out in a number of villages, hardly any peasant farmers could afford to keep their children in school long enough to learn the alphabet of three thousand ideographs necessary for simple newspaper reading. Their general knowledge was also so limited that words describing unfamiliar things were hardly intelligible when spoken or read aloud. Their interest in events outside their farm boundaries was less than the absorption in world affairs which might be expected of a third- or fourth-grader in an American grammar school.

Kuomintang figures for education among city dwellers and others in the non-peasant twenty per cent of the population also seemed exaggerated; the school authorities, like some generals, apparently tried to get more face and funds by reporting they were running a larger operation than they really were. From research I did in several provinces during the Pacific war, I would estimate that in the average community under the Kuomintang much less than half the non-peasant adults, less than ten per cent of the total population, would have gone far enough through school to read a newspaper easily. Those who had gone on through middle school — the equivalent of an American high school — where they could get the general knowledge for an active interest in public affairs would be less than half the literate minority, less than five per cent of all adults.

The number of college graduates would be fantastically small. In my imagined community of some seven hundred and fifty thousand people — obviously a provincial one — I think less than a thousand men and women would be likely to have gone to any kind of modern college. Those who had been able to study in Europe or America, absorbing Western ideas in undiluted form, would probably not be more than ten to twenty individuals, compared with ten to twenty thousand with similar training in the smaller American community.

These estimates are my own guesswork and may be too severe. They do not apply to the few great semi-modern cities where education was farther advanced. Still, I am sure they present a more truthful picture than the American delusion which filled China with many little Madame Chiangs and T. V. Soongs, who would put their country on its feet in Western style as soon as Kuomintang rule could be stabilized with American money and guns.

And when you learned the small number of potential Western-style citizens and leaders, you had only scratched the surface of the problem. Even within this tiny minority, most were influenced by a background which stifled the progressive urges they might have taken from their training.

Before going on to analyze this background, I should explain my use of the word "feudal". I choose the term because it is the commonest English word which most vividly suggests China's traditional society. Marxists give the word special meanings I do not imply. Most scholars do not call the old Chinese society "feudal" because of its differences from the feudalism of Europe during the Middle Ages. Land in China could always be bought and sold, while in medieval Europe it could be possessed only as a fief from a feudal lord. There was no outright serfdom in China; a tenant farmer could abandon his land and go off as a wanderer when he went bankrupt. A Chinese family's estate was usually divided among all the sons instead of being passed on to the eldest, as in feudal Europe.

Nevertheless, the meaning is reasonably accurate for my uses. Most Chinese have always been peasant farmers, bound to their land by poverty as securely as were the European serfs by their feudal obligations. In recent decades, an increasing number of peasants have become tenant farmers who had to pay to their landlords tithes as exorbitant as those demanded by Europe's medieval aristocracy. China's lack of a commercial middle class, and the domination of modern industry and trade by the wealthy minority of landlords and their connections, were also feudal.

The attitude of this upper class was based on the ancient feudal communities where the land-rich lived in their great compounds in the county cities or on the fertile surrounding plains, with the walls of their family houses enclosing a tiny nucleus of ease and security. In the centuries before the impact of the West, the economic difference between the rich and the peasants was not as great as it has been recently, but the social gap was wide and clearly defined.

Like education, government was a monopoly of the small group of landlords. Some imperial officials might win their posts in scholarly competitions, but as there were so few peasant scholars this was still a class government. For the most part it was a personal government too, centered around the top officials, administered by their appointees or "men." Since the landlords and their connections had always been the government without serious challenge, they thought they would always be. They felt free to treat government as a toy or game. It was always run in a maze of intrigue; sometimes this was a necessary result of all the interconnected personal "deals" which were the best kind of security anyone could know in a society where there were so few public safeguards. Sometimes the intrigue was woven for its own sake, as a sort of amusement.

The economic supremacy of the upper class, based on the permanent land, seemed equally impregnable; they knew no other standard of values. The only uneasiness which could have clouded their comfort was the knowledge of all those masses of peasants surrounding them, in the tenant villages and in the poor fields stretching out to the swamps and deserts and mountains. The traditional name for these outer masses was "Lao Pei Hsing" or Old Hundred Names." The "Lao Pei Hsing" were so many, the privileged were so few.

Since land was the basic standard of wealth, money — the secondary one — could also be treated as a toy. Debts and tithes owed by the peasants were part of the land-wealth, of course, and were not to be trifled with, but within the upper class, financial arrangements might be conducted as a game, with cash used only as a token, rather like a pawn in chess. The exact amount of money loaned or returned was seldom as important as the personal relations in the "deal" whereby the money changed hands.

This upper class attitude could be quite evident in modern times, even in reform movements. Director Lu of the CIC at Paochi was probably the most practical, and — in 1941 — most progressive field director in the whole organization, but his subordinates made no secret of the fact that his official finances were a personal tangle of "deals" that only he could understand; money allocated for one purpose would be temporarily put to other uses, perhaps loaned out on speculation, manipulated about from one Co-op to another, in ways which would panic a Western public accountant. Lu was very prone to intercept funds sent through him to the front-line Co-op Headquarters, using the money for a while in his own organization before forwarding it. In later years, when I knew some of the Democratic-Leaguers I heard of cases where personal funds were so mixed with League funds that nobody except the men who had arranged the complications could untangle them again. And in their political line-up as well as their finances, the progressive organizations — like the Kuomintang — often acquired a superstructure of intrigue undertaken for personal advantage or perhaps simply through habit.

All these traditions of the upper class naturally made for a more unrealistic kind of life, in view of those multitudes of peasants standing around the edge. Consciously or unconsciously, the privileged group built greater walls to guard its security — which might also be insecurity.

Perhaps the most conspicuous of these safeguards — which might work to just the opposite end — was the cruelty of class relations, as shown in an artificially enlarged famine. The ruthlessness of the landlords could be explained only as a form of panic among men who themselves felt insecure because they were so greatly outnumbered.

Like some Western colonists the Chinese upper class also made a fetish of its leisure status, and tried to mark itself off from the "Lao Pei Hsing" by holding physical labor and discomfort a disgrace. In the Co-ops I knew organizers who, realizing they had to gain the good will of the workmen they were teaching and leading, still could not bring themselves to share in the physical work of the Co-ops. Later, during America's participation in the Kuomintang's wars, I heard from disgusted U.S. Army officers of their Chinese colleagues who seemed sensible and capable leaders, aware of the weakness of feudal military ways. Nevertheless, when a stream had to be crossed in battle, they would refuse to slosh through like the Americans; they wasted time arranging for servants or soldiers to carry them over dry.

Aweing the illiterate peasants still further, the privileged class made a fetish of its literacy. In many parts of China, the superstition has survived into modern times that a piece of paper with writing on it is sacred and must be burned, never put to dirty uses. The old Chinese tradition that the scholar is the highest form of human life is often admired in the West, but much of the old scholarship was abstract philology. To a deadly degree, it was the study of ancient literature and the further refinement of an already complicated written language.

Some of the impracticalities of the Chinese language in the modern world are well recognized. Though it is a rather easy language to speak — a foreigner can soon learn enough to chatter it in a rough way — its complexity as a written language hinders literacy. It can take years for a Chinese to learn to read and write his ideographic language, while it may take only months for an illiterate Western adult to learn to read and write his phonetic language. Also, the loose structure and the imprecision of Chinese make the language awkward for use in modern technology.

Less well recognized is the chance that the exclusive nature of the Chinese written language has helped impose a whole pattern of thought and action upon the élite who were its masters. Even in modern times, there has been a common tendency among upper-class Chinese to regard the writing, reading, or speaking of words as an activity which need not always be related with the facts the words describe. In their thinking, the words themselves can take on an independent existence just because they have been written, read, or spoken.

In an argument, for example, once something has been said, it must be accepted as partly true. Within the argument, the fact that it has been said must be classed with the original facts which gave rise to these exercises in language. Even if you know your opponent's stand is not supported by real facts, and you know that he knows that you both know it, you do not imply he is a liar. You accept what he says as part of his strategy and pretend it is true. You adapt your strategy to include the lies or truths which will neutralize it. This can be done because the argument need not necessarily uncover facts or establish the truth: its purpose may just be a compromise — a personal "deal." If the compromise suits both sides, it need not correlate with the actual facts. Language need not be used as a means of direct expression or investigation, but can be used as a tactic or toy.

Of course this happens in all countries, all languages, but in upper-class China it reached an unusually stylized pitch. The nature of the Chinese written language, in which each word is a different ideograph and each ideograph a sort of picture — usually abstract but always with enough individual style to give it a certain life of its own — undoubtedly contributed to it. The most grandiose modern example of word mummery has been the way the Kuomintang was able to run a government and a war against Japan, later a civil war and post-war reconstruction, all having large sections which never existed except on paper or in speeches.

Allied to this habit of accepting the symbol for the fact is the Chinese concept of "face." Ancient China held few of the activities which dominate the workaday world of the modern West. Most of the Chinese who were not producing food on farms were working to fill other household needs, making clothes, furniture, pottery, and so on. Much of China's national trade was in tea, salt, spices, dried seafood, and other specialities for the table. The whole country's business life was a sort of housekeeping.

In the West today, the superstructure of industry, wholesale trade, non-personal government, mechanized war, scientific and other research, law, medicine, and the other professions has not only obscured the housekeeping nature of civilization, but has given rise to new standards of value. Our idea of efficiency is probably the most important of these. We more often want an object to work and be cheap than to be tasteful and costly. We usually admire men who can get things done more than those with inherited position.

As far as housekeeping goes, we Westerners may have lost a bit by our new ideas and methods. In the recent past, a wealthy Chinese family would eat, dress, and generally live with more comfort and assured style than a comparable family in the West. But for running the complex kind of civilization we have developed, our new standards are indispensable, while the Chinese upper class has clung fatally long to the worst side of a housewife's view of the world, an attitude which can be summarized by the word "face." A Western housewife who has these fancies can be recognized by her address — better than her husband can afford — and her guest parlor full of elaborate furniture her family is never allowed to use. She values the appearance above the reality.

Since the traditional world of the Chinese upper class had practically no machinery, no laws, nothing that could not be operated by the human technique of "deals," its members were predisposed to take modern Western inventions and institutions and make them into tokens of face, just as they had already made toys of their own politics, money, and language. The pressure of centuries of tradition was so strong that it would really be a loss of face for them seriously to try and learn the mechanics of anything that came from outside their family walls. It would imply that they were ignorant, like the peasants. The ultimate example of this was probably given by the last Manchu Emperor, Pu Yi, in the nineteen-twenties when he was imprisoned in the Forbidden City of Peking: he was given an automobile, and after the gas was gone and the chauffeur ran away, was content to be pushed around the palace in it by a team of coolies.

Over and over again one finds the upper class valuing Western innovations, not for their intrinsic worth or usefulness, but for the prestige ownership brings. It was because a family could somehow increase its reputation as a Westernized, progressive one by purchasing a humidor with a picture of an airplane on it that the dry-goods stores of the provincial cities looked so much like toy shops for adults. Any car salesman who has worked in modern China can attest that novel upholstery or a musical horn might sell more cars than a good engine.

Similarly, Western ideas have been treated as tokens or toys. It was no accident, for instance, that for years after its introduction, the new word "Democracy" was often translated not by meaning but by sound. It was *"Te-Mo-K'eh-La-Hsi-Ya,"* a string of unrelated Chinese characters which made an intriguing noise and gave an exotically Western, modern, cachet to the speaker.

This attitude is harmless enough when applied to housekeeping but the old upper class in China consistently applied it to government and war. A city could be made theoretically clean and modern with New Life hygiene posters instead of a sewage system. An army would be strengthened with mud-and-timber forts patterned after pictures of the Maginot Line, rather than with well-trained, well-treated soldiers. The Kuomintang's assumption that it could neglect other aspects of its strength after it began receiving American weapons — glittering tokens of great face — has been a perfect example of this foible. In the past, when the superficial approach to political or military affairs produced a failure so great it could not be ignored, face could be saved simply by new orders abolishing the causes of the failure. Of course these new regulations need be observed for only a token period, long enough to save government face.

The habit of convenient indirection, the custom that assertions and assumptions be accepted in place of facts, the exaggerated concern over prestige, have been general enough throughout the upper class to color almost everything it tried to do. It has been a cause for so many Westerners leaving China, quite unjustifiably shouting that all Chinese are cheats and liars. Naturally it affects Chinese progressives as well as reactionaries, since it derives from the innermost processes whereby thoughts are placed into words and related to facts or turned into action. Co-op reforms could exist just as completely on paper as Kuomintang victories.

Precedent suggests that any attempt to fight the Chinese Communists through use of the old upper class may rapidly acquire a plausible façade behind which the real structure is quite different, or hardly exists at all.

Perhaps the basic idea I am trying to approach here is that in a society like China's, revolution can be a fundamental and entirely natural fact of life, as hard to slow up as a pregnancy.

Americans are in a bad position for examining such an idea, because we have never needed a real revolution ourselves. Our eighteenth-century War of Independence which we call Revolution was more a regional rebellion against a distant tyranny. It developed ideas of freedom and equality which became revolutionary when applied in older, more stratified countries — France, for example — but our own theories did not drastically affect the social or economic structure of new and fluid America. Wealthy Americans were more inclined to be Tories than were the poor, but the split between the pro-British and anti-British camps divided our society from top to bottom, in a zig-zag. It caused no lasting horizontal cleavage between the classes. The leader of our rebellious armies, George Washington, was one of the country's largest landowners, while some Tories were farmers who had as little property as British peasants.

Our Revolution was not more serious because it did not have to be. America was an expanding country, with a western frontier beyond which the riches of half a continent beckoned. Class barriers were usually not very high and troublesome in this burgeoning society, and most Americans had some reason to think they could improve their position through their own work. By the time we filled our territorial limits, a growing industry and trade offered new opportunities. Our expansion allowed many abuses and produced great inequalities, but it also brought a slow rise in the general standard of living. In most parts of America, it brought an increase in public education, making the process of democratic self-government stronger and surer.

According to Marxist thinkers, all this American progress is a temporary illusion. As America is a capitalist democracy, they maintain, our inequalities must steadily increase now, in somewhat the same way as in Koumintang China. We will move suicidally toward greater monopoly — by private interests since this is a capitalist country — with fascist controls to protect it at home and imperialist expansion to support it abroad. This must produce a great new depression which will tempt us into starting a preventive war against Russia. It will bring on a Communist revolution in America.

I cannot accept such a theory. Although plenty of powerful and violently anti-Communist Americans are doing their best to jerk the country into the pattern the Marxists expect, I do not think they will succeed. Even if they resort to conspiracy and an American version of the "Big Lie," I am sure we have the best possible chance to avoid the road to monopoly, aggressive war, collapse, and revolution. Too many Americans already have a stake in our existing society, and know how to protect their interests — through voting, unions, and other collective action. Whatever our final goal proves to be, I am sure we can move towards it gradually and without violence, by legislative action which expresses the will of the majority.

Thus, in America, where a future revolution does not appear to be necessary or likely, the revolutionary group is small and tends to attract mavericks and misfits who are at war with society for personal reasons. The Communists are the only revolutionists I know of in America; I was once told by a European Communist that the American Communist Party was one of the dismays of the Comintern.

But in China, where revolution has been so badly needed, the people who worked towards it could be of a different sort. Most of them, though not all, tended also to become Communists or to co-operate with the Communists. This was quite natural. After the Kuomintang purges following the Shanghai coup in 1927, the Communist Party was the strongest surviving revolutionary group in China; it was the only one with its own territory and armed forces. During the later years of Japanese invasion, the Chinese Communists began to show themselves very successful in gaining support among the peasants, who had to be the chief source of strength for any revolutionary movement. To many politically minded — educated — Chinese who thought revolution necessary, the Communist program seemed the quickest way of bringing it about. While the doctrinaire aspects of Communism have repelled those who are of a tolerant and relaxed temper, and suspicions of Russia alienated others, the Chinese Communist Party has been able to attract men of a calibre at least equal to that of the leaders in America's major political parties.

By contrast, to judge from the personal histories of the men I knew in the CIC, and later the Democratic League, I would say that the Chinese in Kuomintang territory who have been available for public work and liberal non-revolutionary politics along Western lines were usually mavericks: either exceptional and non-typical individuals, or the products of accidents of environment. Some were members of the small, non-typical upper class in Shanghai and the other large cities, where Western-style business did produce educated families with slight feudal connections. Some were the sons of landlord families who happened to gain liberal ideas instead of commercial materialism from Western education. Some were wealthy men who came to differ with the usual outlook of their kind because of accidents in their personal lives. Some were the sons of the poor who, through missionary scholarships or other strokes of non-typical luck, were able to get the education they needed for a liberal Western attitude.

I suppose the political meaning of all this is that for our own safety Americans must quickly realize how different other countries can be from America, particularly in ancient Asia where modern politics are colored by heritages from a long past which has no parallel in America. Judging from the example of China, an infinite amount of study will be necessary before America is able to behave towards such countries in ways which benefit both them and America. Wherever study shows that a revolutionary situation is approaching, America will have to adopt revolutionary policies, otherwise that revolution is bound to go Communist and may anyway. As in China, a policy of military suppression can succeed only temporarily.

I have enough valued friends in the group of non-party Chinese mavericks not to wish to belittle the immense effort and loving care which Western-style reformers have spent on projects like the CIC, the Chinese Red Cross, Jimmie Yen's Rural Reconstruction program, various missionary enterprises, and even some directly sponsored by the Kuomintang. But looking upon their scattered and meager work as the final result of a century in which the West had every chance to help China move from feudalism to democracy, their attempt at Western-style reform too much resembles the industrialism which — in the interior — was most conspicuous in toy shops for the landlord class.

I remember as the best symbol of this failure of the West a Chinese woman I met at the CIC headquarters in Paochi. She had just returned from several years study in England, where she graduated from the London School of Economics. Short, stout, flashingly bespectacled, she was a woman with Western "know-how." She was in charge of an adult-education project among the peasants in the villages around Paochi. Her detailed plans were beautifully drawn up in Chinese and English, on imported paper with diagrams in colored ink. They looked fine. I asked her what success she had had in getting them into operation.

"Oh, we've already had to abandon the schools," she said.

"Why?"

"We found the peasants were too ignorant."

I was reminded of the Empress Dowager, the next-to-the-last Man-chu ruler, no doubt a secretly frightened and bewildered woman, who had found it reasonable to use Chinese Navy funds to build a marble pleasure barge in the lake of her summer palace outside Peking.

In the early spring of 1941 Rewi Alley planned to go back from Paochi to Shuangshihpu, "Twin Rock Village," the crossroads settle-ment in the mountains where his house was to have been, then he would make a field trip farther northwest, to Tienshui and Lanchow. At the Press Hostel in Chungking I had been warned that if I applied for permission to travel too widely in the North I would probably not be allowed beyond Chengtu; the Kuomintang was reluctant to allow stray foreigners into controversial areas and no foreign journalists had traveled in the extreme Northwest since the blockade against the Chinese Communists was thoroughly clamped. I later found this was mainly because no foreign journalists had really tried, but in the meanwhile, I had no visa for Tienshui and Lanchow.

Since the CIC in Shuangshispu had been preparing some caves for Rewi to take the place of his unlucky house, he offered me the use of them as long as I wanted to live there. In the first week of March we climbed into another decrepit CIC truck and rattled back into the mountains of the Szechuan-Shensi border. Rewi stayed in Shuang-shihpu for about ten days before going off.

As I had in Paochi, I followed him on his inspection trips to the Shuangshihpu Co-ops. It was a little like going with a perpetual-motion machine. When he was not striding rapidly across the slopes, his short, muscular figure almost squared by his many shabby sweaters and sheep-skin mackinaw, he was walking in and out and around and sometimes over the objects of his inspection, poking, peering, snapping photographs even when there was no film in his camera — it flattered and heartened Co-op members to think their effort was being pictured. Always, he crackled with compliments, criticisms, and suggestions in Chinese, sometimes with sarcasms and side comments in English for me: "Will you look at this rapturous latrine they have dug, right beside their well? Remind me to get them to move it, as soon as I have settled the small trouble of the bank loan they seem to have disappeared with." . . . "These smiling bastards are so pleasant because they don't want to bother making their cloth exactly the same width and color as the Paochi Co-op cloth; we can never become a really big business unless we get our stuff standardized." . . . "Now they are asking why they can't have a CIC bank in Shuangshihpu. Seems they want to borrow from within."

There were no limits to his working hours, and in the evenings, in the Co-op schoolroom we inhabited since his caves were not ready, he held levees for CIC people with problems, serving them quarts of his precious coffee. Later he wrote advisory letters to Chungking and the seven Regional Headquarters. He wryly admitted that many would probably be memoranda to himself. In his travels he often found his old letters in the action-pending files; he would then act

himself, and report it to the letter's point of origin, where, on his
further travels, he would find the later letter and act upon that.

Even when all his letters were written, and the schoolroom was
deserted by his court of CIC children, his attention was seldom far
from the Co-ops. As he went to bed or got up, shaved or ate, he
constantly thought aloud: "Remind me to ask for some cold cream
next time I write to Hong Kong. Those refugee mechanics from the
Shanghai swamps are worried because their kids' faces get so chapped
in this desert air. Must keep the mechanics happy and learn more
about them; they're the kind we're going to have to work with when
we go back to the coast, after the war." . . . . "This old Chinese trade-
guild tradition helps us get workmen together in Co-ops, but it makes
them secretive as fools. Can't get it through their heads that the
other Co-ops aren't their enemies. They won't teach their methods to
the others." . . . . "Dammit, these people have a sense of co-operation,
if they only knew it. How do you think China has been irrigated for
thousands of years? Irrigation Co-ops, of course. And how were
the fields guarded? Crop-watching Co-ops. By the way, those crop
watchers were the foxiest ones. They just put whitewashed stones in
the Co-op members' fields, then nobody would really have to watch,
because nobody else would dare steal; when they saw the stones they
wouldn't know who *might* be watching. . . . "

Even when he was thinking and talking in English, he retained
some of the staccato volubility which marked his Chinese, and he had
a Chinese peasant's fondness for pithy, semi-proverbial phrases. In a
rather Chinese fashion, his speech also rattled with emphatic expletive
sounds and repetitions — "Huh? Huh? Ugh!" — and the effect could
be hypnotic, particularly since his favorite phrase was "Yo ban-fa!" —
There is a way! In the usual conversations of that period in the Kuomintang Northwest, the more common phrase was "Mei-yo ban-fa" —
There is no way. He also had an extremely un-Western vagueness
about times and places, distances and numbers, but when I complained
about it, he just laughed and said: "What the hell? You'll never
believe you can change anything unless you think the world is fluid."

Only on the evenings when he was very tired did he show that
under all his busyness he might not be a contented man. His traveler's
life had to be a lonely one, and during the United Front period both
his adopted sons had gone to Communist country. He did not hide
that he was bothered because he could not see them. His cheerful
monologues in the schoolroom sometimes gave way to long silences,

and more than twice he ended one of these by saying: "Ah, I sometimes wish I had invested in three or four more kids, instead of buying all those books in Shanghai." Then he would carefully point out that anyone who got too fond of a few people cared less about the rest.

Though he did not like to admit it, he was acutely conscious of the CIC's uncertain future. As early as 1941, he seemed to have it in a seldom-uncovered part of his mind that the CIC might fail, but he pointed out that this was no reason to be discouraged. Whatever happened to it later, it was giving a livelihood to some people, education to others. Both could help whatever came after the CIC.

He was also aware that the men who called him a "new imperialist" and a foreign meddler were gaining the strength which would probably oust him. He was afraid that those who wanted to turn the CIC into another ornament to Kuomintang paternalism would try to use what he called the "Living Buddha technique" on him, recalling him to Chungking for a bureaucratic job with much face and no work, or worse still, sending him abroad to lecture. A number of the CIC letters he was always writing to Chungking were arguments why he had to remain in the field. "Got enough Living Buddhas down in Chungking now," he would mutter as he sent them off.

If he were to lose his traveling job, he realized that as a foreigner he had no business interfering in the CIC's difficulties with its government, so he wanted to devote himself to its other basic problem: lack of suitable personnel. In Paochi, Shuangshihpu, and Lanchow he had already set up training schools, named for Joseph Bailie, an American missionary who had been a pioneer advocate of the humane industrialization of China. In the Bailie Schools promising apprentices from the Co-ops, boys from orphanages, sometimes destitute refugees Rewi picked up on the roads, were given an education like one in a manual-training school in America.

They learned how to operate and care for machines, how to repair them and build them from plans. They were taught enough of several kinds of work — carpentry, electricity, auto mechanics — to give them that casual, adaptive, general handyman's skill which is so common in mechanized America but has been very rare in China. They learned enough of their own language to read newspapers. Some learned enough English to continue technical studies in this language. All were taught a certain amount of history, geography, economics, and other general subjects. Perhaps more important, they were taught the habits of mind — curiosity and scepticism, reliability and self-confidence —

which might help them attack the ancient dilapidations of their country.

They would be a new variety of Chinese: partly educated men who were not ashamed to work with their hands, men with some Western "know-how" who could not be made futile by uneasiness over those vast outer masses of peasants, because they themselves were part of the multitude, members of laboring families. With them, Rewi hoped to reinforce and replace the badly qualified utopians or opportunists who had been prominent in the CIC until then. For him to concentrate on these small schools for small boys after his current position would mean a great loss of prestige but he thought that if the Kuomintang climate became much worse, it was the only thing left him to do. He believed that if each year the schools could turn out even a hundred young men of the kind China needed, the effort would not be wasted.

The last I saw of him that year was on the afternoon his truck left for Tienshui. As was expected, it broke down on the first hill, at the western exit of the valley about a mile from Shuangshihpu. From the mountain where I had gone to walk I could see it all clearly: the smoking engine, the mechanic who rushed to put stones behind the rear tires, the passengers who dispiritedly climbed down to watch. Rewi was recognizable even at that distance, and not only because of his stocky, padded figure and red hair. He leaped from the top of the truck, looked under it, poked into the engine, rallied the other passengers to push, hurried to the engine, hurried back, pushed again, and generally circled and lunged and waved his feelers like a busy brown ant, until the wabbling old vehicle was eased out of sight over the brow of the hill.

I saw him briefly twice again in the next two years but as what he feared might happen to the CIC and his own position in it did begin to happen, he came down from the Northwest less and less. Even before he was forced out of his job as national field secretary, he began to abdicate because he felt he could no longer be effective. As he had planned, he concentrated on the Bailie Schools; a flute-cane and a taste for bizarre sunsets would never have satisfied him. In 1944, when there was a Japanese-invasion scare and the Shuangshihpu and Paochi Bailie Schools evacuated to Shantan in the deserts of the extreme Northwest, near the Turkestan border, he followed and went into a self-imposed exile.

Some time before this book went to press, in the autumn of 1949, the

Chinese Communist armies occupied Shantan. As far as I have been able to learn, Rewi was still there. Though it was chronically short of funds and its annual graduating class never exceeded a hundred, he had made his Bailie School one of the few promising spots left in the wreckage of Kuomintang China.

It was of course a tragic waste that the years of work and experiment by Rewi and his Chinese and foreign colleagues should result only in a tiny school on the edge of the Turkestan desert. While Kuomintang China was so desperately in need of all kinds of reform, it was a greater waste that the whole CIC movement should have been allowed to wither. The final irony of its decline may be that the same factor — foreign influence — which made the CIC possible seems to have been a major reason for its failure.

As a New Zealander, Rewi is a British subject, and it was the British Ambassador, Clark-Kerr, who in 1938 gave the early CIC its greatest official boost; the American State Department refrained from action and indeed took no notice of the CIC until five years later. But unofficial American support was always an important reason why the CIC was able to keep alive. Between 1938 and 1949, private American contributors sent about four million American dollars to the Co-ops. This proof of American public interest helped keep the Kuomintang from disbanding the CIC.

In recent years, however, as the Kuomintang became more dependent on the American government, British attitudes and unofficial American attitudes became less important to it. Although in 1943 the State Department sent an advisor to look into the Co-ops, and he arranged for some of them to work for the U.S. Army on a purely commercial basis, the American government never expressed encouragement to the CIC with money. Of the several billion dollars spent in the effort to bolster Kuomintang territory during and immediately after the Japanese invasion, not a penny was allocated to the CIC. This let the Kuomintang feel free to continue reducing the Co-ops, whenever and wherever they became successful, and the liberals in the CIC were given cause to wonder how the American government helped Chinese liberals.

9 · *The Sealed Cave*

A DOZEN odd centuries before I lived there in Rewi's caves, when Tang Seng, the Buddhist saint, passed through Shuangshihpu on his way to India to bring back the Buddhist scriptures, the village must have been a very small place indeed: probably just a tiny knot of shops in the forest, selling tea, paper, and amulets to travelers on the ancient stone-paved pathway between the North and South. But I think it already existed, for modern Shuangshihpu had its own story of Tang Seng's passing, quite different from the national legends which have collected around his name.

As Tang was so holy that one bite of him would give immortality to the biter, he wore a special lamp on his head. He could not be bitten as long as the lamp was lighted and the lamp would not go out as long as he had no impure thoughts. By the Shuangshihpu story, two fox-fairies — evil spirits which usually appeared as foxes, though they could take other forms — were living in the ravine above the village when Tang traveled through. Hearing he would pass, they changed into beautiful naked women and lay in the stream at the bottom of their dell.

Tang arrived and took one look. His lamp flickered.

He turned away. His lamp burned brightly.

He looked again. His lamp flickered dangerously. When he turned away, it revived only weakly.

He looked a third time and his lamp went out. The fox-fairies — now bold and sharp-toothed and completely furry again — rushed him into their cave where they prepared to cook and eat him.

Tang usually traveled with a pig for company and a monkey for protection. At the time of the Shuangshihpu capture the monkey was away in Turkestan on business of his own, but he sensed something was wrong and hurried back in somersaults a thousand miles long.

With his wand and his special power against foxes, he got Tang out of the cave intact, and the local people walled it up with the evil ones inside. The mouth of the cave was still carefully, fearfully, bricked over when I spent March and April in Shuangshihpu in 1941.

At first the gnarled little legend seemed to have as little to do with modern Shuangshihpu as the Saxon tales of Beowulf and Grendel's mother would with my home town in Connectuct. More than any other village of its size in the Northwest, this one was part of the flimsy net of semi-modern towns and roads which the wartime retreat had flung loosely over the interior provinces. It stood at a main highway junction of unoccupied China, where the single motor road north from Chungking spilt, with one branch leading northeast to Paochi, Sian, and the northern fronts, one west to Lanchow and Russia. In the first years of the invasion, refugees following the Sian road down from the coastal cities had swelled Shuangshihpu's population from one to three thousand. In some respects it compared favorably with the average American or European village. It had a street of shops, several inns and restaurants, a bank, a bathhouse, and three schools, though two were private. The CIC was eager to make it a center and showcase — a smaller Paochi — so it had sixteen Co-ops and a water-powered CIC generator for street lights. It was just the kind of progressive-looking Kuomintang village which foreign visitors to China were enthusiastically writing about in those years. It was, in fact, *the* one that a number of them visited, briefly.

There was no denying that Shuangshihpu itself was a cheerful place. Most of the refugee settlers came from Honan and Hopei, and the winding main street had the air of purposeful bustle I remembered from before the war in the prosperous parts of the coastal north. There was always the noise of hammering on wood or metal, the clack of shuttles, the whir of sewing machines. Beside the houses lay a wide stretch of white sand and gravel where two green mountain streams united as the Chialing River and started south toward Chungking; on sunny days the beach was even busier than the streets. Here the camel caravans camped on their way from Kansu to Szechuan. Upstream, the village women washed their clothes and food. Along the sands the dyers dried their long strips of new blue cloth, and the shopkeepers sunned tea and grain and tobacco on sheets of clean matting. On other mats the sewing women sat. In the late morning the boys from the refugee middle school for officers' children played

basketball on the sand. In the afternoon the kids from the CIC kindergarten tottered about in a vaguely military column, shrieking the
chant which taught them numbers:

> *ONE* walks *two* or *three* li,
> Past smoke from *four* or *five* farms;
> Enjoys the view from *six* or *seven* spots,
> And picks *eight, nine* or *TEN* flowers!

One end of the beach was also the chief place of contact between
the busy, well-to-do refugees and the creatures from the denuded
Tsinling Mountains which walled Shuangshihpu. This was the fuel
market, where the native farmers who unprofitably tilled the steep
slopes brought their huge burdens of logs, kindling, bark, roots, straw,
and thorns: every stick and shred they could tear off their land.
Shaggy and grimy as their loads, they sat mute and forbidding while
the village women, the plump wives of the merchants, innkeepers,
and chauffeurs, sallied out among them holding their money before
them like female animal-trainers brandishing whips and kitchen chairs.

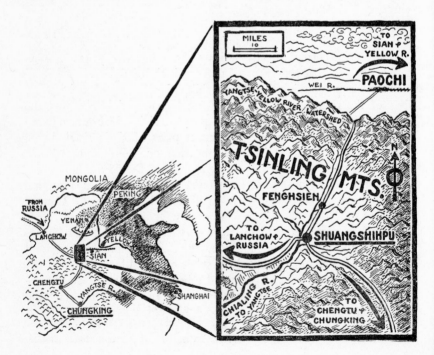

Soon after Rewi left I moved from the schoolroom to the big house which was to have been his, on the opposite side of the river, then into his three caves, higher up the hill. They made very comfortable quarters, their barrel-vaulted tunnels dug deep enough into the dry loess clay to be warm in cold weather, cool during the heat. Their floors were gray brick, their sides and ceilings whitewashed. They were in the southern slope of their hill, and all day the sun shone through the latticed paper windows which covered the entrance walls. I settled in with two puppies and an eagle, the unwelcome gift of the manager of the CIC hostel, who hoped I was thus bound to paint his portrait.

Even at this short distance, the citified village looked shrunken, a narrow line of houses along the brilliant river, dwarfed by the vast, naked, tiger-striped slopes above. Beside the caves were three decaying farmhouses typical of pre-refugee Shuangshihpu, and the more I learned from their ragged inmates, the more I saw on walks higher in the mountains, the more did active modern Shuangshihpu with its Co-ops and cigarette stalls, its garages and barber shop, diminish.

It soon seemed that the proper place to view it was from the highest summits, where the cluster of painted buildings looked tiny as a lost toy in a quarry, its roads raveling away like frail white strings. From the outer rim of the Shuangshihpu Valley, for miles in all directions, extended a sea of red and purple mountains checkered with farms. However thin they might be spread, the men who scratched their living out of the mountain patches vastly outnumbered the refugee villagers, surrounding Shuangshihpu's little compartment of cheerful pragmatism with a huge, dim limbo of ignorance and superstition, half-understood poverty and pain. The village was a perfect model of China's traditional society, with the lucky few in their central enclosure and the multitudes of peasants standing around it.

The full moon rose a few nights after I moved into the caves, while I was having dinner over in Shuangshihpu. As its light whitened the mists on the river, the quiet streets turned to bedlam, with children screaming, women beating pots, men slapping the mudguards of busses, soldiers shooting their guns into the air. A shadow was cutting into the moon, the start of an eclipse. The sophisticated villagers knew the shadow would come and go; they did not make their noise very long, and as they did, they laughed like adults on Hallowe'en. But long after the village was silent, from far up in the dark mountains, the tiny clanging of kettles and pans came with the fast, persistent beat of fear. The night was not quiet again until all the farmland was bathed in the full light of the restored moon.

Next morning I asked Lao Hsiung, the farmer who lived closest to Rewi's caves, if the people in the mountains made an uproar because they were really afraid of a celestial dog eating the moon.

"Of course they weren't afraid of a dog!" He laughed condescendingly. Then he thought soberly for a moment. "But perhaps they were a little uneasy about the dark." It seemed that the fox-fairies' cave could have been sealed up less than a dozen centuries ago.

From the first day I climbed one of the rocky, thorn-bordered paths leading up out of the village, the darkness which threatened the mountain people was evident, lying like a pall on every field and farmhouse. The land was dying and its people with it. The first Westerners who traveled through Shuangshihpu and wrote about it, early in the nineteenth century, had reported that this was wild empty country, heavily wooded with pines, holding only a few farmhouses along the torrential mountain stream. Now there were wretched little farms right up to the summit of the mountains. Except for the cherished domestic trees around the farmhouses, only a scruff of second growth was left on the most inaccessible steps. Already, the thin red and yellow soil of the hilly fields was clutched on every flank by jagged erosion gulleys. The two large streams which joined at Shuangshihpu still ran joyfully full of lime-green water from springs in the higher mountains near Paochi, but the smaller valleys were choked with white boulders through which only sluggish rivulets trickled. The pool in front of the fox-fairies' cave had been reduced to a stagnant puddle. The few acres of good farmland in the flatter valleys were slowly being covered by dry deltas of gravel and boulders, tumbled out of the ravines by the fierce, brief rains which came in the summer when they could also harm the mountain fields, washing out the new crops.

If the bounteous fragrant woods in the early travelers' tales were not exaggerated, these mountains had been deforested in four or five generations. Old farmers I talked to could remember that as children they listened to very old men who had maundered about great forests where bear and deer and snow leopards lived, but I was never able to make sure how the trees disappeared so rapidly. Peasant memories for such facts did not go beyond two or three generations, and no economic history has ever been written of China, telling how and when

great poverty came to stay in all the different villages. The usual
Shuangshihpu explanation was: "Soldiers took the trees away." There
had been much movement of troops on the north-south road during
the warlord campaigns of the twenties and probably the foraging of
firewood for the armies, and perhaps commercial lumbering by some
officers, had destroyed the last real woods.

But the cause of general deforestation must have been simply the
increase of the farming population. Judging from the few peasants
who remembered anything of their family history, this had come
through immigration, mainly from the Yellow River Valley farther
north. Some migrants were fleeing droughts and floods, some had just
lost their farms to the monopolists who were destroying the old balance of rural feudalism.

The final stages in the slow murder of the country proceeded inex-
orably all the time I was there. One of the paths from the mountains
wound down across the bluff in which Rewi's caves were dug, and
every day farmers would stumble past, weighted down with huge
stacks of kindling and brushwood to sell in the village. Sometimes
soldiers from the garrison climbed up with laughter and axes, and
returned with great logs which showed they had "confiscated" another
farm-yard tree as firewood. Sometimes the farmers themselves carried
fine big logs down to the fuel market, tokens that they had been
forced to sacrifice one more guardian of their fields. Because of the
decreasing fertility of their land, they could not afford not to cut and
sell their trees, even though they were dimly aware that it meant bad
luck — worse crops.

In recent years, since the influx of urban refugees had sent up the
price of cloth and other things they must buy in the village, they had
been cutting more and more. The refugees at least enlarged the market for wood. Most of them were middle-class city-people who not
only used fuel for cooking but liked to keep themselves warm all
day. In one small mountain village I climbed to that spring, every tree
— fifty or sixty in all — had been chopped so recently that the stumps
were still pink and the chips smelled of resin. In a few more years
there would be no trees anywhere on the mountains, but as Lao
Hsiung said when I asked what he thought about it: "If that should
happen, there will be plenty of time to worry about it then. This
spring's wheat is more important now."

The older farmhouses, down in the valleys, were tragic monuments
to the region's past, magnificently built of brick and heavy joined

timbers. Their sagging roofs were decorated with ornaments of metal and tile, and in the dark interiors, under soot and cobwebs and broken farm tools, were panels of fine carving. Great holes now gaped in many walls and roofs, and around the houses were drifts of broken brick and tile. Their inhabitants not only could not afford to build such houses now; they could not keep them in repair. They had also lost the skills their ancestors knew. Hopelessly patching the tiled roofs with thatch, or the smooth brick walls with slovenly balancings of fieldstone, they seemed as unlucky inheritors as the Yucatan Indians who built their huts on the platforms of the jungle-grown Mayan pyramids. The newer farmhouses, higher in the hills, were little more than kennels of mud and straw.

Except for the Co-ops and other wartime structures in the village, the only decent new building in all Shuangshihpu was an ornamental gate house before the Buddhist temple which crowned the cone-shaped hill overlooking the village. It had been built the year before by craftsmen brought from Sian: not even the professional carpenters in the village could do such fine work any longer. Funds for the temple had been dunned from the peasants by the priests, with the implied threat that mysterious disaster would overtake those who did not contribute. While the refugee villagers might regard the mountain farmers as dwellers in a dark surrounding world which stretched to the limits of any life definable as human, the farmers in turn thought they lived in an inner compartment surrounded and menaced by a larger, darker world, of ghosts and mysterious powers, to be sealed off in the appropriate ways, such as giving money to the priests or keeping a cave bricked up.

On the mountains, the homes of the living were outnumbered by the mounds which housed the dead and the shrines to appease local spirits. Each new grave, always placed in a good field, took more farmland from the survivors. The other shrines were scattered up and down the slopes, wherever some great rock or strange configuration, some ancient accident or evidence of grace, had roused the hope or fear that the place had hidden meaning. The older ones were built in the style of the old farmhouses, with tiled roofs and carved images. The newest shrines were just pieces of wood or fieldstone, crudely daubed with the names of the spirits they were to appease. Because they had to, the gullible had come to believe the spirits were gullible also, and might be turned benign by whatever makeshift a bankrupt farmer could devise.

But these people who hoped to trick their way past calamity were as engulfed by it as any I have seen. Apart from the grinding poverty which kept them in rags, unwashed except at birth, marriage, and death, they suffered an unknown multitude of ills: none could afford the refugee doctor in the village and there had never been a public medical service here. Some limped, some walked sidewise, some winced at every step, many had peculiarities that approached lunacy. But they knew nothing of the broken bones or adhesions, the traumas or obsessions which handicapped them. When they were sick, they were "sick with pain," when they died, they "died of sickness." The insides of their bodies and minds were a dark world, walled off as completely as they hoped to seal away the outer universe of supernatural threat. They had learned from their elders that there must be a connection between two darknesses; when they sickened, they did various things with colored paper, smoking punk, chicken's blood, fresh pine branches. Then they stubbornly sealed the pain away inside and went on with their work until it should pass or overcome them.

To an outsider, two of their misfortunes were horribly clear. Shuangshihpu lay in the belt of western mountains where goiter was common, and two or three in almost every family had it. Generations of it seemed to have brought a high birth rate for cretins, dwarfs, and monsters.

I well remember the first strange one I saw flopping about in a field, who frightened me as much as I alarmed him. The moment he saw me he dropped his hoe and came toward the path, loping, then crouching, then loping again. I was the first foreigner to live in Shuangshihpu for any length of time and as this occurred in a remote valley, I may have been the first light-haired person he had seen. As he came near the path, he bent almost double and wove his body from side to side, his long arms swinging. When I was a few feet away he crouched motionless, peering up through his matted hair with animal suspicion. His neck was one great blob of goiter, his swollen face a cluster of smaller blobs.

I took one more step, quite uncertainly. He leapt into the air, waving his arms and gobbling like a falling bomb. As I ran back down the mountain, I could see him scuttling off in the opposite direction. Whinnying and screeching, he crashed through a thorn thicket and passed out of sight. When I began walking among higher mountains, I came across whole families of such misshapen idiots, stubbornly applying what little was left of their minds and strength to a travesty of farm work.

The last snow of the year fell on a night in late March and all next day lay glistening on the red and yellow hills. The winter wheat in the valley fields was already high enough to show as a jade-green fuzz above the white. When days of sunlight followed and the rare water from the melting snow reached its roots, it quickly grew tall enough to ripple in the fresh winds. The few fruit trees left by the farmhouses blossomed pink and white, and among the thorns on the untilled steeps the wildflowers opened: forsythia, violets, tiny poppies. In the thickets there were flashes of unfamiliar wings, striped and speckled with gray, yellow, red, blue, olive, as the southern birds arrived to join the dusty pheasants and magpies and the countless raucous crows which had wintered here.

The farmers began their spring plowing, each with an ox and a mule harnessed single file like figures on the wall of an Egyptian tomb. Those who had eaten all their last year's grain shivered in light summer dress, since they had had to pawn their winter clothes to buy seed. The carters' scrawny horses out at pasture wandered forlornly over the hills looking for the last scraps of last year's grass among the thorns, and took to following each other to eat the fresh dung. Along with the birds, two human migrants arrived from the south, a father and a ten-year-old son who wandered in along the road from Szechuan and settled in a hollow they scooped out of a bluff by the river. The father was a taciturn man who said only that he had been a tenant farmer until his wife died and he decided against a settled life which always brought more debts. In a few days he found work as a coolie over in Shuangshihpu and made just enough to keep them. The child was too near birth or death to do anything, and sat unmoving in the chilly little hollow all day, unable or unwilling to speak to anyone who questioned him.

As the days lengthened and grew warmer, the peasants up and down the valley lived and died in their special fashion. On a hill behind Rewi's caves, the father of one family died. Since his wife had been failing and the family was very poor, they decided not to bury him right away. Perhaps the old woman would die, too, before really warm weather came and the old man began to smell. Then they could save by burying both with one funeral. The old lady agreed, so they stored the coffin in their darkest, coldest room, the old woman's sickroom, and piled stones on its lid to keep the dogs out. The sons started seventy-day beards as a sign of respect for their father.

From a village some miles away came the story of a pretty farm girl whose family had been forced by debts to sell her as a concubine to a usurer in Fenghsien, the county seat. The girl tried to kill herself by swallowing a gold ring the moneylender had given her. Gold was thought poisonous and so few people in the villages had gold to trifle with, it was easy to see how such a superstition could survive. Of course the ring only reappeared a day or two later, and the usurer took it back.

In Shuangshihpu itself, one of the local landlords prosperous enough to live in the village, aping the city ways of the refugees, had bought a farm girl as a wife. In early April he murdered her with a knife because he suspected she was carrying on with another man. The manner of her death was a very public secret and her parents were preparing to walk the ten miles to the county seat and complain when friends of the husband came and said: "She is dead and it won't help her if he is killed too. Why don't you just let him give you some money?" They were too poor to be anything but reasonable, so they accepted seven thousand Kuomintang dollars — about three hundred and fifty American dollars. That was the end of the matter, except for the girl's funeral on a hillock over the village one evening, cynically witnessed by a shabby crowd on the mountain above, standing silently with folded arms.

In April a much poorer husband, working a tiny farm on the eastern side of Shuangshihpu Valley, became disturbed about the barrenness of his second wife. To her humiliation, he sold his pigs to buy an iron chain which he pegged down around the grave of his first wife, to contain her jealous ghost. Of course the expensive chain was stolen as soon as word of it got down to the non-superstitious refugee loafers who hung around the garages in the village.

Later a young wife on the other side of the valley gave birth to her first child. She had not even a midwife to help, so she bungled the job and the baby died in two weeks. During the second week, she left it every evening and wandered for hours on the dark hills with a lantern, wailing and pleading with it to change its mind and live. It was believed that infants had little will power and died because spirits had persuaded them to; there was a chance their feeble impulses could be turned back again from death.

High in the most desolate mountains above Shuangshihpu, a family of tenant farmers — the "Hairy Kuos" as their neighbors called them — decided they could not go on farming under their increasing burden of rents and taxes. They climbed down the mountains laden with baskets and boxes, and trudged off toward Paochi, where they hoped to find work as coolies. For the tax- and rent-collectors who would eventually have to climb up there, they left on the door of their deserted house a placard with the traditional farewell of all North China farmers who abandoned their land in desperation and contempt.

> If this place refuses hospitality,
> Other places will not spurn our working strength.

But this departure was almost the only crisis I heard of in the mountains that spring which did not in some way involve superstition. It was impossible for an outsider to learn much of the tokens and ceremonies hidden away in the dark houses and dark minds, but even the visible signs showed how completely every act of life was affected Over the farmhouse doors, pictures of the Yin and the Yang and the Eight Signs were hung to bring prosperity. On some outer walls, white circles were painted to keep away wolves. On many nights, sticks of punk smoldered at the corners of the fields. In the mornings little offerings of food could be found near the mountain shrines.

One day, every farm family visited its graves and tied white papers to the grass and bushes growing there.

Superstition was the only way these worried and ignorant people had been taught to cope with their problems. There was a government-supported primary school in the village but few of the mountain farmers were able to send their sons, since a child old enough to learn was old enough to work. Ironically, one factor keeping the farmers in such poverty that education was an impossible luxury were the land taxes they paid to support the school and all other functions of the local government.

The temple at the north end of the village was more important to the farmers than the school. It had been built in memory of a good-natured member of the local gentry, an opium smoker whose ghost was supposed to have been seen after his death. He had been kind to his own tenants, so the belief had grown that his ghost would intercede with the evil powers on behalf of all farmers. Some bright young organizers in the Shuangshihpu CIC had pasted sarcastic inscriptions on the temple gates — "Give a catty of chicken and all questions will be answered," "Give a half-catty of opium and all requests will be granted" — but the farmers, who could not read, still stubbornly came to burn incense and on holidays to sacrifice food out of their meager stocks.

In the evenings of early April the mountain people started burning the grass on the mountains; all night the lines of fire crept and writhed among the summits. In some parts of China it was sensible to fire the underbrush on the heights at this time of year, to improve the summer's grazing, but here there were no flocks and the fires blighted the young trees and bushes which might reclothe the naked slopes. Most farmers I talked to would admit no reason for setting the fires, beyond the fact that the mountains had always been burned in April. Perhaps they had some unworded folk-memory of the centuries before the Emperor Ho Lu taught men to ride on deer and unicorns, before Yu Tsao taught them to build nests, when humans barricaded themselves on the hilltops and annually burned the underbrush to make their outside paths safer from the beasts of the forest.

Only one could give a more specific reason. He was a stumpy little old man with a wide hare-lipped grin, almost as much of a natural as that first crazy hunchback.

"Why do you set these fires?"

"For fun!" he laughed wildly as he piled more burning straw in a cranny where several seedling pines had been struggling to live.

The mountain farmers were fearfully reticent about politics, and many appeared really ignorant, even of their own village government. In their vague way they seemed to regard "government" as a mysterious and menacing abstraction, very distant and different from themselves — "the people," the Lao Pei Hsing — and consequently impossible for "the people" to understand. Following what I later learned to be a peasant tradition of centuries' standing, most of them disliked and mistrusted "government" automatically, and tried to know and talk about it as little as possible.

Down in the village, however, among the more secure and voluble urban refugees, I was able to learn a little of the mechanics of local rule. There were two branches of government, one handling the people-to-government debts and responsibilities, the other supposedly handling the government-to-people responsibilities. The first and stronger branch, the people-to-government one, was the Kuomintang's revival of the ancient Pao-Chia system.

Here it was entirely appointive. The top official, the Lien-Chang, had been selected by the county Magistrate in Fenghsien, and had picked his Pao-Changs, each of whom had appointed his own Chia-Changs. It was unmistakably a tyranny, but the most grotesque thing about it was that it was a tyranny among paupers.

Its greatest beneficiaries were hardly able to maintain a standard of living equal to that of the refugee shopkeepers. The rapid deforestation and destruction of the land had kept even the landlords in poverty and the trend toward great land-monopoly had been impossible. In 1941 the biggest landlord in the village was reputed to own only forty acres. Still, the inequalities were great and growing. To a mountain farmer who had just been forced to pawn his ragged winter jacket to meet some new requisition, the fact that the Lien-Chang down in the village had two padded-cotton overcoats seemed as much of a luxury as if he had a limousine.

Beside the demands of the Pao-Chia system in Shuangshihpu, all other functions of government, those handling the government-to-people responsibilities, were dwarfed. Because of its highway importance, the village was called a Cheng, or town, and had a Cheng-Chang, or mayor, appointed by the county magistrate in Fenghsien.

He supervised the primary school and the garrison or police force of provincial militiamen, whose chief work was to see that the Pao-Chia exactions were peacefully collected. These functions were supported by the land tax, in theory dunned from the landowners, but since this was a government in which authority and privilege always went hand in hand, the tax was often collected, wholly or in part, from peasants who farmed the land as tenants. Except for the schools, there were no public services, not even a volunteer fire department. The village families looked after themselves, guarding their interests by their personal, feudal "deals" with other families.

Orders had come from above that the village was to train a "Self-Protection Corps" in case the Japanese came, but the mayor felt he was far enough from the front to ignore the command most of the time; in the two months I was there, I saw the "Corps" only twice. It consisted of fifty or sixty of the poorer village men, procured through the Pao-Chia system, who drilled on the river-beach with willow wands instead of guns. Though I never saw one, I was told that rarely, after orders had come from above, the mayor would convene mass meetings — attendance conscripted through the Pao-Chia system — and would lecture the people on foot-binding, queues (still worn by some mountain farmers), public health, morals, or the necessity of hating the Japanese and the bandits (Communists).

Still more rarely, a stray fragment of the modernization and uplift which the Kuomintang in Chungking was always publicizing would seep down through the government bureaus between Shuangshihpu and the capital. The Mayor might order, for example, that coolies must wear coats to market, that children older than twelve must not relieve themselves in public, or that the playing of mah-jong must definitely cease. If any of these national orders did apply in Shuangshihpu, there would be a flurry of reform-enforcement lasting two or three weeks, long enough to preserve the government's face, then the novelty would be abandoned, having convinced a few more of the "people" that "government" was a hopelessly mysterious abstraction.

Down in the village, among the urban refugees, and in the highway traffic which connected them with the rest of China, there were already some signs of the stormy times ahead, which were to visit on the national middle and upper class many of the problems and miseries which as yet were known only to peasants. The two larger secret-police organizations in Chungking had agents in Shuangshihpu, spying on transients who were outside the decreasing circle of political favor. All major Kuomintang banks and monopolies had offices in or near it, busily cornering the trade that passed through, and at the main corner stood an official cargo-inspection and toll station, one of the many that were driving private merchants off the roads. Non-official trucks, mostly old hacks converted to burn charcoal or vegetable oil, were obliged to stop as much as half a day here, paying squeeze as well as taxes. The trucks of the official monopolies would wheel up in the clean odor of gasoline and whisk through with no more than a knowing smile exchanged between the chauffeurs and inspectors.

Private smugglers' trucks were usually the only ones which could vie with the monopoly cars in prosperous appearance and favored treatment by the tax officials. Their trade was no secret, for the Japanese and puppet tax stamps were still on their crates of goods. When they spent the night at Shuangshihpu, the smugglers would swagger into the restaurants like princes, with powerful Japanese light bulbs which they screwed into the restaurant sockets as long as they were feasting with their guests, the inspectors from the Kuomintang toll station.

Nearly all trucks, official as well as private, approached and left the village under a staggering burden of "Yellow Fish," as illegal passengers were called. Most trucking offices sold tickets to no more people than the trucks could carry, but then the habit of personal, extra-legal "deals" would enter in. Underlings in the office, the chauffeurs, the mechanics, and their assistants or "men" would privately sell passage to as many people as could possibly be fitted in or on a vehicle. These trucks quavered up to the outskirts of Shuangshihpu like human pyramids. The driver would stop to let the Yellow Fish off, then proceed to the inspection and toll station. When his legal cargo had been cleared, he would drive to the opposite end of the village and wait for the Yellow Fish.

The whole business was stylized, with the Yellow Fish boldly carrying their luggage past the inspection station through the side streets or over the bluffs, where the inspectors could easily see them. Except for brief periods when the inspectors had received new orders from above, telling them definitely to be severe with Yellow Fish, or when their squeeze from legal tolls was too low, they did not bother with the evaders. Everybody wore that secret smile.

Because of Yellow Fish delays, few vehicles ran on schedule. The steep hills were dotted with trucks which had broken down under their extra loads. Whenever I was walking on the highway and was passed by one of these fantastic cars, careening down a slope amid noises which told of its coming disintegration, with its dozens of passengers clinging to its sides or writhing about on its roof, I thought that here went a veritable model of the modern Kuomintang, speeding through China's traditional landscape, on the way to its necessary end.

The human cost of this cruel joke of a government could be seen most clearly in the military traffic which passed through Shuangshihpu on foot. Armies on the move came over the mountains often while I was living there. Every time, their order of march was the same.

First came the commander on horseback, with his tasseled sash and ornamental sword. Next came his higher officers, afoot or on horseback, with their gear carried by orderlies. Then, between an armed guard of junior officers or trusted enlisted men, came a long line of peasants kidnaped to carry the field ovens and other heavy equipment.

The enlisted men followed the carriers, sometimes walking in step, sometimes just slogging ahead in the uneven, rolling motion of a mob. They were always burdened with field equipment, plus whatever bedding or furniture or food they personally owned, but I never saw them carrying their guns. The weapons followed in conscripted farm carts, safely out of reach of the men. The escape of any enlisted men was guarded against by as large an escort of armed officers and trusties as watched the peasant carriers.

It was easy to see that they might want to escape. Except for a sprinkling of lean, leathery veterans who would boast they had been campaigning since the years of the warlords and were satisfied with the only life they knew, almost all passed with faces marked by pain or worry. Usually their limbs were emaciated, thickened at wrist and ankle by undernourishment. Their eyes were mattered or feverish, their swollen feet often bound with bloody rags.

Behind the last of the armed guards followed the scarecrow march of the very weak, sick, or dying soldiers. They need not be guarded. Unless they had the strength to catch up with the others, they would be no use to the army. And the more hopeless their condition, the less likely their attempt to escape, since there was less chance that they could ever make their way back to their distant families or anyone else who would care for them. It was a well-established Kuomintang policy to send new conscripts into armies so far from their homes that they could not desert with much hope of getting back. For miles after the main column, the road would be littered with wretched men, tottering and even crawling along, in the effort to keep up with the field kitchens which were their only source of food.

These were seldom troops who were suffering their way to the front to throw their last strength against the invaders. They were more often provincial armies who never had faced the Japanese, and probably never would. They were pawns juggled back and forth in the Kuomintang's dreary game of internal power-politics, and the purpose of their suffering was to reduce the strength of this or that regional nabob, to build up a garrison of outsiders in some rear area, to increase the national weakness and disunity from which the Kuomintang drew its strength. The guns carted along with them were to awe and quiet the peasants where they were sent.

Several times that spring, batches of new conscripts were herded through Shuangshihpu, and since they had not the training which gave a soldier's life a minimum value to his masters, they were treated with a more casual brutality. The worst group I saw was about one hundred and fifty men who had already been goaded up several hundred miles of highway from Chengtu and had another hundred or more ahead of them before they reached their "training camp" in Sian.

I shall never forget the afternoon they were herded into the village. It was splendid sunny weather, the hills burning red and green, the sky like peacock glass, snow rimming the highest summits. Slowly around a bend in the yellow road staggered the long line of spectres, their flapping black rags thick with dust, their faces gleaming pale as the distant snow. They were roped together, of course, and they cruelly jerked and cut each other as they lurched about. Many seemed delirious, staring wildly and talking to themselves. Some inhumanity toward conscripts was usual enough to go unremarked but this was a surpassing case, and there was a startled hush on the busy Shuangshihpu street as their guards drove the groaning, panting, gibbering creatures into the barns which had been requisitioned as their night's lodging.

That evening there was much gossip, interested if not indignant, and the stories of those who had talked to the conscripts or their guards were widely circulated. It was said they were opium smokers, beggars, and other riffraff cleaned off the streets of Chengtu for the New Life Movement. They had been sent on this walking trip with the idea that most of them would die and the rest of them become real conscripts. The villagers who lived near the requisitioned barns reported they were given no bedding. Coming from frostless Chengtu, dressed in thin cotton, many had already become sick during the freezing mountain nights. It was also reported they were fed nothing but a little porridge made chiefly of water. Some said the guards had admitted to underfeeding them by policy, to make them so weak they would not try to escape.

But the conscripts still had one way out. Next morning, before the party was whipped off again, the guards laid out on the riverbank, then thriftily stripped, the frail bony corpses of four starved and exhausted men.

As a general rule, the refugee villagers paid little attention to such signs of national collapse. They were still contented ducks, quacking and eating their snails and minnows while the leopard in their park finished off the chipmunks and robins and smaller chickens.

Most of them had settled here more or less by accident, while on their way to Chungking, but soon they realized they had stopped in a good place. The three roads leading into Shuangshihpu began buzzing with emergency war traffic and any man with sense and a little capital could make a success of a restaurant or other business for transients. Though private traffic had begun to fall off by the time I lived there, Shuangshihpu was still quite prosperous.

Since the refugees rented their land in the village, they were exempt from the land tax, Shuangshihpu's single regular tax, but they could send their children to the school and enjoy the police protection purchased by the tax. They had to register in the Pao-Chia system, but those with money could bribe their way into a favored position in it. Even those with little money could commonly avoid being victimized the way the mountain farmers were; they were city people, with more prestige and skill for making personal "deals" with the country Chia-Changs and Pao-Changs; also, as Easterners together in the Northwest they had a certain esprit-de-corps, and more fortunate refugees could and would help the others. The Pao-Chia officials were not particularly severe with them as long as they could still get all they wanted out of their traditional victims, the mountain farmers.

The refugees themselves had in the poverty-stricken mountains a reservoir of cheap labor, full of peasants who were pleasantly easy to bilk and intimidate. By and large, their relations with the local people were like those which old-fashioned Western colonists used to force upon natives of darker, presumably inferior, races. As members of the

middle class, they despised the uncouth and backward peasants. They had more skills and experience, and most of them had more money, than Shuangshihpu's own landlord class. By 1941 they had taken over almost all stores and crafts in the village. Such urbanities as the restaurants, the barbershop, the brothel, were run by and for refugees. Even the few local landlords who could afford to eat and dress like the refugees did not have the money or training to compete with them in business, or to mingle with them socially. There was not a single enterprise jointly owned and operated. Only four or five intermarriages had taken place, and these were regarded by the refugees as unfortunate misalliances. Not a single local workman had the skills and capital to qualify as a member in any of the Shuangshihpu Co-ops.

The general economic rôle of the refugees was also that of short-sighted, temporary colonists. According to pre-war surveys, this county of Fenghsien was minerally one of the richest in China, with copper, coal, and iron already mined on a small scale by the peasants, and the presence of several other metals indicated; on the basis of the published surveys, Rewi had decided to make Shuangshihpu a Co-op center before he left Shanghai. The two rapid little mountain streams offered excellent sites for hydroelectric development, and Shuangshihpu's position on the highways made it certain that as West China developed, the place would grow in importance.

But no refugees I heard of had made an effort to invest in Shuangshihpu's permanent possibilities. They preferred short-term commercial investments. Even the Kuomintang banks, with offices in the village, had ignored the prospects for productive enterprise, preferring the quicker profits of trade and hoarding.

Up in the mountains the farmers used to grumble about the refugees because they "cheated the Lao Pei Hsing" and drove prices up. They looked forward with pleasure to the day when the annoying city people would go back where they had come from. It was the same down in the village. The refugees happily anticipated the day when they could start back home. I never met a single one who planned to stay after the war was over. The notion that this was a temporary interruption to Shuangshihpu's slow history of poverty and decay, that after the war the mountain farmers would be able to look down on the smokeless chimneys of the abandoned refugee houses and shops, tickled the refugees just as much as it did the farmers. This was a very different situation from the one currently described in the Kuomintang's propaganda abroad.

Among all the ducks I saw in the village and on its roads that spring, I remember only three people who seemed to have a sharp sight of when and where in history they were living.

The first was a small middle-school girl, just beginning her education, whom I watched one morning at the toll station. She had come through on a truck from the south, traveling by herself to re-enter school at Sian. Usually the police here made little political investigation of passengers, but her bus had a flat tire in the station, and as no other vehicles came in during the hour while the patch was vulcanized, the bored police amused themselves with the effects of the marooned travelers. Eventually one discovered the diary of the twelve- or thirteen-year-old girl and the whole crew of armed and bemedalled government servants crowded around, first to admire the pressed flowers between the pages, then to read the entries with mounting suspicion.

Apparently the child had copied from her schoolbooks quotations from Sun Yat-sen, with her own naïve questions as to how his ideas applied to what she saw around her. The highest police officials were called out to squint into the notebook and after a conference they decided she had "dangerous thoughts." As I left, the chief was copying excerpts from the diary to send with a letter of warning to the principal of her school. The little girl was frightened, weeping as the police tore apart her carefully packed suitcase in the search for more subversion, but she seemed to realize how silly a tableau this was, for occasionally she burst into fits of hysterical laughter.

The second maverick was a young man whose political education was well under way and seemed likely to kill him. One noon in the village I had noticed a group of boys sitting listlessly in the dust before a restaurant where several army officers were dining and wining. They were nearly as ragged and miserable as ordinary conscripts, but they were not roped together and wore the remains of flimsy, home-made pieces of military gear: knapsacks, map cases, and so on. Crossing the river on the way home, I saw some other boys showing their difference from peasant conscripts by painfully washing their clothes and bodies in the icy water.

After lunch one of them came over to the caves. He said his group were students from Shanghai, persuaded by Kuomintang underground agents to smuggle themselves into unoccupied territory on the promise of education at the Officers' Training School in Sian. They were being marched all the way to Sian, the long way round through Hengyang, Kweiyang, Chungking, and Chengtu. Some months before, this boy and two of his friends had got into a roadside conversation with Rewi, who had told them to come and see him when the group reached Shuangshihpu. Since then, one of his friends had died, the other run away, and he was tragically sorry to find Rewi was not here.

He was about sixteen, middle class like all his companions, the son of a baker in the French Concession of Shanghai. He was thin as a bird and must have been feverish because he trembled incessantly. But he parried all questions about his health with apologies for his filth, which seemed to obsess him. His clothes were loathsomely crusted and his gray skin was splotched with the welts and rashes of scabies.

"Don't think I am used to being like this!" he said, his chin quivering. "I always kept myself clean when I could! In Shanghai I took a bath every two days! In Shanghai my father would beat me if I wore dirty clothes! In Shanghai . . ." When I asked if he would like a bath and clean underwear and socks he burst into tears and refused until I showed him how he could lock himself into the kitchen-cave and nobody could possibly see how dirty he was.

He ate enough supper for four and when I invited him to spend the night he asked for a pencil and paper. He stayed up for hours, writing and rewriting, then left before daylight to rejoin his group. On the desk I found this note:

Don't think I cannot stand trouble but I want you to know what has been happening.

On days when we do not march we have only two meals of porridge — no solid food. On the march we have nothing but water and that is dirty river-water. Out of our whole group of seven hundred who gathered outside Shanghai, less than four hundred are left. The rest have run away or become sick or died. Most of those who have gone are dead.

Now I have only the clothes I am wearing and my rice bowl, but I think perhaps I have enough strength to reach Sian.

You know all our friends who died had parents who loved them. But now they are dead. Brothers and sisters and friends who loved them. But now they are dead. They wanted to fight the war of resistance. But now they are dead. They wanted to free China for their countrymen because they loved other men. But they are dead. Now we who are not dead want to give our blood and youth and energy for something more than this.

The boy didn't have his rice bowl any longer; I found he had forgotten it in the kitchen. Later I had several letters from him, saying he reached the Training Camp and was physically comfortable there. As I did not think he should get letters from a foreigner at that school, I never answered, and after two years his letters stopped coming. His case remained the neatest and most disagreeable example I ever saw of the Kuomintang's ingrown trend toward self-destruction.

He and his companions had been just the kind of young men the Kuomintang needed if it were ever to establish an effective government. I imagine that whoever arranged to get them out of Shanghai had realized this, and the original plans for their travels must have included reasonable comfort for them while they marched from Shanghai to Sian. But in this idiot government by patronage, all levels of officialdom conspired together to preserve one another's face and rackets. It was too easy for these boys to find themselves marching under army officers who starved them for profit.

The third maverick I met that spring had survived all the political education he could take from the Kuomintang and had gone on to postgraduate work of his own devising.

He was an old ex-official, with an active political record dating back to the days when he helped overthrow the Manchu Empire. A Manchurian, he had emigrated to Shensi Province after the Japanese invasion of his homeland in 1932, when the Manchurian Young Marshal was blockading the Communists. The Young Marshal had had him appointed Magistrate of a county near Sian, but his position became shaky when his protector was imprisoned after the Sian Incident. Like many Manchurians, this old man had become cynical about the Kuomintang in the years before the Japanese invasion, when the Generalissimo and his group appeased the Japanese and consolidated their monopolistic control of the country. Unlike many, he was not timid about saying so. Not long before he came through Shuangshihpu, he had been relieved of his Magistracy.

He was famed as a wit. On the night I had dinner with him he seemed tired or ill, for he sat silent and detached, but his friends and the CIC people who were our hosts giggled and whooped like schoolboys, recalling his historic sallies. Just before he lost his job, he went to a Kuomintang banquet in Sian. He must have realized he was on his way out, and decided to commit political suicide in style.

One of his most self-satisfied colleagues had sent an official car to fetch him to the dinner. It wasn't much of an automobile but its owner had just been assigned it and thought it increased his face.

"How did you like the car?" he patronizingly asked the old man.

"It's a remarkable one," the old man said. "It has a noise everywhere except in the horn."

Another guest at the banquet had been a newly arrived Kuomintang man from Chungking, an enthusiast who had not been heard during the Party's perilous earlier days but had been on the bandwagon, shouting his devotion, ever since 1927 when the Kuomintang became safe and successful.

"Why don't you join the Kuomintang?" the visitor asked.

"When it was an underground party I was afraid to," the old man said. "Later I was ashamed to."

It was one of the highest dignitaries of the Shensi provincial Kuomintang who had brought on the final chill.

"Are there many 'erh-liu-tse' (Shensi slang for professional loafers) in your county?" he inquired.

"Not now," the old man said. "They have all joined the Kuomintang."

That evening in Shuangshihpu, he began to rouse himself towards

the end of dinner. He was on his way south, presumably to a comfortable retirement. Though he had a good name as an official he
must have salted away a fair amount of the moderate squeeze which
was so customary it was all but legal.

"What are you planning to do now?" someone asked.

"I don't know," he said with mock pathos. "I'm an old man. I've
lost my job, now I have nothing . . . "

He developed a wicked twinkle. " . . . except a little money!"

Then he told a story which seemed a fine example of that Chinese
"old roguery" which some writers have extolled to the West, without
explaining its use as a defense against insupportable circumstances, intolerably far beyond personal control.

In a county near his, the old man said, the Magistrate was a young
man, foreign-educated, and unusually full of ideas of honor and
responsibility. A legal question was brought to him by two old-
fashioned landlords. One litigant decided to send a pair of suckling
pigs to the Magistrate, but his lawyer was horrified and explained
that this was a new kind of official; to try bribing him would certainly make him decide the case against the briber. The question was
duly tried and decided in favor of this landlord. His lawyer was
surprised, as he thought their case had been the weaker one.

"Of course I sent him the pigs," his client placidly explained. "But
I sent them in the name of my opponent."

By the middle of April my farmer neighbor, Lao Hsiung — "Old"
Hsiung — had lost enough of his distrust of a foreigner to talk a little
of his life, even of some of the dark facts he sealed off from his
ordinary attention with stubborn endurance and painful laughter.
Only when the conversation approached the local Kuomintang and its
methods did he devise an excuse and wander away with an amiable
smile.

He was called "old" because that was the commonest and most
affectionate peasant nickname. Actually, he was a very young man to
be head of a family but his father had "died of sickness" three years
before, and his older brother was an idiot with strange periods when
he had to be locked in a storeroom; sealing the mad ones away at
home was the only remedy the mountain farmers had for the insanity
which so frequently cropped out in their families. Lao Hsiung's left
eye had been "sick" when he was a boy and he could no longer see
through it, but otherwise he seemed healthy as a yearling ox. When

we talked under his big oak tree in the warm noon hours, he would bring his infant daughter out to play in the sun, naked except for the red wool bows in her hair. He was devoted to the child and when he tossed her in the air or paddled her small dusty feet against his solidly muscled chest, their laughter was one of the few sounds of delight I remember from those barren mountains.

Though they seemed typically wretched to me, Lao Hsiung claimed his whole family were better off than their neighbors. They had meat once a month, he boasted, and often ate vegetables with their potatoes, corn, or wheat. They had twenty mou of land, four or five acres, ten of it mountain land, ten on the richer flats. They had once owned two houses, until soldiers of the village garrison evicted them from the larger one, several years before. The Hsiungs at that time moved into their smaller house, evicting a tenant whose financial balance as a farmer was thus upset; he wandered off down the road with his family and nobody knew what had become of him.

"How much rent do the soldiers pay?"

"Rent!" Lao Hsiung was amused at the very idea.

The chief question for the Hsiung family that April was whether their wheat from last year would be enough for seed and for food until the next crop was in. Each day they fearfully checked the emptying bins. If there were not enough, they would have to pawn some of their essential equipment — they had nothing else — or borrow money from the bank or the usurers in the village.

They dreaded this. All farmers recognized that the smallest loan was the first link in the chain of increasing debts and mortgages which had gradually barred many of their neighbors from their own land, forcing them off into the uncertain lives of tenant farmers or vagrant laborers.

"Once a farmer gets in debt he will never in his life get out again." Lao Hsiung would sagely repeat this observation, so often heard in rural China it was almost a proverb, then he would laugh as if it were a joke he had made up himself.

As it happened, the Hsiungs were lucky in 1941. Warm weather brought on planting time so early, they had quite enough wheat for seed. They thought that if they ate sparingly, they could make their remaining wheat and potatoes last until they could grow more food.

Year in, year out, the Hsiungs were also lucky because they were comparatively free from the conscription worry. Of three sons only the youngest had been taken. Only one son in a family was exempt, but last year when the conscription officers came with the Chia-Chang to collect another conscript, the idiot older brother had been in a plausible period and Lao Hsiung was able to send him. It was common for the hard-pressed peasants to try to trick the Pao-Chia requisitions in any way they could; sending their idiots, invalids, and cripples into the army, mixing the army wheat with sand, and so on. Lao Hsiung's brother's madness must have made him take risks no sane man would venture. He never would tell how he had got away, but he came back less than a week after he had been led off shackled to his fellow conscripts. With luck, he would be in a plausible phase when the officers called again.

The youngest brother had been conscripted so long ago, Lao Hsiung said, that nobody except the mother thought of him now. He could not remember exactly, but thought the boy had been sixteen or seventeen when he was taken away. Of course he had never written back. He was illiterate, and private's pay did not afford the use of professional letter writers. Whether he was alive or dead now, he was not expected to return. No conscripts except those who escaped in the first month or two, before they were marched too far away, had ever reappeared in Shuangshihpu. "Government" had never informed any local families of the fate of their soldier sons. For his family, a conscript's life usually ended on the day he disappeared down the road, shackled to his fellows.

But the Hsiungs had no misfortunes to ensure them against taxes and requisitions. With twenty *mou* of land their taxes were in the fifth and next to lowest class, but they had to pay between ten and twenty Kuomintang dollars every month. It was a comment on government efficiency that in this very accessible village, half a year after the national government had ruled that its taxes were to be collected in grain, the land tax was still collected in money. Though Lao Hsiung boasted of his prosperity, his family could usually pay their land taxes only if he and his idiot brother spent some days a month working as coolies over in the village. If they were unable to pay what was asked — and the tax collector never warned ahead when he raised the tax — the soldiers with the collector took whatever grain or equipment they judged to be worth as much as the arrears. Last month the Hsiungs had been a couple of dollars behind, so the soldiers took two cooking pans of the old quality no longer available.

Lao Hsiung was rather vague about the Pao-Chia requisitions which were levied in addition to the land tax. He said it was hard to remember about them because they came so irregularly — whenever the local Lien-Chang, the magistrate in Fenghsien, or any transient officers decided they needed goods or services from Shuangshihpu. His most vivid memories of the way the Pao-Chia system worked were of the spring when his family's seed grain had been requisitioned to help

feed some passing troops, and of the winter week when he himself had
been taken as an army carrier, helping drag a field kitchen all the way
to Paochi before he was released.

With his day-to-day problems so pressing, Lao Hsiung had little
interest in anything beyond his own fields. The outside world was a
vast misty space about which he knew little and cared less. Anything
more than three miles distant was "far far away." Anything which had
happened more than three years before was "long long ago."

He knew nothing of his family's history, where it had come from
or when it came to Shuangshihpu. He did not know who had built
his house or when, except that it was before he was born, long long
ago. There was the ruin of a handsome carved-brick gate a few feet
from the north end of his house but whether there had ever been a
wall for it to lead through, he neither knew nor cared. The only thing
he did know for certain about his house was that the family could
never afford to make repairs on it.

He did not know how the family had got their fields. They had
never had papers of ownership until last year, when officials came over
from the village, looked at the mountains, and gave papers to all the
farmers. The Hsiungs did not like the idea of papers; they never had
them before. They left them out in a room where the children played
with them until they were torn up.

"Why should we need papers?" Lao Hsiung laughed. "Nobody
else would want our land. It's too poor!"

Lao Hsiung knew that the Japanese had invaded China and that
there was a Generalissimo named Chiang, but that was all he knew of
the war or politics. He did not know how long the war had been going
on, though he was sure there had been snow on the ground the first
time he heard about it; that would mean he heard about it five or
six months after it started, if he heard about it the year it began. He
knew the names of none of the battles, not even Taierhchwang,
China's one clear victory. He had not heard of the government's epic
retreat from Nanking to Chungking, indeed he was vague about where
and what any national capital or government was. He knew the names
of no members of the Kuomintang government except the Generalissimo, and he was not too sure who or where he was.

"Have you heard of Madame Chiang?"

He looked blank for a moment. "The Generalissimo is a man so I
suppose he must be married," he said calmly.

He didn't know for sure if the Japanese killed people, they were far,

far away, but he had a vague idea they were bad and cheated the farmers. When he learned that he couldn't remember, though he was sure
he hadn't known it as a child.

"Don't you know it spoils your land if you cut down all the trees?"

He laughed. "Everyone knows the farmers only cut down the trees
because they need money. The best trees are stolen by soldiers anyway."

"Don't you know your fields would be richer if you didn't dig all
last year's roots out of them?"

He laughed. "If we didn't dig up the roots for the stove, we
would have to cut down more trees to cook our food."

"Do you know if you eat more salt, it may prevent goiter?"

He laughed. "Salt costs so much now, we can't afford to eat any
at all."

"Why don't you dig your graves on the hills, where they don't
spoil the fields?"

This was a sober answer, after some thought. "I don't think the
dead would like it if we buried them in poor land."

Of recent events in Shuangshihpu, only a few survived clearly in
Lao Hsiung's memory, such as the year the motor road came through.
The day the first car arrived was a great one, with farm families
rushing down all the mountains to crowd around the machine. They
were not frightened because they head heard descriptions of cars from
the road workers, conscripts from Honan, and they had already seen
airplanes. More important to Lao Hsiung than the wonder of the car
was the fact that in the year of the road, several families had been
forced to leave their land and wander off. Some had had too much of
their land confiscated as right of way. Some had had their topsoil,
painstakingly fertilized through the investment of generations, carried
off as fill.

Lao Hsiung also remembered the year the Communist army came
through on its Long March — it must have been six or seven years
before, long long ago. The county government had sent speakers to
call meetings and tell the farmers the Communists were bad, so on
the morning when Lao Hsiung heard the people farther down the
slope screaming that the Communists had come, he took his family
and ran up into the mountains. As they climbed they could see many
Communist soldiers running out of the valley nearest the village. The
villagers were running up the mountains in every direction. The
poor who lived in the village wore blue clothes like the mountain

farmers, but it was summer and the village officials and ten or fifteen of the bigger landlords were dressed in white like city-people. The Communists all wore gray uniforms. The men in gray chased and caught those in white but let all the people in blue escape.

Lao Hsiung and most of the others in blue hid in the mountains until the ones in gray moved on, about a week later. Returning, they found their houses and everything in them unharmed, but all the white-clad bodies lay on the river bed where they had been shot.

Lao Hsiung was noncommittal about the executions. He knew some of these men had been bad because they cheated the farmers but about others he was undecided; he had heard they were kind. We were getting too close to subjects he refused to discuss, and I could see he was preparing to leave.

"Did any people from Shuangshihpu go away with the Communists?"

He laughed with all the pride of a landed farmer; then spat contemptuously.

"Only a few beggars!" he said.

With a most amiable smile he shrugged his ragged coat up over his shoulders, and led his little daughter off to their ruined house.

One day towards the end of April a line of military trucks thundered into Shuangshihpu along the road leading down from Lanchow and Russia. Under their tarpaulins hulked the unmistakable outline of cannon. Trailing long plumes of dust across the valley, they wheeled

through the village and disappeared up the road to Paochi and Sian.

More and more came during the next week, in long convoys of forty or fifty. Some stopped in the village overnight and it was learned the cannon had come from Russia and were French guns from the First World War. One rumor said the Russians got them when the French gave them to the Poles to fight Russia in the early twenties. Another rumor said the Russians got them more recently, capturing them from the Finns. In Shuangshihpu there was more interest in where they were going. Sian was a Kuomintang base for two fronts, one against the Japanese, one against the Chinese Communists.

All politically minded travelers who had come through in recent weeks brought rumors of impending civil war. Marginal Kuomintang-Communist hostilities had continued since the New 4th Army Incident in January. That April, reports of the new Russian-Japanese Neutrality Pact were received in Shuangshihpu just as the Russian cannon began passing through in Kuomintang trucks, perhaps to the front against the Communists, and in the village a cynical interpretation was put on the whole business. It was believed that the Russians had secured themselves against any threat from Japan by an agreement which would allow a joint Japanese-Kuomintang campaign against the Chinese Communists.

Civil war was thought a certainty when General Ho Ying-chin, the famously pro-Japanese, anti-Communist Minister of War, came through Shuangshihpu from Chungking, on his way to Sian. Several months before, General Pai Chung-hsi, the Generalissimo's Chief of Staff, had travelled north to confer with the Communists in an effort to settle the differences which later resulted in the New 4th Army Incident. His trip had been surrounded by the greatest secrecy but the Japanese had bombed and strafed the road while he was on it. General Ho's trip was more like a royal progress. He stopped for an hour or two in Shuangshihpu at the best inn, the CIC hostel, and after inspecting the kitchen and toilet like a good member of the New Life Movement, he held a levee for the local officials. He had done the same in every town he passed and his visits were reported in the press, but the Japanese sent no planes over the road while he was on it. Instead, a guard of Ho's own troops, who had marched in just before his passage, were stationed every few hundred feet on the highway, facing out into the country. They were élite soldiers, well-enough fed and clothed to be entrusted with guns even when they were strung out like this and had every chance to escape.

Among the young CIC people who were my friends in Shuang-shihpu, these omens produced a furtive emotionalism. They preferred not to talk politics when I was with them but as soon as I left I could hear the discussion mounting. I remember one party when a very young organizer got himself drunk in a restaurant and began singing a popular war song from the United Front period, describing how the Kuomintang and the Chinese Communists would unite to defeat Japan. The other guests were embarrassed, rather frightened since two men at the next table wore black uniforms without insignia and might be secret police. His friends finally quieted the singer by dragging him outside and dousing him with cold water.

Believing civil war might soon replace the war against Japan, I made plans to go up to Paochi and on east to Loyang, in Honan province, near the front. There were Japanese, Kuomintang, and Communist armies north of Loyang and it should be a good place to see what would happen. If there were no civil war, the area was still the best place to cross over into Communist territory, which I was anxious to visit since no foreign journalist had been there in two years. It was hopeless to try to cross the tightly guarded Kuomintang-Communist blockade line north of Sian, but near Loyang, in northern Honan and southern Shansi, smuggling had made the Kuomintang frontier against the Japanese so lax that it was supposed to be easy to cross into occupied territory, where you could find guerrillas who would guide you back into the Communist districts.

All through April the weather in Shuangshihpu had been relent-lessly sunny and by the time I left, rain was badly needed. The wheat on the mountains had already been damaged and the crops in the valleys were threatened. A week before, the peasants had decided to begin a partial fast to bring rain. They would not eat meat, which they could seldom afford anyway, nor would they sell meat for any-one else to eat. They would not eat or sell onions, considered as bad as meat for making the breath offensive to the powers which needed propitiation. This was the only time I saw the mountain farmers impose their will on the well-to-do village; no price could budge the farmers from their superstition, and the refugees, even the Kuomintang officials, were forced to be content with meals of turnips, carrots, and potatoes, like the poorest mountaineers.

The day I left was another sunny one and though the Hsiungs were more cheerful because their cow had calved the day before, they spent much of the morning out in the fields, looking apprehensively at the weather and their crops. On my way to the bus station, I walked down to the river behind a pair of goiterous mountain farmers leading a thin black mule which stumbled along under a great load of firewood, the remains of a fine tree. The beast was muzzled, but lunged at every clump of grass or wheat by the path. The farmers explained that when the animals were too hungry they had to be muzzled, otherwise they could cause trouble by grazing on other people's richer fields down near the river. They laughed about that, and one of them kicked the mule.

Under the bluff by the river the little boy from the south still squatted in his hollow. About ten days before, his father had "caught a sickness" and died; for a few days I had been able to get the boy up to the caves to eat, but he did not like leaving his hollow after his father's body had been buried by the nearest farmers, who were at last offended by the smell. Apparently the child simply decided against life; he stopped coming up to eat and sat huddled in his rags in his darkest corner, staring resentfully at anyone who came near. As I learned when I returned through Shuangshihpu next winter, he died shortly after I left, and nobody except his father ever did know whether he could not or would not speak.

Over in the village, while I waited for the bus, I watched some carpenters from Paochi building a restaurant, skillfully sawing, fitting, and hammering. In the hot sunlight their new lumber filled the whole street with the sharp, clean odor of construction. At the crossroads

the tangle of carts and trucks, the shouting of the carters and the roar of engines, gave the fine morning the excitement of arrival and departure, of change and growth. The shops of Shuangshihpu's busy main street made an even better façade for a new China than they had when I came to the village; in tribute to a Chungking drive for reforestation, seedling shade trees purchased with county funds taxed from the mountain farmers had been planted in a neat line along the gutters. Over the door of the bus station was a glossy new poster of the Generalissimo, staring into the distance with his bland look of decision.

Another convoy of trucks with cannon from Russia was entering the village as the bus finally got underway and roared up the little knoll hiding the road to Paochi. Over to the left, on the cone-shaped hill part way to Tang Seng's cave, a straggling line of blue-clad farmers was climbing to the temple to pray for rain, carrying their candles and incense and strips of colored paper. At that distance the wheedling of their horns, bells, and drums was inaudible, but some of the sophisticates in the bus — "guerrilla merchants" and other shabby urban types — noticed the procession anyway and leaned out the bus windows, waving and jeering until we reached the spot where our Yellow Fish waited.

10· *A City Falling Apart*

THE TRIP from Paochi past Sian to Loyang — a little more than three hundred miles — was one of the few in unoccupied China which could still be made by train. The towns were on the pre-war Lunghai Railway and on the first leg of the journey, travel was even luxurious for the Lunghai had a few Wagons-Lits sleepers, delivered from Europe in time to be brought west in the great retreat. These immense cars might move over an uneven single track, stopping at the mud huts of village stations, but their interiors, gleaming with mirrors, tropical-wood veneers, and chromium fittings would have caused paroxysms among the foreign thing-worshipers on the South Bank of trainless Chungking. All the fine coaches were used in a deluxe "Special Fast Express" which, because of the extra weight of the imported cars, was the slowest train on the line.

Twenty hours east of Paochi, ten east of Sian, the "Express" stopped at dawn on a dusty flat at the foot of the vertical granite pillar of Hua Shan, the sacred mountain which had inspired many classic fancies of Chinese landscape painting. The passengers for Loyang flung their luggage out the windows and doors, bargained for carts and mules, and like a cavalcade of pilgrims cantered briskly eastward through the milky morning light. At the top of the first low hill, the path came out above the Yellow River, beside its great right-angle bend. To the left, the wide sandy stream approached down the shallow mountain trough which brought it straight from north to south for some five hundred miles. To the right, it flowed off east through a widening valley, towards the ocean which was another five hundred miles away. Below and straight ahead, on the near shore of the sharp bend, lay the ruined and partly deserted city of Tungkwan, its painted gate towers hulking medieval and forlorn over bomb- and shell-pocked walls. The railway passed through a corner of the city and inshore from it the road to Loyang skirted the hills. It had been dug into a deep trench, and the crowding travelers moved around Tungkwan between walls of earth, like the Children of Israel through the heaped waters of the Red Sea. On the opposite side of the Yellow River, Japanese forts, flags, and sentries were clearly visible.

For three years Fenglingtu on the north shore had been Japan's deepest point of penetration in this part of China. Japanese troops moving southwestward down the railways from Peking had reached it in the first push of invasion, and built forts from which they could shell the railway and road on this side, the main arteries of east-west travel for the northern half of Kuomintang China. From time to time they tried to cross and completely block traffic, but the current was bad here and they had always been beaten back. Their own position at Fenglingtu was not too secure, for the Kuomintang still held flanking positions behind the Japanese salient, in the mountains on both sides. There were also Chinese Communist armies behind the Japanese lines all over North China.

By the time I passed through, the Tungkwan front was as stylized as could be with live ammunition. Passenger traffic had been stopped on the railway within reach of the Japanese artillery but freight trains crossed regularly at night; the Japanese usually exercised their cannon only in the late afternoon. Passengers could go across the railway gap by day in handcars, whenever a traveler arrived with enough money or prestige to wangle one; the Japanese seldom wasted ammunition on small targets. As Tungkwan city was within range of enemy guns the

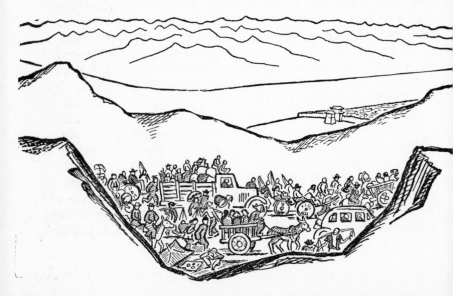

wealthy had moved out, but the farmers in the dangerous surrounding fields, and those in the city who felt they would lose more than they could gain by going, had stayed. In plain view of the sentries across the river, they went stubbornly about their business.

Later, when the Kuomintang became our ally and distinguished Americans came out to inspect the war effort, Tungkwan was the Kuomintang front they were taken to see. It was ideal for the purpose. An honored guest could reach it comfortably by "Special Fast Express," look at live enemies through field glasses, then move behind the Tungkwan hills and watch Kuomintang troops demonstrate an attack on imitation Japanese lines.

I crossed the railway gap by handcar as guest of an old gentleman who had shared a compartment with me from Sian, though whether this was lucky I could not decide as the car sped across the sloping fields in front of the Japanese forts, popping in and out of the bright spring trees like a tin duck in a shooting gallery. My host said he got the car because he was an ex-official and still had friends on the railway. Like the Magistrate I met at Shuangshihpu, who proved to be another friend of his, he was a Manchurian and had lost his job to a central "man" from Chungking. His response, he frankly admitted, was to become a smuggler. He was on his way to Chieh-shou, the busiest smuggling port in Honan.

That was a wonderful place, he claimed sarcastically, where more than a million dollars' worth of smuggled goods passed through daily (over U.S. $50,000 then). Bank notes were plentiful as leaves in Chieh-shou, and the firms which brought the goods up from Shanghai were so rich they kept free restaurants for their customers, serving finer food, Chinese or Western, than the best places in Chungking.

He looked successful himself, with smart luggage, a body-servant, and a supply of American cigarettes smuggled from Shanghai, but he feared the days of a free-lance like himself were numbered. The Kuomintang monopolies, particularly H. H. Kung's Central Trust, an affiliate of the Central Bank, were entering the trade on such a scale, and could get such favorable terms from the customs officials and the military who taxed smuggled goods, that the smaller private operators could hardly compete.

I had traveled from Paochi with a young CIC secretary who took a stern view of the cynical old man and when we reached the ruined station where we were to wait for the train to Loyang, he firmly made excuses for both of us and led me out into an orchard full of travelers napping in the shade while they waited for the train. Though this section of track was safe, several miles of it farther east were just within range of Japanese artillery and trains came to pick up passengers after dark. As we talked with the idlers here, it became clear that this was one of those queer Chinese journeys in which a few days' travel from one province to another put you not only in a world of different scenery, architecture, dress, and customs, but into a new climate of war.

As was feared in Shuangshihpu, the guns from Russia seemed not to have been sent east against the Japanese. They would have had to pass through Tungkwan and nothing had been seen of them here. Perhaps they were being hoarded in Sian or had been sent north against the Communists.

In Tungkwan, a possible Japanese attack on the Chungtiao Mountains, across the Yellow River, caused more worry. This range stretched through southern Shansi and northern Honan for nearly two hundred miles and held the Kuomintang's flanking position east of the Japanese at Fenglingtu. In some ways it was the key to the defense of the whole northern half of Kuomintang territory; as long as it was in Chinese hands it was risky for the Japanese to cross the Yellow River at either end of it. The Kuomintang had garrisoned the Chungtiao with some two hundred thousand men and armored it with forts so elaborate that they were called the "Maginot Line" of North China. The Japanese had already made thirteen unsuccessful attacks on it.

The gossipers in Tungkwan feared a new try because smugglers coming south from Peking reported three fresh Japanese divisions had arrived along the railway north of the Chungtiao. Smugglers going north had disgustedly returned to unoccupied territory, complaining the Japanese would not sell tickets to Peking, and this was thought to mean heavier troops movements were afoot. In Tungkwan, it was so widely believed the Japanese were building the new roads they needed for an all-out attack on the Chungtiao, and were paying good wages for labor, that many coolies and peasants from this Kuomintang side of the river had gone across to work for them.

When the train from Loyang arrived in the evening to pick us up, it seemed that even though the Yellow River made it safe to have a railway here, I had returned to the neglected, partly dismantled outer wastes of Kuomintang China. These cars had no plush carpets or chromium hand basins; many were converted cattle cars, and the few real passenger coaches were in the last stages of decay, their broken windows boarded over, their corridors feebly lit with vegetable-oil lamps.

On that night's journey we shared a compartment with company which must have been more painful to the CIC secretary than the old man of the hand car. They were an armed gendarme and a battered-looking man in his twenties, shackled together at the wrist. As soon as the lamps were blown out for our trip past the Japanese batteries, the gendarme began snoring and his captive spoke to my

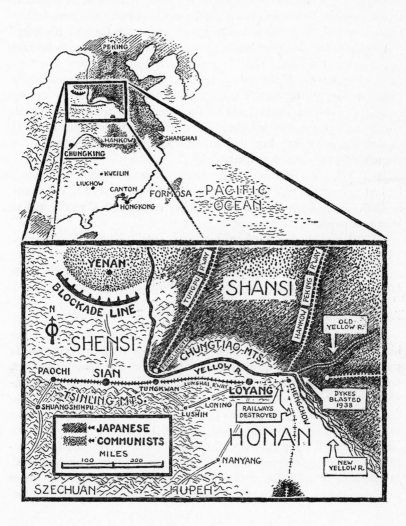

companion, whose CIC badge he had noticed. He asked after a few people he knew in the Co-ops, then said he was a hospital clerk since he could not afford to train as a doctor; he had thought of joining the CIC for an assignment to public health. After a silence while he bent closely over the gendarme to make sure he was asleep, he quietly explained he was on his way back to a Kuomintang "Thought Correction Camp" in Loyang after trying to escape on parole.

He had been sent to the camp because a fellow clerk accused him of being a Communist — in hope of taking over his job, he thought. In the camp he had been beaten with whips and poles and once had to lie face down while a board was placed across the back of his knees and jumped on. He confessed he was a Communist, though he said now he really wasn't. Then he was given good food and quarters, allowed to mix with the other students, and forced to attend daily lectures. Except for the youngest and weakest students — "crying girls," he said — he found most of the others uncorrected, unmoved, sardonic about the easy life they had without work or expense. Their studies were nothing but the Kuomintang rituals which had been dinned into them since primary school.

That was why he tried to get away. It was so boring. Though he had never been told how long he would have to stay in the camp, he had already been there a year and feared his escape would add at least one more.

"What will you do when you get out?" The CIC secretary whispered.

The other young man laughed softly. "I am going to get the most crooked job I can find," he whispered. "Make a lot of money."

It was dark enough so I could not see their faces.

In Loyang next morning, the low, richly wheat-covered hills behind the railway station, the solid gray buildings with full green shade trees before them, the crowds of city-people in pale summer clothes, were as distant in character from the red summits and blackened farmers of mountain Shuangshihpu as a thriving city in Illinois or Ohio would be from the most remote and benighted community in the Ozarks. Loyang's more timid industrialists had evacuated three years before, when the Japanese first threatened the city, and most productive enterprises still found capital hard to get in such an exposed area, but none of these blights showed to a new arrival. Loyang was a depot in the growing smuggling trade, and its commerce could hide indus-

trial depression. It was also capital of Honan, the richest wheat-grow-
ing province left in Kuomintang hands, and through it was taxed or
marketed much of the grain which fed the armies and bureaucrats
and city-dwellers of all the Northwest. Its one or two square miles of
old brick and tile houses, laced with a few streets of semi-Western
shops, sheltered well over a hundred thousand people, clattering about
the routines of Chinese urban life in fair prosperity. Its medieval walls
had been torn down to deprive the Japanese of protection if they took
it, but the lines of the old moat were still there, and outside them the
usual adjuncts of a semi-modern provincial capital were still operating:
railway suburb, official compounds, Catholic missions, Protestant missions, airfield, power station.

This was a pleasant surprise, since I had expected to find a corpse-
city like Wuchow and the other towns so close to the southern front.
But they were on the navigable West River, up which the Japanese
could easily attack, while Loyang had the wide, shallow, treacherous,
almost unnavigable Yellow River flowing partly around it, between it
and the Japanese. The river passed a little more than ten miles north
of the city, and about sixty miles to the east, beyond Chengchow,
where the dykes had been blasted to stop the Japanese, it swung south
across a wide swath of ruined farmland, rimming the whole eastern
boundary of the province with a belt of streams, swamps, and quick-
sands which the enemy had never been able to cross.

Another reason for Loyang's normal look was the Chungtiao
Range whose fortified summits, visible on clear days, rimmed the
north bank of the Yellow River where it flowed near the city. Beyond
the river and the mountains, the closest Japanese were some fifty miles
away.

Nevertheless, when I reached it at the end of April, Loyang was
beginning to tremble with rumors more alarming than those at Tungkwan, for a drive on the whole province from all the occupied areas
surrounding it was feared. Though Loyang was well protected against
a limited drive on the city itself, Honan was vulnerable to a larger
invasion, since it was a flattish, low-lying province, outside the mountain fortress of West China, cut off from the supplies and reserves of
the west by rugged mountains through which only three roads led,
one the bottleneck at Tungkwan, swept by Japanese artillery; the
other two, crude mountain trails. Unoccupied Honan had an area
larger than Denmark and roughly seven times Denmark's population —
about twenty-five million Honanese — but with these shaky strategic

prospects, the people of Loyang quite naturally told each other scare-stories. It was said the Japanese were not only building new roads approaching the Chungtiao in the north, but also in eastern Honan, beyond the flood-zone of the wartime Yellow River, and in Hupeh, the next province to the south. Worst of all, in the east they were rumored to be mending the blasted dykes near Chengchow; this could turn the Yellow River into its pre-war course farther north and open the whole eastern flank of the province to them.

It was reported, incidentally, that the Japanese officer in charge of the dyke-repair crews had sent a truce delegate to the Chinese commander on this side of the breach, asking him to stop his shelling because the Japanese were only trying to help the farmers in the flooded areas. When the Chinese commander refused, Japanese planes scattered leaflets on the flooded districts, claiming the Japanese wanted to mend the dykes for the farmers, but were being prevented by the Kuomintang. In 1941 this seemed just another capricious incident of a confused and peculiar war, but it made an unwhimsical memory in 1944, when the Japanese did take all Honan, and mobs of Chinese peasants attacked sizeable groups of Kuomintang troops, disarming and sometimes lynching them.

When I was in Paochi, I had planned to cross the Yellow River near Loyang and travel in the Chungtiao while I waited to see what would happen. As soon as I reached Loyang, it seemed wiser to wait there, and perhaps get a new pair of shoes for an emergency return to Paochi. Then, from May 3 on, it was borne in on everyone in Loyang that private decisions about personal futures might be a lost privilege.

The city began to have constant air raids. Hordes of troops slogged through it toward the Yellow River. Though the local Kuomintang press remained noncommittal, the rumors and refugees which began trickling in from north of the river told that something mystifying and disastrous was taking place in the Chungtiao Mountains. The Japanese had launched their fourteenth attack against the "Maginot" on May 3, but instead of being repelled as before, they broke through immediately. Their advance into the mountains was quicker than any since the most unprepared and panicky weeks at the beginning of the war. By May 11 they had infiltrated the range and occupied the northern side of all important Yellow River ferry crossings. Their front was now hardly ten miles from Loyang.

The official news continued to be reassuring, but Japanese artillery could be heard from the streets of Loyang. Thousands of refugees clogged the roads down from the Yellow River. The air-raids upon Loyang and the Lunghai Railway increased enough to suggest they were a softening-up for further invasion. It was rumored the Japanese at the river had already brought up parachutists and amphibious units for a crossing. In less than two weeks this city which had sheltered behind the vaunted Chungtiao defenses like an ants' nest under a log was uncovered and thrown into multifarious scurryings.

At first Loyang's change into a city of flight was obscured by its troubles as a city paralyzed by air attack. The weather remained perfectly clear, and five or six times a day the planes came, usually to scout and make small bombings in the mornings, mass attacks in the afternoons. This very compact town had only a few obsolete anti-aircraft guns and there could be no pretense of carrying on normally during alerts. The alarm sirens had no variety to tell what planes were coming, so at the approach of a single reconnaissance ship, the city would prepare for a real raid. Panic soon crept in when the alarm system broke down with the loss of lookout stations in the Chungtiao. The planes were often not spotted until they crossed the Yellow River, and by the time the sirens could make one quick crescendo, they were overhead.

The brief frenzies which convulsed the city when the sirens began growling up momentum were like those trick sequences in old movie comedies, in which a slowed-down camera suddenly changes an avenue of normally moving traffic into a lunatic street full of jerky black figures racing crisscross. One moment the dusty main street

would drone with its usual tempo of leisurely confusion. Just one cry of "Ching Pao" — Air Raid! — from someone with sharp ears, and the wooden shop shutters would clatter, the carters' whips crack, and the ground rumble with running feet. Each person tried to reach his home dugout, so they ran helter-skelter, bumping head on and catching one another's clothes in the things they were carrying. They clutched what they used for their parts in the regular life of the city, and in the dust and the terror, whose sound the mounting scream of sirens seemed to be, the homely objects had the same air of cruel comedy as the collisions and spills. The farmers with their twin baskets of tufted vegetables hung from carrying-poles, bobbed and ducked like mechanical toys. The cloth merchants charged past streaming armfuls of colored fabric. A comb seller would jitter crazily up the street, flailing the wand from which his wares jangled on strings. A caterer's apprentice jogged past, balancing a tray with a bowl of soup from which a boiled fish leaned to inspect the living panic with dead eyes.

The soil under Loyang was firm but malleable loess clay, and early in the war deep dugouts had been cheaply built under almost every house and shop. As the wail of the sirens sank from hearing, the people of the city sank from sight, scuffing down the steep steps and ramps into the tunnels. In the deepening roar of the planes the sun-baked streets were empty except for the policemen, peering uneasily from their corner pillboxes, shouting and sometimes shooting at stragglers.

But the clay dugouts were not proof even against near hits; after

each lengthening raid, the clean-up squads carried more straw-wrapped bodies through the streets. Nor were the dark, smelly caverns proof against rumors and other ills. Those who came coughing and gasping to the surface became slower to go about their business, preferring to talk apprehensively by the dugouts. Each day fewer shops re-opened, fewer people ventured on the big streets.

By May 11, when the Japanese had taken the Chungtiao and more planes were free to come to Loyang, the city was dying and its people knew it. The electricity failed because the powerhouse was bombed. The schools shut. The price of wheat went down as hoarders dumped their stocks to prepare for flight. The price of fresh vegetables went up when the farmers learned that if they came to town, they might be conscripted to help evacuate the official compounds. The price of real-estate, machinery, furniture, and all non-portable goods went down. The price of gold, jade, and small valuables which could be concealed as well as carried went up.

The raids spread over more and more of each day and the city began to have the shabby, dishevelled look I had known in Chungking the autumn before, with tangled wires and scatterings of rubble on the streets, posters and paper windows hanging in shreds. In the shops, the mirrors and glass show windows were taken down, the latter replaced by netting to keep out thieves. The merchants began moving their stocks into their cellars or out into the villages, and filled their shelves with empty boxes and a token display of the cheapest goods. Now the big streets were usually deserted from dawn to dark, except on one day at the height of the raids, a lucky one by the old calender

for weddings and funerals. Between bombings the little processions with their spangled red coffins or bridal chairs hurried furtively through the city, the musicians carrying their medieval horns and drums but not pausing to celebrate on them.

By the middle of the month, many streets were quite empty even at night, dimly lit by red and white lanterns and a nearly full moon. From behind the wooden shutters of shops came the sounds of packing and crating; from behind those of offices and banks jingled the counting boards of clerks clearing up their final accounts. Towards morning, when the moon went down and the lanterns guttered out, the black main street became a river of creaking, lowing, tolling sounds, as the farmers' belled oxen dragged the heavily loaded carts of the evacuees out of town.

During the first two weeks of May I went out into the country only briefly, but was struck by the gap between the lives of the city-people and the country farmers, just as great as in Shuangshihpu. No bombs had fallen outside the city limits and most peasants were not frightened by the threat of invasion. Some did not know of it. Many were not interested. Most planned to stay if the Japanese came. It seemed that the international war, with its air raids, battles, and evacuations, was a luxury for the city-people to monopolize, along with their newspapers, theatres, and leather shoes.

The Loyang peasants had a great enough worry of their own. However much richer it looked than the mountains of Shuangshihpu, the Honan plain was in the early stages of drought. As last year had been drier than normal, famine was likely if this crop and the autumn one were poor. The peasants of Honan, farming good wheat land, had to pay extra-heavy taxes and levies. Their grain reserves were almost gone.

Thus, while the city-people fearfully scanned the sky for planes, the country-people hopefully looked for clouds. Every day during the raids, banner-carrying delegations of old bound-footed peasant women came into Loyang, on their way to burn incense in the city temples where favorable weather was besought. Some had come tens of miles in the country buses which terrified them and made them sick. Dressed in their market-day best but without knowledge of public dugouts, with red embroidered shoes on their stumpy feet which could not run, they hobbled obstinately in from the suburbs under the sky which held no hope of rain, only the threat of steel. In the cities and the country alike, great famine in the following two years was to kill more Honanese than the whole Japanese war, but now the city-people, who could still afford to buy grain, were as little worried by the peasants' drought as the peasants were by the city's danger. Lolling at their dugouts, they laughed and mocked at the old country-women as they tottered by.

On May 16 I went into the country west of Loyang with a CIC organizer, Lao Tu — "Old" Tu — who was running the evacuation of the Loyang Co-ops. I know I began remembering that day vividly because it brought the heaviest bombings Loyang ever had; the alert lasted from five in the morning until after five in the afternoon, and some hundred and ten planes dropped at least seven hundred bombs. Later I thought of that day whenever I heard of another Chinese city trembling on the brink of dissolution. It gave a terrible picture of a community falling to pieces, partly because of external pressure — invasion — but also because of internal pressures, some inevitable, some the results of Kuomintang rule.

The first alarm sounded while it was still dark, and as the sky paled to a faint gray which might be cloud, a reconnaissance plane puttered like a sewing machine over Loyang and its suburbs. No bombers came, so at six Lao Tu and I cycled out over the flattened remains of the old city wall. The sky had brightened into perfect blue and the air was so clear that the Chungtiao Mountains could be seen, a faint lavender ridge above the low green hills hiding the Yellow River. On the long summit of the nearest hill the huge royal grave mounds, relics of Loyang's time as a national capital two thousand years before, were already sunlit. Streaked with mist, the threatened land had a deceptive air of freshness and fertility. The new leaves on the poplars and willows were not yet dust-coated and glistened darkly over the pale wheat; the fields which had been ruined by drought were bleached pale gold among the green. Everywhere the sloping plain stirred with city-people in light summer clothes.

Our way led along the main road west through Hsi Kung, the official suburb, but before we got there the reconnaissance plane came down along the road, very low. We put the bicycles in a ditch, covered them with grass and flowers, and went into a sparse little grove where two or three hundred people from the city were wandering among the trees or sitting on the small modern grave mounds. In

the center of the trees a new grave was topped by an elaborate funerary creature tethered to a pole, a long dragon of purple and white lace
paper. Food vendors had set up shop and several families were wolfing
noodles or eggs boiled in rice wine.

As we waited Lao Tu told me that the old temple across the road,
now used as a government office, was built on the site of the palace
of Yang Kwei-fei, the only fat one of China's famous beauties. She
had stayed in office for a record period as concubine of a Tang Emperor, by wearing garters and underpants so loose they were always
falling off and giving the Emperor opportunities to help her back
into them. She was also such a toper that the palace wits suggested her
epitaph should be: "Drunk But Still Drinking." Lao Tu took great
relish from the fact that in the ninth century Yang Kwei-fei had been
famously raped at the same hot-springs resort outside Sian — in Lin-
tung — which was the scene of the Generalissimo's abduction during
the Sian Incident.

When the reconnaissance plane returned to the grove and circled
over it, the eating and chattering and laughing stopped. There really
were too many people in so small a grove, particularly since the dry
weather had kept the foliage thin. Everyone lay down, curling in
heaps around the tree trunks, and each time the plane returned it sent
a new wave of the panic-stricken out into the wheat, awkwardly
crouched over and hopping like kangaroos. The paper dragon rolled
and tossed in the light breeze, waving a lacy tail at those who fled.

The reconnaissance plane made off to the north but before its puny
noise faded, the air grew thick and powdery with the roar of heavy
bombers. In the grove the recumbent people looked seriously at each
other, then began pulling at leaves and grass to throw over themselves.
Off to the east a tangled clot of people were frantically rushing north,
to the south a line of carts were whipped towards the east. By the
railroad tracks a scattered crowd running up a bare slope vanished
suddenly, into fox holes in a flash. All over the plain the people standing in the fields dropped into the wheat.

The sky was so radiant with mist it was impossible to spot the
bombers, but their thunder rolling smoothly from all sides told they
were close and low. Then the falling bombs fried and flapped and
down the whole half-mile length of Hsi Kung, a few fields away, the
explosions punched up, white and crinkled and solid-looking as giant
cauliflowers. The wheat rippled under the concussions as thirty-three
planes wheeled and passed overhead. Fires showed above the trees,

sending up fat columns of dirty brown smoke which drifted and thickened into a great dark slab. Then the slab tipped down and the acrid smoke poured rapidly out over the bright fields.

Lao Tu decided the best exit to the safer country beyond Hsi Kung would be through the narrow bottleneck between its southern walls and Loyang's small river, the Lo. As we passed, a horde of shaken soldiers was pouring out of the bombed official compound, their faces glistening with sweat, their guns glinting yellow in the blackened sunlight. In the narrowest part of the bottleneck, a mill stood at the mouth of a canal with its water wheel revolving thunderously. One soldier began to run, and all who were close enough to the mill not to know that no planes were audible ran too, and threw themselves into the wheat. Within a minute they noticed the farmers working peacefully in the silent fields farther away; then their own foolishness cheered them so much they abandoned their flight a few hundred yards farther on and gathered on a bridge to watch a fisherman on homemade water skiis, herding his flock of fish-catching birds, tame cormorants. In a dilapidated pillbox overlooking the bridge, a party of soldiers who had come out of Hsi Kung before the bombing were sedately playing cards with a couple of tarts.

This was out of the smoke and at a noodle stand under a tree Lao Tu and I stopped for breakfast. When all the garrison troops from Hsi Kung had recovered their breath, they seemed to think the bombings and the chance of invasion a lark. They were not local men, they said, so they had no families to worry about here. If the Japanese

came, they were sure they would not have to fight; they would go west, protecting the flight of the government. Since they were guards, not warriors, they were élite troops, well equipped and apparently well fed, with their jackets and pants comfortably full in the warm sunlight. Most of their conversation was extravagantly unprintable. While we waited for the noodles, one of them gained loud popularity with a Lamaist joke.

On a mountain of the Tibetan border lived a Lama Living Buddha, a minor one, and on the next mountain a Lama hermit. One day when the Buddha was old and sick, the hermit came scrambling down the mountains and sprinting to a village. He rushed to the first woman he saw, a young shepherd girl, and told her to lie down. She said her mother had told her never to lie down for strangers. He told her to go ask her mother again, so she trotted home. Her mother said of course she must do anything the holy hermit asked. Trotting back, she found him sitting dejected on a rock, all his haste gone. He pointed to the next field, where one donkey was mounted on another.

"The Living Buddha has just died, and I wanted to reincarnate him in human form," he said sadly. "Now the job has been done differently."

This was beginning to sound like one of those mornings of carefree air-raid chatter on the hills around Liuchow and other southern towns, hundreds of miles from the front. But these soldiers at the noodle stand, and a few others who had no settled life in Loyang, were the only adults I saw really entertaining themselves that day. Near a city only a few miles from a threatening front, a community beginning to scatter and lose its shape, even the pleasantries and obscenities over the noodles had a sinister ring.

Unlike the public conversations on the Liuchow hills, they might not be merely an innocent way of passing the time; they also seemed a first outcropping of that irresponsibility or nihilism, often cruelly humorous, which could overtake soldiers and other rootless ones during a crisis which dissolved the fabric of society. When the break-up had proceeded far enough, the spirit of detachment could lead beyond jokes, into looting, rape, and murder.

The plain where all this was happening was two or three miles wide, inclining gently upward from Loyang through Hsi Kung and on for three or four miles to the first range of western hills. On one side lay the low slopes hiding the Yellow River, on the other meandered the small Lo River, in the drought hardly more than a brook seeping over a wide bed of gravel. All the wheat-covered plain was splotched with compact little farm villages, standing in their groves no farther apart than single farmhouses would be spaced in America. Between the villages, the fields were broken by smaller round islands of trees, shading the grave mounds with which the centuries had burdened the land. Across the center of the plain, a straight line of trees marked the one motor road leading from Loyang to the comparative safety of the western mountains.

After the big dawn attack on Hsi Kung, the bombers began visiting Loyang itself, diving on it in threes or sixes every fifteen minutes or half an hour. Since no Chinese fighter planes appeared during the whole series of Chungtiao raids, it was safe for them to come in small numbers. Because their airfields were so close, they had gasoline for a leisurely selection of targets. All day they circled and dove like bees pestering a mole, and the sky at the eastern end of the plain, over the city, bulged with smoke and dust. Sometimes this plumed up in many single columns, sometimes it sagged down in one wide mushroom. In the morning, when the sun was on the other side, it seethed like a heap of gray and cream-colored gauze. In the blaze of noon it was almost invisible, except for thin streaks of scratchy black. In the late afternoon, when the sun struck it from the west and the air was full of dust from many feet, it thickened and brightened and seemed to expand, polluting half the sky with bands of yellow and orange and brown.

All day under the trees, tens of thousands of people from the city wandered or sat, marched or ran. There were single people and groups of all sizes: families, military units, the staffs of shops, and of entire government bureaus. Some had just come out for a day away from the noisome dugouts; some had moved their things into the villages and were preparing for their final flight; many were already on their way into the mountains. In the morning, when the trees cascaded silver in the fresh light, they moved about quite methodically, or quietly watched in the groves while their children amused themselves. By noon, when the trees floated still and greasy over their inky shadows, the heat and the buzzing and snarling of the planes and the merciless pounding of explosives in the city began to have its effect. When the planes flew over, they were more inclined to bolt, rushing crisscross in and out of the groves, scattering into the wheat. Along the moter road, scare rumors passed from mouth to mouth.

Yellow River artillery was intermittently audible all day, and more and more fearful glances were cast toward that low slope in the north, and beyond it the Chungtiao Mountains, now shimmering cobalt in the glare. By midafternoon, some people would start to run for a while even when no planes were near. Some hastened back toward the city, to risk salvaging what they could before what they thought was happening did happen. More hurried out along the road to the mountains. It seemed as if a steady wind were pushing over the slope from the Yellow River. As yet it was strong enough only to send a few stray leaves tumbling, but behind it was power which could billow all the leaves away, flatten the forest, and blow the ponds empty, exposing the hidden creatures of the mud.

By the end of the afternoon, when the wheat fields were solid yellow in the hot slanting light and the farmers who had been imperturbably harvesting them all day were starting back to their villages, the road to the west was filled with people slowly moving away from Loyang afoot or in carts, rickshaws, wheelbarrows, and automobiles. Over the trees by the road, the long straight snake of dust raised by their passing stretched all the miles from the towering smoke in town to the edge of the hills. In the fields a little distant from the road, their shouting, wailing and cursing, merged into a low, quavering, continuous sound, like the moan of a stricken beast pouring out its blood in a long, fatal stream.

In the morning of that day, after our breakfast of noodles, Lao Tu and I had cycled to the CIC's evacuation headquarters in a machinists' Co-op in the village of Chiliho, "Seven Li River" on the western road about a mile beyond Hsi Kung. Here some of the thousands of problems underlying the vast spectacle on the plain were being discussed, vociferously or sadly. The CIC planned a more thorough evacuation than the average Kuomintang organization — it would move all its workmen as well as its officials — but even so, the Co-op evacuees were torn by conflicts and confusions.

The Chiliho machinists caught Lao Tu into their troubles as soon as he arrived. They wanted to return all the bank loans the CIC had arranged for them, since they were of peasant stock, associated banks with "government," and feared that if the invasion interfered with their payment of interest they would be cruelly punished. Reassured on this point, they began to discuss whether to evacuate as a Co-op or go to their family village and become farmers again.

The shoemakers' Co-op which came through during the morning was in the throes of a savage argument whether to continue evacuating; some members wanted to wait in Loyang until it was conquered, then move to one of the bigger Japanese-occupied cities farther east, where business was supposed to be better.

The women's Co-op, for spinning and needlework, later arrived in complete confusion, stampeded by the dawn bombing of Hsi Kung. Most of its older members already wanted to go back to Loyang, uneasy because they were farther from their homes — nearly three miles — than ever before, and frightened to be going into strange country with an organization, not a family. Only the youngest girls, the most enthusiastic at rallies, were happy. While the organizers tried to persuade the older ones from going back, these junior misses delighted the machinists — who had washed and put on their best clothes as soon as the women began arriving — by briskly inspecting the Chiliho Co-op and asking questions about profit and loss, markets and raw materials, with an absurdly professional air. Then they borrowed tools and metal scraps from the machinists and set about making themselves crochet hooks. Later they burst into tears when, despite all pleas, an older member with two small children decided to rejoin her husband and started back towards Loyang.

The printers' Co-op which came through with its press and type loaded on oxcarts was the only single-minded group. Its members were mostly boys twelve to sixteen years old, and to them the crisis meant that all the remote talk they had heard at CIC rallies, about *Building for Resistance* and *The War of Attrition*, had suddenly become immediate and thrilling. With the pomp of much smaller kids playing motorman-and-conductor, they cooked and ate their late breakfast, reassembled their caravan and disappeared down the western road, boasting of the great things they would do as guerrillas if the Japanese came.

Towards the end of that sun-struck morning, I cycled out the western highway beyond Chiliho. In the corridor of choking dust which boxed the road, the outcroppings of savagery among the masses of other evacuees made the disagreements within the Co-ops seem like fond family tiffs. Whenever the crowded traffic tangled on itself, there was unnaturally fierce shouting and sometimes fist-fights, almost unknown in placid times in China. There were bitter quarrels wherever food was sold, or transport bargained for. The keepers of restaurants and food stalls were profiteering to the limit before they had to

flee west themselves; prices were four or five times higher than usual. Carters, barrowmen, and rickshaw men were charging whatever they thought the traffic would bear, and their prices climbed steadily.

Though its flight had been on for days longer than that of most private citizens, the Kuomintang government was still foremost in this turmoil. Nearly all the automobiles and perhaps half of the carts were piled with the families, furniture, and files of the provincial capital's great civil and military bureaucracy. The government was also the chief contributor to the air of hasty, brutish, self-preservation which hung over the road in a miasma as choking as the dust. Its carts were conscripted, or sometimes "confiscated" without any payment, and were dragged or driven by peasants as closely watched by armed guards as if they were convicts, or army conscripts. Many of the roadside fights were caused by government people or soldiers who attempted to "confiscate" more or better transport for themselves, or were using their authority or guns to buy whatever they wanted at prices below the fair, non-profiteering ones. In the panic of removal the government was even beginning to savage itself; the spiral of monopoly and exclusion was tightening so rapidly, within the privileged minority, that its results were visible.

The many vehicles of the bigger officials and the more important offices were the most raffish, for the powerful could commandeer all the transport they wanted. Their cars and carts were loaded with household goods complete to hat racks, porch hammocks, and potted palms. Some carried broken furniture, odd lumber, strips of old matting — the kind of junk that collects in a cellar. The human cargo on these carts was as motley a jumble: special guards, servants, their families, poor relatives and other courtiers, their families, their friends and friends of friends, and all the illicit riders the marginal passengers had been able to smuggle on through personal "deals," or for a price. Heading west in defeat and retreat, these caravans seemed an even better symbol of the modern Kuomintang than the Shuangshihpu trucks with their cargoes of commercial Yellow Fish.

There was a small middle stratum of semi-important officials evacuating with one family, a modicum of luggage, and a couple of trusted servants loaded on each cart. Then came the wagons packed with the proletariat of the privileged class: the petty bureaucrats, the accountants, the clerks. They jolted west with angry faces, because they had to abandon all that would not fit into one suitcase, and many husbands had to leave their families to wander west by themselves. Along the side of the road trudged the dispossessed of the official minority; many bureaus had reacted to this uncertain time by firing the less influential people who formed the outer layers of their pearl. The rejected ones were fleeing west on their own savings, hoping that in the western mountains their offices would begin rehiring help.

Naturally there was bitterness on every level. The people afoot cursed those in carts, those with one cart complained about those with six, those with unlimited carts resented the ones who could evacuate to Sian by special train. Those on the train had no doubt grumbled about the smaller élite who could go out by plane.

In later weeks, when the Chungtiao invasion and the evacuation were being rancorously recalled, it began to seem that the rôle of the Kuomintang government, exemplified in this opportunist flight, had been second only to the Japanese army in shaping Loyang's troubles. No doubt any community in any country would have shown signs of dissolution when it suddenly realized that a threatening enemy front had come so close. In Loyang the trend was hastened by official action.

During all the first days of crisis, the Kuomintang had used its news outlets to promote a false sense of security in non-official Loyang. Of the Chungtiao, the local paper usually printed only the brief, incomplete, optimistic communiqués supplied all over China by Central News. The Loyang papers thus had a more coherent account of the current Nazi attack on Crete than of the nearby Japanese invasion. Editorially, the papers warned the citizens not to talk about the local military situation, lest that "cause the people to become restless." Meanwhile, "government's" own flight in its conscripted carts was getting underway.

After the Japanese reached the Yellow River, the papers carried a few official warnings about parachutists; non-government gossips guessed this was mainly because Nazi use of parachutists in Crete had made them seem glamorous, and "anti-parachute precautions" would look well in bureaucratic reports to Chungking. No effort was made to inform non-official citizens of the more routine facts of their danger, nor to advise them when, where, or how to evacuate. Private evacuees who went up the western road soon began returning to Loyang, saying that living conditions in Loning and Lushih, the cities in the mountains, were impossible. The earliest official evacuees had already "confiscated" all available quarters and cornered the food supplies, driving prices beyond the reach of all except the richest.

In effect, at the first sign of insecurity, the Kuomintang had abdicated its position of leadership and responsibility. By May 16, with the government in full flight, this threatened community was actually in a state of anarchy. So far, officials were the ones who had most openly adopted the ruthlessness needed in an anarchic struggle for survival, but a slight increase in panic could infect all the leaderless with the same spirit. The police were leaving as hastily as the rest of the government. If it could become known, for example, that the Japanese had crossed the Yellow River, there were no restraints to keep the whole Loyang plain from being disfigured with a monstrous enlargement of those brief air-raid panics in the city. What was left of orderly life could crack apart and be engulfed in the passions of a mob running crisscross, colliding with itself. The cruelties which often marked Kuomintang panic-retreats were collisions of a sort, between abandoned people who might all be equally terrified.

On that sixteenth of May, with the Kuomintang's own evacuation still incomplete, the western road was thoroughly guarded by soldiers and only the thinnest edge of this danger showed through the bright surface of the day. The crisscross motion was already established, however. The main movement was always westward, but a number of disillusioned private evacuees were returning from the mountains, while others were going from side to side, looking for secluded villages where they could be conquered with some hope of safety. Violence was also beginning to show; within a few miles of Chiliho, I saw a stripped corpse in a ditch, its throat slit from ear to ear. In the tea shops by the road, uneasy conversations told of the beginnings of greater collapse.

. . . "Don't try to ride as a 'Yellow Fish' on a military convoy. One of them came through yesterday, taking as many as it could carry. When it got out in the country, the soldiers drove the Yellow Fish off and looted their baggage . . . "

. . . "These restaurant keepers should be more careful how they put up their prices. Down the road one tried to double his price while his shop was full of customers who had ordered but had not paid. They beat him up and broke his dishes . . . "

. . . "He was a professional carter and had been hired by a merchant to take his things up to Lushih, but when he was passing an official convoy which had one broken cart, the soldiers stopped him, threw the merchant's things into the ditch, and made him join the convoy. The merchant had already paid him for the trip to Lushih but the carter didn't like being kidnaped anyway. That night he bribed the soldiers with some of the merchant's money and escaped, with part of the official luggage still in his cart . . . "

. . . "Beyond Loning, be careful to sleep only in big villages. Two nights ago, some armed men — deserters or farmers — raided a small village full of refugees and robbed everyone. Two men and a child were accidentally killed . . . "

Three years after this, in the spring of 1944, when Loyang finally fell to the Japanese, friends of mine who were there told me that the trend toward social disintegration did burst into open anarchy. Along the western road, the evacuees robbed and murdered one another in the struggle to escape. On the hills, bandits, deserters, and farmers — who by that time had been through two years of starvation — roamed in hordes, pouncing on the road whenever they saw groups of evacuees weak enough to attack. After the Japanese surrendered and the civil war began, Loyang was the first former provincial capital within China proper to fall to the Communists, in the spring of 1948.

Certainly the first reason why the Loyang plain was not the scene of utter chaos on that May day of 1941 was that the Japanese did not cross the Yellow River. Secondly, the Kuomintang troops which had been defeated in the Chungtiao were bottled up there by the early loss of the Yellow River crossing places. They could not flee south, spreading disorder and terror as they had after too many other lost battles.

A third reason was the calm of the peasants, perhaps stupid, perhaps sensible. The tens of thousands of nervous city-people wandering in the country could always see greater numbers of matter-of-fact farmers and their families, busy with their ordinary tasks. It was as if the toiling peasants in all the fields were connected by invisible ropes which spread a net over the country, preventing unrestrained running and despair. "Government" — the lofty and paternal abstraction which promised to do good things for its people when they had proved themselves worthy — was leading the trend toward confusion and lawlessness. It was the lowliest and most despised of "government's" national children — the peasant "people" — who supplied adult stability.

In the afternoon of that day Lao Tu and I visited a few farm villages on the edge of the hills, where some of the Co-ops were to move temporarily, and there it seemed that the one problem of crisis which really interested the farmers was the Kuomintang conscription of carts. This had been done through the Pao-Chia system, and while the exactions varied from place to place, the average demand had been for thirty carts from every Pao, approximately every hundred families. As the poorest families had no carts, and some carts were shared by two or more families, this was at least half of the transport of most villages. Payment for use of the carts also varied greatly. Unlucky farmers got nothing. The luckiest got ten Kuomintang dollars (fifty American cents) a day for use of a cart, two oxen, and two men to handle them. This was not enough to feed the men and animals on their western trip. They were paid nothing for their return trip. To Lushih and back took more than a week by oxcart.

In most villages the farmers had started pools so the cost of the government evacuation would be shared by families lucky enough not to have had their carts taken. But everyone was worried, because the harvest was now started. It was a serious problem to get the crop in with so many carts and men gone; old people and children had already been pressed into service in the fields.

But even in the villages crippled because of the Japanese advance, there was surprisingly little knowledge of the invasion. Some farmers did not know that the Japanese had already reached the Yellow River, that some of the explosions they heard were artillery, not bombs. If questioned too closely about the war, they would laugh their amiable, non-committal laugh.

"In the city they know about such things," they would say, politely moving away.

As I was beginning to learn, the peasants all over Kuomintang

China could be curiously neutral, regarding the war as a distant abstraction, like "government," vaguely connected with themselves but
too complicated to understand. This was natural enough. By 1941 the
Kuomintang had abandoned even its superficial, United Front, campaign of war-propaganda in the villages. The kind of news which terrified city-people had to percolate into the villages slowly and indirectly. Also, the constant traveling back and forth across the fronts
had informed the peasants that many farmers in occupied territory
were not so much worse off than themselves. Some were better off.
Consequently the war to them had none of the emotional character
it could acquire among more prosperous people. It was more like a
kind of bad weather which might pass over a farmer's fields. His wise
course was just to stay home, trying to prevent or repair the damage
to his own holdings. Because so few farmers left their land, incidentally, I believe the Kuomintang's claim that eighty million people
emigrated west during the early years of Japanese attack was greatly
exaggerated. I doubt if the real figure exceeded twenty million.

The peasant attitude to war was shown in the way those who
were ignorant of politics and battles could be informed of any war
measures which directly affected themselves. Such news traveled by
village bamboo-telegraph and rapidly spread over hundreds of miles,
on both sides of the front. One example, from before the Chungtiao
battle, was the way good Japanese wages for roadwork had been
reported south of the Yellow River, attracting laborers from Tungkwan and other places in unoccupied territory. In the Loyang villages
on May 16 I heard two other items of unpublished news which had
traveled more than a hundred miles.

One was that officials near Nanyang, in southern Honan, had become so frightened of invasion that they ordered all farmers within
half a mile of the motor roads to destroy their houses, to keep the
Japanese from using them as forts if they occupied the roads. The
Loyang farmers were worried that the same might happen here. The
second story was that only a few days ago on the Lunghai Railway
between Loyang and Tungkwan, a train full of peasant conscripts
had been bombed and burned. The line had been under constant air
attack, but the conscripts were locked in freight cars to prevent their
escape. About two hundred were burned to death. Some farmers
around Loyang feared their sons had been on the train.

Under all these threats and fears they still went about their daily tasks with their patient industry. As Lao Tu and I went back from the villages to the motor road, we passed an old farmer resting beside his harvest. He was watching the road with its long cavalcade of fleeing city-people. As we came up, he laughed and gestured toward them.

"Ta-men mei-yo ban-fa," he said contemptuously. "They have no method."

He waved towards himself and his village, "*Wo-men* yo ban-fa," he said proudly. "*We* have a method."

On the way back to Chiliho in the blazing midafternoon, Lao Tu and I stopped to rest in a tiny grove of three and a half trees sheltering a well and two and a half drunks. The man with the bottles said he was a street merchant who had tried to evacuate with his small stock of coat hangers, belts, and other sundries loaded on a hired wheelbarrow. The barrowman would only bargain for one day at a time and each day farther west had charged a higher price. Finally, during an air raid, he had got away with the barrow and the goods. That was enough evacuation for him, this merchant decided, and started back east. He planned to cross the front to his old home in occupied territory, and set up as a street merchant there. When he found he could not pass through Loyang today because of the raids, he had bought a couple of bottles of pei-k'arh — raw white whiskey —

and a supply of cigarettes, and settled under the trees to enjoy himself.

Propped against the half-tree was his only dependent, an old uncle, happily half-conscious, clutching a broken bird cage stuffed with his other pair of shoes, his towel, his toothbrush, and his tattered copy of the ancient classic, *Tales of the Three Kingdoms*. The second full-drunk was a country peddler of needles, buttons, and notions, who had stopped off the road as a stranger earlier in the day, scenting a free drink. Since he carried his business in a tray and had not slept in a bed of his own since he left his father's home as a child, he too was free of the pressures which drove the crowd on the highway.

They had made the grove their own, prodigally tossing away half-smoked cigarettes until the grass seemed spangled with white flowers. From the tinfoil in the cigarette packages they had twisted an army of tiny wine goblets, marshalled on the beaten earth at the lip of the well. They offered us drinks, and in the afternoon heat, a gulp of alcohol made the grove an island remote from the alarms of the mainland.

To the eye of one sprawled stomach-down in the shade, the coarse overhanging grass with its multiple joints and spears, the squadrons of tiny crinkled goblets beyond, the glittering black ants which investigated both, made a world as large and important as the distant one containing the burning city and the dishevelled crowds on the tree-lined horizon. By this time all anti-aircraft fire in Loyang had petered out and the Japanese planes ignored the spatter of rifle fire which followed their approach. While we lay there, three came in from the north, wheeled overhead and followed the motor road east for their run over the city, so low that the little bristly pilots, distinct behind their glass, were seen as queer creatures halfway between the sharp insect world and the hazy world of men.

In the grove the castaways were having a wonderful time. When we came up they had been rolling with laughter because of a man in the village where the liquor was bought, who had been so frightened by the dawn bombing of Hsi Kung that he jumped down the vent hole of a dugout — a twenty-foot, vertical drop — and broke both legs. The merchant, a hairy little man, round and hard as an apple, tried to kick his uncle awake to tell a story he liked; when only snores resulted he told it himself. I later learned it came from *Strange Tales from a Chinese Studio*, an ancient collection of fables.

"It was at the end of one of the dynasties, I forget which. The cities were decaying and there were bandits in all the hills. In one city a young man inherited a sword from his grandfather, a fine sharp sword, the kind they didn't make any more. With it he got a good job in the 'Bandit-Suppression Corps.'

"Once the 'Corps' caught six bandits and took them home to cut off their heads. One bandit had lived in the same street as the young man and knew how sharp his sword was, so he asked him as an old neighbor to cut off his head himself.

"The other bandits had their heads chopped off by men with poor new swords, who had to hack and hack. When this bandit put his on the block, the young man with the good old sword took only one slice. The head almost jumped from the body, and rolled along the ground, shouting:

" 'What a sharp sword!' "

When they finished with the delight and the drink that went with this one, the peddler wiped his stringy face on the back of his hand and paid for his next several drinks with another story.

"It must have been about fifteen years ago, in the villages between the railway and the Yellow River. There were two kids the right age and their families made an engagement for them. The boy was about eight, the girl a year or two younger. But before they were old enough to marry, the boy was taken off by some soldiers who came through. His family never heard from him and after a few years they decided he was dead. When the girl grew up she was so pretty her father had no trouble arranging another match, with the son of a rich landlord. The father was a poor farmer and the marriage-contract included enough money for him to settle his debts.

"Just three days before the wedding, the first boy came back. He had been in the army in Sian, was a corporal, had a nice uniform, and had grown up strong and good-looking. When he came and asked for his bride, though, her father explained she was promised to someone else, and the family would be ruined if she didn't keep her second bargain. The boy hadn't seen her and hadn't heard how pretty she was, so he agreed and started back to his own family village.

"But the girl had been at home when he came. When she heard a strange voice outside, she wet her finger and worked a peep-hole through the paper window. She liked what she saw so much better than the landlord's son that she slipped out by the back door and caught up with the corporal in the fields. She said she thought she was still engaged to him and asked him to take her away. He liked her looks as much as she liked his, so they secretly went to the railway station and took the train to Sian.

"When he heard the girl had disappeared, the landlord's son collected a gang of relatives. Armed with scythes and pitchforks and bird-guns they went to look for her at the corporal's house. It happened nobody was home there except a maiden aunt, and she was in bed with the teacher of the primary school. He hid in a cupboard while the aunt threw on her clothes and went to answer the pounding at the gate. When she saw the crowd with their guns, she lost her wits. She thought she was already found out and it was useless to hide anything.

" 'Where is the person?' they shouted as they rushed in.

" 'The person is in the cupboard!' she replied, thinking they wanted the schoolteacher.

"They swarmed to open it, but she screamed: 'The person has no clothes on!'

"Naturally they thought the girl was inside. They tied ropes around the cupboard and carried it off to the bridal chamber in the landlord's house. The maids of the family took off the ropes and tried to coax the person out. They brought soap and perfumed water and silk clothes from the wedding chests, telling the shut cupboard everything they did. Then they went into the hall and coaxed through closed doors.

"But the room stayed silent. When they went in again, of course, they found only the poor old naked primary teacher. He had just hanged himself from a rafter with one of the silk bridal sashes."

Lao Tu seemed very thoughtful, knitting his thick eyebrows into a single line across his big Aztec-looking face as we walked our bicycles back toward Chiliho through the evacuee traffic.

"His story reminds me of another hanging," he said at last. "It happened last year, very near here. The machinists at Chiliho told me about it.

"Just beyond their village were twenty mou of land owned by an old man, a widower. His sons were dead and he was too weak to farm, so he rented his land to tenants who paid him half their crop. He was supposed to pay all taxes out of his half. In a normal year the land gave three hundred catties of wheat a mou, but last year his fields were dry and the crop was a failure. The tenants reaped only about twenty catties a mou, and the old man got little more than two hundred catties altogether.

"Soon after the harvest, the Chia-Chang came with soldiers and told him his tax of army grain came to two hundred catties. As he had already eaten some of it and didn't know how much was left, he brought it out sack by sack for the collectors to weigh. When he had brought almost two hundred catties he went in and did not come back. After waiting and shouting, the Chia-Chang went into the grain room which he found empty except for the old man, dead, hanged from a rafter."

As I had been learning ever since I left Chungking, many young men like Lao Tu, born and educated in the modern coastal cities, but now in war jobs among the peasants of the interior, had placed themselves in a life as alien from their own as an American city dweller from the Atlantic seaboard might find among the Indians of Arizona or New Mexico. Out of interest or boredom, almost all had become amateur sociologists.

Of course their position as strangers from the east coast was far more difficult, even tragic, than that of any New Yorker in temporary trouble on a Navajo reservation. Here they themselves were the isolated and freakish minority, bred in the treaty-ports which were the reservations of their kind. The primitive villagers with their hard ways and cruel troubles, surprising and shocking, were in fact the undiscovered people of all the rest of their country.

Most of these modern young men as yet had little idea that the underlying insecurity and brutality of life in the interior could affect their own lives; their village stories were just odd trinkets to roll around and compare in conversation. About Lao Tu I was not certain. He was older than most of his colleagues in unprofitable public work in this late year of the sagging war. On the road to Chiliho he looked long and sharply at the people hurrying away from the disintegrating city before he went on with another story, of the break-up of one family:

"At the Co-ops in Kunghsien, down the road to Chengchow, I heard about a farmer and his wife who lived there with their only child, a twenty-year-old son. Because of their debts the family had lost all but six mou of their land; five are needed to feed one adult here, and they would have starved if it weren't for their son. He had a job in a coal mine and they were just able to get by.

"Last summer the whole village was surprised and pleased when the old wife became pregnant again. She was over forty and had not thought more children were coming. When she had a baby boy, her husband sold three chickens to get money for a party.

"Next time the conscription officers came, they reminded these parents that only one son in a family was exempt. Now they had two sons, so the older would have to go. The weeping mother went to the Chia-Chang, the Pao-Chang, then the Lien-Chang, trying to explain this was a special case. If she and her husband lost the support of their older boy, they could never keep up with their debts. They would lose the rest of their land and there was no telling what would become of them and the baby.

"The officials were not interested. They said the law was the law and there was nothing to do about it. She found something to do, though. She went home and beat her baby on the ground until it was dead."

When we reached the machinists' Co-op, Lao Tu found the beginning of another tale for his list. The tanners' Co-op had come in from Loyang and they were so angry they had nearly forgotten to complain about the evacuation. One of their members was a veteran who had fought all through the Shanghai campaign of 1937 and had been wounded twice. When his army scattered after the fall of Nanking, he had been unable to find his officers and went back to his home in Yuhsien, in southern Honan. As his only brother was a cripple, the conscription officers had taken him away again in 1938, then dismissed him because he was still weak from his wounds and his long walk home. When they came next year he was able to bribe them with seventy-five Kuomintang dollars, and when they came in 1940 they were satisfied with a hundred. Shortly afterward, he came to Loyang and joined the Co-op. Now his father had come up from Yuhsien with the news that he was wanted again for the army. Because this son was not at home, the old man had been held as a hostage for two weeks, then given a flogging and sent to Loyang to find him.

The son could go back as a conscript, the old man could go back to jail, or the family could buy a substitute. It was an almost universal practice for families with enough money to buy substitutes to keep their sons out of the army — a middle- or upper-class soldier was a rarity. But with the inflation well under way, substitutes now cost seven hundred to a thousand Kuomintang dollars apiece, and this old

man would have to go into debt to get one. Meanwhile he was evacuating with his son's Co-op, and all the tanners had passionately entered the case. Of course there was no satisfactory answer; they were
still arguing and swearing as they went off along the western road.

Lao Tu had been abrupt with the tanners and before they left, he
shut himself up in the room he had occupied in the machinists' Co-op
earlier in the year, while he was trying to get the Co-op started. He
still kept one of his suitcases here, and when I went in I found him
looking through a photograph album, the kind of personal record I
had seen pulled out of suitcases in barren rooms all over West China.

First came the snapshots of the pre-war childhood, of the Scout
Troop visiting Nanking and Hangchow, the mother and sisters on the
veranda in their smart Western clothes, the pretty co-eds behind tennis nets, the line of racers on the white lip of the pool at the Shanghai Civic Center. After the graduation group-photo came newspaper
clippings with grisly news pictures of the first days of war in 1937.
From Hankow, during the United Front in 1938, came the photographs of giant parades with posters and banners, of groups of eager
sunburned young men and women lined up on the steps of public
buildings, of smiling girls in uniform, posing in a park before iron
models of the Woolworth Building, London Bridge, and the Eiffel
Tower.

Lao Tu looked very slowly through his Hankow pages, pointing
out the faces: "This one died of TB in Shansi" . . . "This one went
back to Shanghai and got a job in the puppet Railway Administration" . . . "This one went over to the Communists" . . . "This one is
making a lot of money on the Burma Road" . . . "This one is in the
'Thought Correction Camp' in Chungking." Toward the back of the
album, in the pages for 1939 and 1940, there were fewer and smaller
and more blurry photographs — of a crumpled girl in a patched uniform, a broken-down bus, a few farm women with crude looms, grin-
ning foolishly in front of a cave. The last pages had no pictures at
all: film had become too expensive, the camera too rusty, the friends
had drifted away.

"I'm fed up!" Lao Tu suddenly shouted. "Fed up! Fed up! Fed
up!" He riffled the empty pages, slammed the album, and scaled it
into a corner.

"You didn't know I was engaged, did you?" he said savagely. "I
have been for three years and I haven't seen her in two and a half,

since we had to evacuate Hankow." He emptied the suitcase on the floor and began violently sorting his things into two piles. "If we have to leave Loyang, I'm through with this damned public work. I'm going right on through to Chungking. My girl's uncle is a big shot in the CC police and I'm going to ask him to get me a job, any kind of a rotten desk job that will make me enough money to have a wife."

When the all-clear sounded faintly from Loyang at half past five in the afternoon, the raid had been going on so long it took the crowds on the plain nearly an hour to readjust to the new idea. The sun was down before any number began pushing their way down the road to the city, along the column of evacuees still streaming west. Flocks of birds wheeled and chittered in the green sky, and up and down the line of feverish, tired, and excited people there was more twittering as panic rumors spread, together with rumors of hope, just as wild.

Near the city the returning crowds fell silent when they passed fugitives of a new sort: bombed ones, covered with dust, hurrying away from their houses with clutchings of useless luggage or none at all. Apparently the whole twelve hours of attack had had little purposes except terror; the railway station was the only military target damaged. Among other things hit were the smugglers' godowns outside the South Gate, full of Japanese goods; Loyang's biggest brothel, called the "New China Study Parlor"; several crates of Bibles smuggled from Shanghai by a Protestant missionary who had them in a warehouse awaiting shipment to Chungking.

In town most of the people from the dugouts seemed feverish, but in the advanced stage where lassitude and stupor set in. Along the dim streets cloaked with smoke and dust, clogged with rubble, there were few public discussions; all were withdrawing into their personal dilemmas too rapidly for talk. They hardly stopped to look when bodies or parts of them were carried past. The Fire Department had been bombed or evacuated, and where there was still any blaze from the bombs, the householders fought it alone, slowly and hopelessly, with splashings of water from dishpans and cooking pots; there was little danger of fire spreading in this city of brick walls, so no outsiders helped. The owners of blasted houses scrabbled among their wreckage, trying to save everything of value before it was dark and the ruins lay open to the many-handed monster they feared might come with the night. Owners of partly damaged houses hastily tried to build thief-proof barricades over the gaps in their fortress. The owners of undamaged houses locked themselves in for the food and rest they desperately needed, or locked themselves out and headed for the western road.

I remember only one man who moved against the tide of that apprehensive evening. Near the big central corner lay a poorly dressed woman who had been in a collapsed dugout. Her husband had been crushed to death, and she had a bad cut on her scalp. She kept sitting up and falling back, working her mouth as if it were full of feathers, feebly calling for her children. They were right beside her, two of them stretched motionless, almost unbreathing, while the oldest, a girl about nine, tried to scrape the dirt from their clothes. A fourth child who had been searching the ruins of their house joined them, weeping bitterly, and vindictively kicking the body of a bombed kitten before him. All the children began to cry.

A few idlers stood about, smoking cigarettes and advising the little girl to take her mother to a hospital. When a broken-down rickshaw pulled by a bedraggled man came past, the child tried to bargain for it. The rickshaw man wanted more than she had. He was moving away when a heavy-set, middle-aged coolie who had just come up, as ragged as the rickshaw man, shouted angrily:

"Take her without any charge! We're all poor people aren't we?"

The idlers laughed, so the rickshaw man could not refuse without losing face. The remnants of the family were loaded into his cart and started on their rather hopeless search for an unevacuated hospital which might take non-paying patients.

That night, soon after the moon came up, the police went through the streets, knocking on doors, warning everyone to go into the country. The air-alarm sirens were broken, they said. There might be a moonlight raid and the city must be emptied now. Nothing like this had ever happened in Loyang before and in a few minutes the dark streets were jammed with a hurrying silent crowd. When they were away from the houses, streaming across the indistinct fields, they exchanged the rumors in whispers: three, four, five hundred planes were coming to wipe out the city; fifth columnists and parachutists were going to take the city; the police were emptying Loyang so they and the soldiers could loot it before they ran away to the west.

Lao Tu and I went out over the railway tracks, into a gully in the long hill on the Yellow River side of the city. In it were a stream and trees, and here lived the farmers who worked the open fields on either side. When the hushed wave of people flowed up and settled in the shadows, filling the gully from rim to rim, dim lights flickered on in the farmhouses and the families began uneasily calling to each other like disturbed birds in a dark bush. The younger farm children unbarred the gates and rushed out to laugh and exclaim, like kids who had got up before dawn to watch the circus come in.

Between four and five, when the moon was far in the west and the sky a vast empty blue, a reconnaissance plane puttered back and forth, here and there, over the city and the surrounding plains. In the gully the fitful dawn breezes rustled the leaves, then died away, rushed again and died. Under the trees it was the same. A gust of whispering would sweep through the waiting mass, then die as every head turned and every ear strained for the first resonance of the deeper roar.

This, I feared, was the moment which had seemed to threaten since yesterday morning. An avalanche hung over the slope and it would take only a cry to bring it thundering down. The calm peasants were in bed, out of sight. If someone should run screaming through the gully, if there were a sudden explosion or burst of flame, the multitude who sat waiting patiently as one creature could disintegrate in the time it took a bullet to pass through one brain. It would rise and scatter as a frantic mob of single creatures, rushing up the gully, down the gully, into the city, away from the city.

But the sun rose and the moment passed. The reconnaissance plane

went off to the north and the sunlight grew hot even under the trees. Slumping against each other, the spent refugees fell asleep, squirming and half waking as they tried to escape the descending clouds of flies. At ten, a weak all-clear echoed from behind the railway station. In little groups, then larger ones, the people beat the dust from their clothes and listlessly trudged back to town.

There was a small raid at noon next day, then no more. The rumors were mixed. The Japanese were said to have tried to cross the Yellow River twice, once with rubber boats, once with parachutists, but had been beaten back so easily they might only be experimenting. Their garrisons on the river were said to be receiving supplies by parachute and that could mean they had trouble with communications in the rear. Their planes continued to stay away from Loyang, and within the week two developments were generally taken as sure signs that the threat of further invasion was over: The Kuomintang newspapers began calling the Chinese Communists traitors and cowards for not having attacked the Japanese in the rear of the Chungtiao, and the Kuomintang government began returning to Loyang. Slowly the city set about reassembling itself.

11 · *Aftermath*

FROM THE SOUTH SHORE of the Yellow River near Loyang, the flag
with the Rising Sun was now visible in the villages on the north side.
In the late afternoons, smoke puffed among the trees as artillery shells
from both banks went whistlng over the wide belt of sandbars and
swift, shallow brown water; the Kuomintang cannon on this side were
rumored to be the mysterious guns from Russia, at last brought to the
front against the Japanese.

Almost every day, incidents of the ebbing battle could be seen
from the bluffs on the south shore. Little columns of greenish-brown
figures followed their red-dotted white flags about on the plain
shelving up from the opposite bank, while other greenish-brown men
on horseback flushed blue-clad figures out of the wheat. Above the
Chungtiao Range, deeper in the newly conquered land, Japanese
planes circled to parachute supplies. The dusty haze at the foot of the
mountains was streaked with smoke from burning fields or farmhouses.
Among the nearest gullies and caves of the conquered shore, fugitives
crept in and out. Every dawn and dusk, a few more ventured across
to safety, clutching bladders or gourds or sealed jugs as buoys in the
treacherous current.

On the south shore the thousands who had already escaped wandered aimlessly, searching for lost families, gathering to peer at the
columns of smoke and wonder if they rose from their own homes.
They camped in huts or lay on the open hillsides, staring with the
blank expression of people who have looked too long into a searing
light. When they talked, it seemed at first as if they had really burned
their eyes blind and could only describe their own fancies. But one
story supplemented another, and their sum was that the moment of
wild dispersion had been reached and passed in the Chungtiao. The
pressure of invasion had joined with all the pressures for internal disintegration. The peasants were swept up in the panic and the coun-

tryside swarmed with defeated soldiers. Screams and running feet had indeed sounded throughout the plain beyond the Yellow River, and each man had found he had no country, no "government" except himself.

I think it is from the old German experimental movie *The Cabinet of Doctor Caligari* that I remember a sequence which began with the screen completely black. A tiny patch of light splashed out in an upper corner and in it a man leaning from a window swung his arm around and around. As his arm circled, a spiral of open screen expanded from it, wiping away the blackness until the strange landscape around him, and all the people rushing over it, were revealed.

The most thoughtful Chungtiao refugee I talked to was a Mr. Kwei, and even after what he had been through, he was too proper to wave his arm above the level of his elbow. As he sat in the shady courtyard of a sedate Loyang restaurant, in his borrowed civilian uniform and borrowed badges, only his cropped hair — not yet grown out from his peasant disguise — kept him from looking exactly what he had been a month before, a small-town businessman with a few official connections, who never expected anything worse than a defaulting debtor to go wrong with him. But as he talked and talked, more and more came clear.

He had been on a business trip to Wangmao, he said, a town halfway between the Yellow River and the foot of the Chungtiao Mountains. There the battle had swept over him with little more warning than a typhoon.

On the afternoon of May 3 he had seen officers from the front in the mountains escorting their families south to the Yellow River. That night he heard artillery in the mountains, and in the morning saw shells landing on the plain. He walked into the country to ask advice at a military headquarters where he had friends, but found the place deserted. Returning, he discovered the Japanese were already close enough to shell Wangmao. He joined a mob of refugees hurrying south toward the river, then narrowly escaped death when it was attacked by Japanese plainclothesmen on horseback, armed with swords.

He spent the rest of the day dodging about on the plain, heading for one Yellow River ford after another, giving up each attempt when he heard each ford was in Japanese hands. There were almost as many Chinese soldiers as refugees on the plain, some fleeing by themselves, some in groups, and going in all directions. Gangs of Japanese and puppet plainclothesmen on foot and horseback were murdering and looting and burning everywhere. He heard that some gangs were really bandits and some were poor farmers from the mountains, but they all looked and acted alike.

After nightfall he decided it would be safer to get out of the crowds on the flat country, and with a few friends he had met in his flight he headed north toward the Chungtiao Mountains. At dawn they reached the top of the first range and stopped at a deserted farmhouse where some remnants of the Kuomintang armies had gathered. There were officers without their men, officers with their families, soldiers without their officers. Many had lost or thrown away their guns and some had already put on peasant disguises. They could see Japanese columns on the plain below, then a party of uniformed Chinese with machine guns came marching around the flank of the mountain toward them.

"Many puppets were our own men who had deserted earlier and they still wore their old uniforms," said Mr. Kwei. "So we could not tell whether these men were friends or enemies. We shouted and asked, and they shouted back but the wind was wrong and we could not hear. We shouted again. They unrolled a flag and when the wind took it we saw it was Japanese. The women and children ran down the mountain and in a moment we men followed. The enemy set up a machine gun and opened fire.

"I fell over a small cliff, nearly crushing a soldier who had fallen before me. We ran downhill together until we came to a temple still garrisoned by a platoon of our soldiers. They had been out of touch with their command since the beginning of the battle and though they had heard firing from all sides, they still did not know for sure if any of the enemy were on the mountain. They thanked us for our news and prepared to leave immediately."

In the Loyang restaurant, Mr. Kwei stared inscrutably at a noisy feast of glossy Kuomintang army officers at the opposite end of the courtyard. On the wall above them was a poster I had once been curious about and had translated. It was a list of orders from the Generalissimo, to improve officials and officers:

No smoking, no drinking.
Sleep early, rise early.
Thrifty life.
Absolutely no gambling.

Absolute obedience to superiors.

All uniforms to be made of cotton.

No office stationery used for private correspondence.

No office badges worn in places of amusement.

No public banquets unless absolutely necessary.

Mr. Kwei went on to tell what he learned of the fighting in the mountains above Wangmao, which had let the Japanese through in hardly more than a day. The three Chinese armies in this sector, he said, had been second-string regional troops from three different provinces. The Japanese came from the northeast, making their first attack on the army which had been stationed in the Chungtiao the longest, and had the best forts and poorest morale of the three. Splitting up into small groups, the Japanese swarmed around and behind the prepared positions. After slight resistance, the surprised army scattered and fled.

When the Japanese attacked the next army farther west, the officers of this second one feared the neighboring army behind them would get Kuomintang orders to cut off their escape route and force them up against the Japanese. Without offering any resistance, they led their troops around the flank of the advancing Japanese. They were going into occupied territory, towards capture, but they had isolated themselves from the brother army they mistrusted. When the Japanese attacked the third army, it was so shaken by the disappearance of the other two that it quickly retreated into the higher mountains behind it.

From what I had already learned through other refugees, I knew this had been the general pattern of conquest throughout the Chungtiao. The Japanese played on all the rivalries and hostilities in the Kuomintang's balance of weakness. Co-ordinated resistance became impossible. When the better central troops were rushed from their safe rear positions toward the front, Japanese planes caught them at the Yellow River crossings and scattered them.

Another reason for quick defeat had been overconfidence in the "Maginot" of earth and timber forts. Since the Japanese had already failed to penetrate this line so many times, it was assumed they never could. The front-line armies had turned into slack garrison troops, and many officers had gone into the business of smuggling.

Near Wangmao, Mr. Kwei said, the Japanese made a test attack about two weeks before the big battle. They advanced against the army with the best forts, the one that later dispersed first. Most of its officers were away on private business at the time, but those who were left sent out a twelve-man patrol. This was captured and the Japanese began bayoneting its members, one by one. When only one was left, he agreed to lead a party of the invaders over unguarded mountain paths to a summit behind and above his army's lines. When the Japanese reached this point, they dug trenches and stationed a garrison. Though the Chinese officers below the summit knew their positions were now partly encircled and were open to enemy inspection, they made no effort to change them. When the major offensive began, the Japanese on the summit made a sortie which ended the last of this army's resistance.

"I shouldn't be telling such things to a foreigner," Mr Kwei added cheerfully. "And I wouldn't if I hadn't spent the last few weeks on the run, wondering who or what was going to kill me." He rubbed his cropped scalp with a ruminating look, lit a cigarette, and went on with his personal story, which was a long tale of confusion and terror in the mountains, incredible complications and narrow escapes, ending with a brief hitch as a puppet soldier, then a swim across the Yellow River. Finally he lit another cigarette and began to generalize again.

"From what I saw myself," he said, "and from what I heard from others in the mountains, resistance collapsed so soon because the Japanese were using guerrilla tactics, the kind we should have used ourselves."

He explained there were half a dozen main north-south roads through the Chungtiao Range. The thirteen earlier attacks had all been directed against them, because the Japanese needed them to move up heavy equipment and supplies. The main Kuomintang forts were built in the valleys and passes, along the roads. The higher mountains, with their net of peasant paths leading around the cliffs and surviving patches of forest, were not heavily fortified. Some were not defended at all. It was believed the Japanese would not risk dividing into the small lightly armed groups which could go through such rough territory.

But by this fourth summer of invasion the Japanese seemed to have learned that the roads and forts and cities, which were all they could take by using conventional tactics, did not make a satisfactory conquest, since they needed large garrisons and did not secure the countryside where the bulk of the people lived. Their intelligence agencies had apparently learned through smuggling ties that conditions in Kuomintang territory allowed a much easier and cheaper offensive.

Thus, in their fourteenth attack, they made their first large experiment with guerrilla war. Throughout the Chungtiao, a wave of plainclothesmen and other irregulars — many of them Chinese puppets — preceded the main attack. Armed mainly with swords and pistols or rifles, though a few had grenades and light machine guns, they swarmed over the mountains on the small paths the Kuomintang had not bothered about, then fanned out through the plain by the Yellow River, spreading panic and confusion. They converged on the riverside towns where there were ferry crossings and captured them by surprise, cutting the Chinese troops in the mountains off from support and escape. Then columns went back inland along the main roads and attacked from the rear whatever forts were still attempting to stave off the main assault.

In the first two or three days the Japanese took all the Yellow River ferry crossings and the main roads through the range. The Chinese armies which had not already been scattered retreated into the higher mountains. Thousands of soldiers and officers, then tens of thousands, began to surrender. Mr. Kwei believed that at least half the Chungtiao garrison — some hundred thousand men — went over to the enemy or deserted and escaped in peasant disguise. Leaving puppet troops in the valleys to negotiate with the hordes who wanted to surrender, the Japanese retired to selected summits and began building forts for permanent occupation.

This victory was won chiefly with the same light weapons the Kuomintang had and could manufacture. Japanese planes were used mainly against cities and communications behind the front, to demoralize the Kuomintang and hinder reinforcements. On the battlefield itself, they served more for supply than for attack. Artillery was used to reduce forts which had already been isolated by guerrilla infiltration. As far as I could learn, tanks were not employed at all. Of course this victory was also won by panic and confusion on the Kuomintang side.

Through the street gate of the Loyang restaurant courtyard where Mr. Kwei and I were sitting, came a family of beggars, laden with tattered bedding, cooking pots, and other household gear. Judging from their dress, they were peasant refugees from the Chungtiao, though most such families had stayed in the country near the Yellow River, waiting until the opposite shore looked peaceful enough for them to return to their land and live under the Japanese. Obviously they were not professional beggars. Instead of whining and weaving about, the adults stood erect and silent, gazing with narrowed, starving eyes at the good food and the people eating it. Their small children stood shyly behind them.

Soon one of the officers at the table across the courtyard noticed them. He picked up a morsel of meat with his chopsticks, called patronizingly to the children, and tossed it toward them. It fell short, landing in the ornamental pool in the center of the court. The children rushed to fish it out, and one of them slipped partly into the water. This amused all the officers, who by now had the flushed faces brought by a long lunch with wine, and they began throwing more food into the pool. The children got soaking wet, and so excited that they sometimes forgot to bring the tidbits back for their parents to hold, cramming them into their own mouths instead.

Then an officer dropped a piece of meat beside his leg and the oldest child lunged for it, splattering water on the man's gleaming leather boot. He roared and kicked the child sideways. All the officers were now rather tired of their joke. They called for waiters and had the beggar family thrown into the street.

Mr. Kwei hurried out and gave the father some money, then returned to his seat. "They look like too many of the farm families I saw in the Chungtiao," he said in a queer tone.

"I wasn't planning to tell you this," he went on quietly. "I thought it was too shameful." He glanced at the tableful of tipsy officers. "I wouldn't be telling you now if those army bastards hadn't played their stupid game with the kids."

"We Chinese have a name for the strategy the Japanese used in the Chungtiao. We call it 'Cutting up the Bean-cake.' But do you know why they were able to cut us up so quickly? Because we helped them. We cut ourselves apart even before they could reach us.

"In the first day or two, while there was still quite a bit of fighting, some of the skirmishes were between Chinese troops, trying to get into the best positions. Later, there was fighting between smaller groups of Chinese soldiers, over the places to hide in the mountains, over the boats for crossing the Yellow River. Other soldiers attacked and murdered officers they hated. The frightened officers began shooting the soldiers they feared. When everybody began to starve, the soldiers would murder the farmers who resisted the looting of their grain. Sometimes they killed the farmers just because they had no food. They often killed farmers to get their clothes, to disguise

themselves. Some farmers formed bands to kill stray soldiers. The life of an unarmed refugee like myself was always a matter of luck. Farmers and soldiers alike took to robbing and mistreating us. Many refugees were killed by their own countrymen. . . ."

I had already heard enough from others not to be shocked by this as Mr. Kwei expected. From what I had seen in the Loyang country-side on the day of the great air raids, I had also begun to realize that panic was an endemic disease of China's collapsing feudalism. This society which contained so little real government — formal laws, organizations of public responsibility — was a kind of anarchy even in normal times. Because of the Kuomintang balance-of-weakness techniques, it was a controlled chaos which must go out of control whenever an outside danger seriously threatened it.

One or two local factors may have made the disaster in the Chungtiao a bit worse than it would have been elsewhere. Even at the best of times, there was little food in these inhospitable mountains. Before the war, the local peasants had to import it, paying for it by mining and a few crude village industries. When the Chungtiao had been garrisoned by so many thousands of troops, their food too was brought in. This was a burden on the mountain peasants, who were conscripted in large numbers as carriers; quite a bit of land had to be abandoned because of the new drain on village labor. Mines and village industries which had paid for imports of grain also had to be abandoned, because of exorbitant army "taxes."

By the time the Japanese started their successful invasion, many mountain farmers were on the verge of starvation. When the Japanese captured the Yellow River fords, cutting the military supply lines, the scattered armies quickly began to starve. Hunger made for greater desperation and ruthlessness. The Kuomintang forces became more inclined to turn puppet. The peasants became hostile to their own troops, who had to steal more than did the enemy; the Japanese had most of their food brought up from the rear or dropped by planes.

Another special failure in the Chungtiao was caused by the mistrust and caution which the nearby presence of Chinese Communist armies aroused in the Kuomintang commanders. Many of the good Kuomintang troops which had checked the Japanese in this part of North China during the United Front period, sometimes by joint action with the Communists, had since been withdrawn from the front against the Japanese, to be stationed in the anti-Communist blockade north of Sian. If they had been in the Chungtiao, they might have changed the outcome of the battle.

Furthermore, there were Communist forces north of the Chungtiao, in a good position to cut Japanese supply lines. But it seemed the Kuomintang would not give them orders to attack where they could best help the Chungtiao defenders, fearing that would allow them to extend their influence too far south. Just to mention this situation now evokes controversies I have not the space to go into here; but in North China in 1941, the well-recognized result of non-co-operation with the Communists was always further defeat at the hands of the Japanese.

With hindsight, however, neither of those special features of the Chungtiao failure seems memorable. More important were the typical ones, which this battle shared with other contemporary Kuomintang defeats, also with those of the later years of the Japanese invasion and the crucial years of the Chinese civil war. I believe the Chungtiao battle marked the point when the Kuomintang, in its retreat from all United Front solidarity and its drive toward complete monopoly, had so confused and reduced its country that it could never again be defended against attack, especially one of guerrilla infiltration.

The Kuomintang was in a bad position to organize a fluid defense in depth, a guerrilla defense against the same kind of attack. Its miserable conscript soldiers could hardly be trusted to scatter into the country. They could not become successful guerrillas, living off the country and hiding in it, as long as the peasants mistrusted or hated their armies. Defense in depth would have called for a large body of junior officers able to go into the field and act on their own initiative; the Kuomintang's paternalist army traditions produced officers of the opposite sort.

This government had to depend on prepared positions, herding its soldiers together into forts or walled cities where they could not escape, where no co-operation from the peasants was needed, where officers acted on orders from above. Its only other hope was to get tanks and airplanes — mobile prepared positions — to be manned by small numbers of élite troops, who could be trusted because they would be given favored treatment. Perhaps the upper-class mentality shared by most Kuomintang commanders, including the Generalissimo, made them satisfied with their handicaps. Forts and cities were the strongest-looking symbols of military strength, with the most prestige or face. Only dirty peasants or foreigners would want to go grubbing about the countryside as guerrillas.

After the stunning Chungtiao success, the Japanese modified their whole strategy in China, relying more and more on guerrilla methods, with increasing success as Kuomintang armies began to molder more rapidly in their prepared positions, and national decay brought the country closer to open anarchy. Their most spectacular triumph was won in South China in 1944, after the 14th U.S. Air Force had built a net of airbases there to give the Kuomintang air support. American planes ruled the skies throughout this campaign, but the Japanese invasion was spearheaded by small units of cavalry and plainclothesmen which could melt into the countryside and were hard to attack from the air. With the countryside in great panic, the Japanese quickly infiltrated around and through the Kuomintang's prepared positions and took the American advance bases, inflicting on us our greatest defeat in Asia.

Later, when the Chinese civil war began, the Communists naturally used guerrilla tactics against the Kuomintang. They had been prac-tising them against the Japanese all through the invasion. Indeed, the Japanese may have decided on such tactics against the Kuomintang because experience with the Communists had taught them that in a huge peasant country like China, prepared positions and heavy arma-ment were not effective against guerrillas.

Whether or not the Japanese had imitated them earlier, the Com-munists' handling of the civil war soon proved they could use guer-rilla tactics even more skillfully than the late invaders. Their decisive sweep down from Manchuria to South China in 1948 and 1949 was largely a fluid advance by infiltration and encirclement. The Kuomin-tang armies impotently retreated to their walled cities and fortified communications, while the Communists took control of the country-side which was China.

The courtyard where Mr. Kwei and I talked in Loyang seemed a microcosm of all that was pleasant and comfortable in China's heritage from the feudal past. In one corner stood a towering heap of pseudo-Western furniture, not yet stowed away after the evacuation, but the rest of the tree-shaded enclosure, with its gray brick walls pierced by banks of latticed paper windows, its gravelled floor dotted with clusters of potted oleadners, its pool and cages of songbirds, had a quiet air of many centuries of settled life. The restaurant tables and chairs and chinaware, and the great metal pots and utensils in the mat-shed kitchen in one corner, were of the sturdy quality and simple handsome design which only a practised and self-assured civilization seems able to produce. The frank, unpretentious manner in which the food was cooked in full view of the patrons — and the food itself, with its subtle combinations of taste and texture — reminded me of the best small pre-war European restaurants. But the European tradition of fine restaurants dated back only a few hundred years. In Loyang there had been shops like this, serving similar food in much the same way, for at least two thousand years, possibly three.

As Mr. Kwei and I made ready to leave, he looked again towards the table of Kuomintang officers, then nudged me back into my seat. I looked over, and saw that the absolutely necessary banquet was finished; the men were gargling tea and spitting it explosively into the cuspidors, or drowsily lolling in their chairs with their uniforms unbuttoned. None noticed half a dozen young chickens climbing about near the top of the stack of furniture which loomed just behind their table.

Such birds were perhaps the first thing a Western newcomer would find uncivilized about a provincial Chinese restaurant. They were allowed to run loose and were thriftily underfed, so they would turn the scraps under the tables into chicken meat which would some day appear on the tables. Until they were caged for final fattening, they were horrible little twists of skeleton and a few dirty feathers. As they scuttled and fought for food, they were an unpleasant reminder of those hungry human mouths massed outside the restaurant's lucky compartment, making this a country where the suffering of birds and animals attracted little sympathy.

The starving chickens themselves would have been more pitiful if they weren't so ridiculous, darting and peering and plotting with bird cunning. Their owners made them look more clownish by daubing spots of ownership on them with bright-colored dyes, so they could be reclaimed if they escaped into the street. These in the Loyang courtyard had scarlet-dyed tails.

When they reached the top of the furniture they balanced in a line on the crowning piece, an armchair. They uttered faint clucks and flapped their almost featherless wings as they teetered in excitement at the litter of rich food below. Then one fluttered awkwardly down on the head of a seated officer, ran along his shoulder and arm to the table, and began frantically eating. Before the men could recover from their surprise, all the others came down like fuddled parachutists and ran impartially around on the table, the plates, and the people.

Mr. Kwei watched with a pleased smile as the officers routed the birds, angrily brushed their clothes, and failed to have their bill reduced on the grounds that they had been jumped by chickens. Then they left in a huff.

"Perhaps they were Communist chickens," said Mr. Kwei with mock ingenuousness. "Did you notice they had red bottoms?"

Loyang was never to regain all the air of busy prosperity it had worn when I arrived, but as June passed with less cannonading at the river and only two or three air raids, its streets slowly took on a more settled look. Most of the evacuees came back from the west. Bomb damage was patched up or walled away. The big merchants replaced their glass show windows, and piled their shops with goods brought back from the country. A new bathhouse opened with great fanfare. The telephone poles were plastered with gaudy advertisements for a new brand of cigarettes, and the little boxes, like mailboxes, where denunciations could be dropped for the secret police, were given a fresh coat of blue paint.

Most stores still stayed shut through the noon hours but now as much for the summer heat as fear of air raids. On the few rainy days — too few for the farmers' new crop — they were shut all day. Along the empty, muddy, steaming streets the shopkeepers could be heard quacking the ritual of their drinking games behind closed shutters. In the evenings, when the air cleared and cooled, the people flowed out and the clamor of Chinese city-life worked up to its shrill, even pitch. Over the heads of the slow crowds, the bats ricocheted like boomerangs, in and out of the radiance of the restored electric lights. At the central corner a line of newsboys shouted papers from Sian, Chungking, and Shanghai; the supply of smuggled newspapers from Japanese territory had failed for only a few days at the peak of the invasion scare.

When the Loyang CIC Headquarters was bombed during one of the late May raids, the staff had moved into a string of loess caves in a gulch on the edge of town and I followed. One morning late in June I was wakened by a flock of schoolgirls in middy blouses and bloomers, skipping down the gulch in excited conversation, fluting the names of countries: Mei-kuo, Ying-kuo, Te-kuo, Su-lien (America, Britain, Germany, the Soviet Union). An extra had come out at three that morning, telling of the German attack on Russia. During the day the price of colored cloth soared; everyone knew the cloth was dyed with colors smuggled from Japanese territory, German dyes which had come through Russia. In the next weeks, the Loyang papers gave much space to this war which was fascinatingly far away, and several Kuomintang editorials bet on the Nazis.

Though it ran second in the press, the local war also got attention. It was officially claimed that traitors had caused the losses in the Chungtiao, and several frightened men who looked like peasants were publicly executed after they had been driven through the streets in display. Some were dressed in yellow smocks and paper dunce caps trimmed with red fringe, like victims of the Spanish Inquisition. It was announced from Chungking that any general who now allowed the Japanese to cross the Yellow River would be shot. Meanwhile, General Wei Li-huang, Commander of this Honan-Shansi War Area, was punished for his defeat when his second-in-command was deprived of his rank, though allowed to keep his job. Wei's own rank and position were unchanged, but this hurt his face.

He soon proclaimed that the Chungtiao experience had "further strengthened his self-confidence." He promised to recapture all lost territory within three months. He conscripted thousands of peasants and confiscated lumber to build more forts and trenches along the Yellow River. He levied two million Kuomintang dollars inside Loyang to build "Mobile Forts," an invention of his own; they were earth forts with wooden cores which could be taken apart and buried somewhere else a little faster than new ones could be built. He announced that "the conduct of the people" in the Chungtiao had shown slovenliness and lax morale. To counteract this, it was ordered a little later that any coolie or farmer or refugee who came into Loyang without a shirt be fined five dollars. Patrols of soldiers marched the main streets in the evening, under white banners with blue ruffles, scolding soldiers and civil officials whose uniforms were not buttoned right.

Another result of the Chungtiao battle was an anti-Communist campaign. Led by the *Ta Kung Pao* of Chungking — the self-styled *l'Impartial*, with its world reputation as a liberal non-party organ—newspapers all over Kuomintang China began accusing the Communists for the Chungtiao defeat, saying they had not attacked the Japanese rear. In cities near the scene of battle, there was a fresh wave of arrests of liberals and leftists; the agitation about traitors gave the police a freer hand than usual.

Now the Loyang CIC came under suspicion when it was learned that some Co-ops in the Chungtiao had gone into the higher mountains where their leaders were organizing guerrilla resistance among the lost soldiers; Communists were notorious for this kind of thing. Friendly officials told the director of the Loyang CIC that his own plans to evacuate the Co-ops during the invasion scare were suspected in certain quarters. Instead of taking them west to the crowded, expensive cities where the Kuomintang was moving, he had been taking them out into the country villages "just as the Communists did."

I had a ringside seat for one of the last flurries of this campaign, because of two American correspondents I had known at the Chungking Press Hostel the winter before, Betty and Jack, who arrived in Loyang during the Chungtiao battle. Since I was already there, they came to stay at the Loyang CIC. Foreign correspondents, of course, were the last visitors the government of the War Area wanted until the defeat north of the Yellow River was well forgotten, and soon after we evacuated out to the loess caves, it appeared we were officially *persona non grata*. Almost every day while the city was visibly filling again, confidently resuming its old habits, petty police officers came to look at our passports and warn us to flee to Sian because the Japanese might arrive at any moment. But we met no real trouble until we went to an evening party at the Loyang Communist office.

The United Front agreement had allowed the Communists to keep open offices in half a dozen provincial cities in Kuomintang territory. Most were closed down after the New 4th Army Incident and this one in Loyang had become so hedged about with hostility that it all but lost its original functions: liaison with the local armies, and purchase of supplies for the Communists farther north. When famine was to grip Honan a year later, and the Kuomintang became more uneasy, its police made an armed attack on these Communists; some escaped while the rest were captured or killed. But in the summer of 1941 they still felt themselves enough a part of the Kuomintang's war to entertain foreign guests, and we were invited.

The party was a great deal of fun, with our hosts as determined to please as Chinese Communists could be in those years when they hoped America might help them if they made the best possible impression on Americans who visited them. After an excellent meal — off an aggressively red tablecloth — we were ushered upstairs through the great landlord's house which the Communists rented, into a hall where a hundred or more of the office staff and guards waited, row on row of scrubbed, and mostly very young, faces. They leaped from the floor where they squatted and followed a cheer-leader in slogans they had learned in English for their foreign visitors, apparently at the last moment. The simpler slogans, like "Down with Japanese Imperialism!" rang as from a single throat, but when they got to larger mouthfuls like "Destroy Foreign Aggression and Promote the Emancipation of the Chinese People!" they mumbled uncertainly after the cheer-leader; all except a small fat girl in a tight uniform who was letter-perfect in a high, fast voice. There was great self-indulgent laughter as everyone squatted again.

The evening's program was much the same as those reported by foreign correspondents who later went to Communist territory. There was a one-act play, an operetta based on farmers' songs, then folk dancing and solo and group singing. The performers were members of the office staff, and their standards of skill were high for amateurs, but the young audience had watched their friends many times and delighted more in the mishaps of amateur production. The play was an emotional study of a Japanese family who turned anti-imperialist when their only son was killed in China. The setting left little room backstage, and the audience chuckled happily during tragic scenes, whenever there was invisible scuffling and the scenery was bumped from behind. The drama ended when the bereaved mother, wailing pitifully, slowly left the empty stage to join a daughter who had already rushed into the Tokyo streets for an anti-war demonstration. From the offstage sounds, the old lady no sooner got out of sight than she stepped in a bucket and fell flat on her face. The audience clapped and roared almost as much as it did at the end of the later musical numbers, when the curtain tangled on itself and the guard who was supposed to draw it shut along its wire by marching from one side of the stage to the other, simply marched across towing a column of bunched-up cloth which left the stage as exposed as before.

The meeting ended when they all sang half a dozen war songs, with a volume which made even the spirit of the CIC rallies, the only comparable thing I had seen in Kuomintang territory, seem subdued. Then we guests were invited back to the red tablecloth for the subversion. A Mr. Yuan, in command of the office, described the Chungtiao battle from the Communist point of view, more quietly than the bitter Kuomintang refugees I had talked to. He said the plan of defense had been good, but spoiled by poor co-operation. He emphasized that the Kuomintang armies had been overconfident because of their prepared positions. Finally, he claimed the Communist armies in the north had attacked Japanese supply lines exactly when and where Chungking ordered. In the second week of May they had cut both major railways leading down from Peking toward the Chungtiao. He added that this had little effect on the battle because the Kuomintang ordered the attacks too late, and too far north, hundreds of miles from the fighting.

After this party, the police redoubled their visits to the CIC caves, hinting that we foreigners should leave town because the Japanese would really treat us as spies if *they* caught us. Secret police were also assigned to watch us; they rented a cave across the gulch and a little down from us, and occupied it until Betty and Jack left for Chungking, a couple of weeks later. I stayed on since the CIC director thought he was already in such hot political water because of his guerrilla Co-ops that the presence of one foreigner could do no added harm. It might be an advantage; the police were rumored to be planning to kidnap some CIC people and they might be deterred by a foreign witness.

A more interesting result of the evening party concerned the Communist claim of attacks on Japanese supply lines. Before Jack left, he and a *Ta Kung Pao* girl reporter, who had also been a guest of the Communists that evening, had an interview with General Wei Lihuang. Wei was the Kuomintang officer in the best position to know about the Communist claims, and had the most to gain by denying them, but he confirmed them. Jack's dispatch to America on it did not get through the Chungking censorship and the *Ta Kung Pao* never printed the story its reporter sent it. I was told several years later that the story had been quashed by the editor-in-chief, Chang Chi-luan, who was close enough to the Generalissimo to be considered a member of his unofficial cabinet. The impartial *Ta Kung Pao* continued to accuse the Communists of not attacking north of the Chungtiao. In Loyang, so close to the scene that more accuracy was necessary, even the Kuomintang-owned papers eventually admitted the Japanese railways had been cut for a while, but they said by the "XXX Army," X being used to indicate censored material.

After I came back to America, I did a little research in old newspaper files to find out how the Chungtiao battle had been reported here, believing the American accounts of a battle I had learned about on the spot would illustrate the press's part in our China blunders. I picked the *New York Times* to monitor, since it had its own correspondents in Chungking, Shanghai, and Tokyo in 1941, and makes more effort than most American papers to get as full a coverage of foreign events as alien censorships and commercial news sense allows. In that Chungtiao month it received a special citation from the Pulitzer Prize committee, "for the public educational value of its foreign news, exemplified by its scale, by excellence in writing and presentation, and by supplementary background information, illustration, and interpretation." But even in the *Times* I found that neither the nature nor the importance of the Chungtiao battle were clear enough.

The Sino-Japanese fighting was not featured once on the front page that May. Perhaps this was to be expected in a month which saw the end of the Allied retreat from Greece, the Nazi invasion of

Crete, the pro-Nazi revolt in Iraq, the flight of Rudolph Hess, many great bombings of London, and a steady series of U-boat successes. But the Chungtiao battle, which involved at least half a million people, did not even get a prominent place in the back pages. Marginal aspects of the Chinese situation, with fresher news interest, were commonly given greater importance than the story of the Chungtiao, which probably seemed just another of those monotonous battles in the Chinese interior.

The annual summer bombings of Chungking began on the same day as the Chungtiao battle, and reports of the damage to American property in the capital, no matter how trivial, were featured as conspicuously as news of the vast turmoil in the northern mountains. The battle was not mentioned at all until six days after it began, and then only in a few sentences near the bottom of a page. At the top of this page was a long and detailed story about a dress which Mrs. Roosevelt had sent to Madame Chiang. Later in the month, all news from China was eclipsed by stories about China Relief Week in New York, which included a "Fashions for Mercy" tea and style show to popularize dresses made of the same material as Mrs. Roosevelt's gift to Madame Chiang. The only neutral evaluation of the fighting in the Chungtiao was given a poorer position and less space than a Chungking story, in the same issue, about Ambassador Johnson's departure from the capital. This piece listed the presents Johnson had received from high Kuomintang officials and described a farewell party given him by the Generalissimo, at which Johnson was jocularly reported to have eaten as many "chao-tse" (meat dumplings) as he had been able to tuck away when he was a young language officer in the Peking Legation and the champion "chao-tse" consumer of the foreign community.

The Japanese had started three smaller offensives at about the same time as the Chungtiao invasion: one in South China, one in East China, one in Central China — in southern Honan and Hupeh Province. The first two attacks appeared to be routine harvest-time raids, for they were later followed by planned withdrawals. The third, also followed by withdrawal, was probably a raid combined with an attempt to divert reinforcements from the Chungtiao, about two hundred miles north of it. In any case, all this activity did finally attract the *Times*. From May 12 until the end of the month it printed some news about the fighting in China on every day but two. On some days there was enough from all fronts to fill most of a column and rate a headline at the top of one of the back pages.

Concerning the Chungtiao itself, enough of the basic facts were published to give an unusually thorough reader some clues to the battle's importance. The *Times* did point out that the Chungtiao was a strategic area, and later admitted the Japanese seemed to have made a quick conquest. Moreover, it quoted Domei, the official Japanese news monopoly, as declaring the Chungtiao was one of the most decisive victories of the war and attributing Japanese success to new "blitzkrieg" tactics.

When the *Times* printed such Japanese claims, however, it usually added that neutral observers were inclined to withhold full acceptance of them. Without qualification, it published Kuomintang counter-claims which happened to be extremely inaccurate. It also seemed to follow the Kuomintang line in trying to deflect attention away from the Chungtiao defeat to the less important campaigns in East, South and Central China, which were followed by withdrawals and could be described as Kuomintang victories.

Toward the end of the month, the *Times* devoted as much space as it had given the actual Chungtiao battle to two questionable after-effects. One was an alleged Kuomintang counterattack, which was not believed in at Loyang. The other was the Kuomintang charge that the Chungtiao defeat was the fault of the Communists, because they had not attacked in the north. The Chungking *Ta Kung Pao* was quoted in a rumor that the Communists already had a truce with the Japanese and might soon become puppets. Although Communist denials of these charges were also published, and one item from Chungking said Communist-Kuomintang co-operation was the probable reason why the Japanese had not been able to invade more than the Chungtiao, the general idea of the whole coverage was that the Communists were at fault. The Japanese, incidentally, tried to capitalize on this, announcing that the Communists had indeed not attacked them, but instead had attacked Kuomintang troops in the Chungtiao. Not even the Kuomintang claimed this.

On May 13, the *Times* reported a speech by the Generalissimo in Chungking. Without mentioning the Chungtiao, he said the Japanese were so exhausted, his government could beat them single-handed if America would supply him with heavy arms. He emphasized that no American soldiers were needed and claimed Japan had neither "the strength nor the audacity" to attack America. He said Japan was just bluffing and her only hope was to create disunity among the peoples of the Pacific.

Two days later, there was printed the *Times's* only neutral evaluation of the Chungtiao fighting. It reported that foreign military observers in Shanghai believed Japan's spring offensives, including the one in the Chungtiao, were only a continuation of tactics which had stalemated the Japanese for thirty months. The Japanese armies in China had a job as futile as trying to make a hole in a sandpile by poking a stick into it. As soon as the stick was pulled out, the sand flowed back and filled the hole. The Japanese had lost their initiative two years before, when they reached the limit of their ability to hold and police occupied territory.

During this whole month, the *Times* printed only two editorials on the fighting in China, and both followed the Kuomintang line. The one on May 16, called "The Human Sandpile," was based on that news item mentioned above, and approved its ideas. The other, four days earlier, likened the Japanese position in China to that of a greedy boy with his hand in a candy jar — stuck, unable to get his hand out unless he relinquished everything he had grabbed.

The only Far Eastern stories which consistently made the front page that month were reports of America's negotiations for an understanding with Japan. Though China was mentioned as one point in question, the general emphasis of these stories was less on the need for stopping the Japanese in China than for keeping them out of the colonial countries farther south. Only one story devoted solely to China appeared on the front page. It came from Washington, D.C., and its headline read: JAPAN IS SEEN AIDING CHINESE COMMUNISTS, LETTING THEM MARCH INTO THREE COASTAL PROVINCES.

It was signed by a correspondent who had not been in China for some time, who when he was there had preferred to do his research in the finer hotels of the coastal cities. He began his story with an admission that so far there was no proof of Russia's supplying the Chinese Communists by overland routes — all those supplies were going to the Kuomintang. Then he pointed out that the Russian-Japanese Neutrality Pact in April had made it meaningful that a Soviet Consulate had reopened in Shanghai and Soviet ships could sail between Vladivostok and Shanghai. The Russians could be supplying the Chinese Communists through Japanese-occupied territory, with

Japanese connivance. As proof that such traffic might exist, he cited the three-year-old fact that Communist guerrillas were present behind the Japanese lines in three coastal provinces: Hopei, Shantung, and Kiangsu. He did not mention, or may not have known, that they were present in at least four other Japanese-occupied provinces, not counting the Manchurian ones. His article was printed on May 17, at the time the Kuomintang was beginning to drag the red herring around to deflect attention from its failure in the Chungtiao. My own guess at the story's original source would be the Kuomintang Embassy in Washington.

In sum, I imagine the average hasty reader of the *Times* got this impression: "There was quite a bit of fighting in China this May, but as they always seem to, the Chinese beat the Japs back. In one place — the Chungtiao Mountains, I think — things looked pretty bad for the Chinese for a while but after a couple of weeks they counterattacked and got behind the Japs and stymied them again. I guess the Generalissimo can go on forever if those Communists don't stab him in the back."

I have not dredged up these old stories for the sake of belittling the *Times*. The American press as a whole gave the same impression of China that year. For the very reason that the *Times* is one of our best papers, its failings show clearly the weakness of our press. Like the State Department, it has simply been too slow in adjusting to our new position as a world power.

The Chungtiao battle and other 1941 campaigns informed the Japanese that they could win against the Kuomintang with a far lighter and cheaper offensive than before. If they hadn't known it already, the confusion in the Chungtiao must have taught them that the danger of a Kuomintang counterattack on a national scale was negligible. Since their new guerilla tactics combed through the countryside so intensively, destroying most pockets of resistance, they found they could hold and police their current conquests with less strength than they had needed in earlier years. In the Chungtiao they also used Chinese puppets on an unprecedented scale, as plainclothesmen and regular combat troops and later for garrison duty. The Japanese consequently learned they were free to move large numbers of men and weapons out of China. It was important news for them in those last months before Pearl Harbor. It was equally important to America, yet no mention of it was made to Americans at the time. Americans were encouraged to hold precisely the opposite opinion.

It was partly because of our false idea of the Sino-Japanese War that we were unprepared for Japan's attack upon us. It was equally because of our ignorance that we later gave China air support before maneuvering the Kuomintang into the reforms which might build up the ground strength to protect the American airbases; this resulted in the South China debacle of 1944, when the Japanese easily took our advance bases. After the Japanese surrender, American public opinion was still so confused that it was possible for a small group of politicians and generals to launch us on our doomed attempt to re-establish Kuomintang control over all China. This brought on the extra, American-supplied years of Chinese civil war, which could only result in continued Chinese suffering and eventual Communist victory.

The Communists, of course, claim the American press distorts the news because it is owned by capitalists. Obviously that is not the answer. But since American newspapers have to sell to survive, our editors do sometimes seem reluctant to give unpopular facts or ideas the emphasis they deserve. Also, as the American public is not yet as interested in world affairs as it must be if America is to succeed as a world leader, our papers cannot afford as full and objective coverage of foreign affairs as is needed.

12 · *Town and Country*

By July the last echoes of the Chungtiao battle faded away in Loyang. More than half the money I brought to China was gone, and I had learned nearly enough for a book. The new Japanese conquests temporarily closed off Communist territory. I knew I would have to go back to Chungking soon and decide when and how to return to America, but first I planned to stay in Honan until autumn.

This four-year-old war now had seasons almost as predictable as the weather, and September, the harvest time, was an invasion month, being dry and cooler, with the ground firm for maneuvering. Loyang's summer rumors boded dire events for the autumn, and whether or not the Japanese would launch a major drive, they were likely to exploit their gains in the Chungtiao by a new series of standard harvest raids, to steal or destroy the crops. I wanted to see if the Chungtiao disaster had been an accident of the time and place, or whether it had set a pattern for future Kuomintang resistance.

After the alarms of May, that was a relaxed summer for Loyang. For me it was an anticlimactic time, since my future road would lead back on itself. But it was a pleasant season. In writing about the miseries underlying life in Kuomintang China and the stresses tearing it apart, I may have given an impression of ever-present grimness and despair. If so, I have been misleading. In a provincial capital like Loyang, there were tens of thousands of families like the refugee villagers of Shuangshihpu, not yet crushed by the war or their government, confident they never would be. Thousands were still profiting. Even so close to the front, the surface of life could seem stable and attractive.

Perhaps the chief reason for this was the basic anarchy which made times of panic so ugly. Since they had little formal government to lead or protect them, the Chinese had to be unusually resilient. Their long tradition of civilized living gave them the customs which ran an orderly community life, whether or not the government could supervise it. When no outside pressure brought terror and wild dispersal, a provincial city seemed able to bumble along in peaceful autonomy just as it had during the centuries of imperial rule. Occasional air raids, an inflation, a nearby front, were taken more calmly than in a country where people depended more on their government.

In the summer after the Chungtiao battle, the indomitable old habits mended Loyang as automatically — and it sometimes seemed as unconsciously — as a body repairs its wounds. Even the rather shabby amusements were soon restored. There was one barn of a movie house showing pre-war Chinese films or American thrillers many years old, while three or four theatres presented traditional Chinese operas. Sometimes one of them housed a modern play, given by a troupe founded to propagandize the peasants early in the war but now, for lack of government support, presenting plays commercially to city-people who could afford tickets.

There were four or five excellent bathhouses, with attendants who could scrape and beat and massage their clients skillfully enough to make bathing an entertainment; placing a towel over the client's toes, they could itch a case of Athlete's Foot so well that some sybarites were said to have caught it on purpose. At the edge of town were mat-shed teahouses with professional storytellers, chanters of the boisterous and satiric "big drum" songs from Shantung and Hopei, and singers of the shrill but haunting Honan "chui-tse" — long ballads with a flavor of yodeling. Other teahouses had little orchestras which used their ocarinas and flutes and fiddles to jazz old folk tunes in a somewhat Dixieland style. In the center of town were half a dozen large restaurants like the one where I had listened to Mr. Kwei. Their food always ranked as an amusement.

And apart from the bought pleasures, life in Loyang or any other Kuomintang city was agreeable for a number of things that were free. One was freedom itself, at least in small matters, surface matters. There was great freedom of curiosity; anything that took place in public was public property and Western-style rebukes for undue staring or listening were unknown. There was great freedom of movement. I had lived in New England near some of the nicest woodlands in the United States, all marked "Private Property: No Trespassing under Penalty of the Law." In a city like Loyang, private houses were unequivocably walled away from public view, but the country outside, the hills and fields to walk through, the streams to bathe in, were open to all.

There was great freedom for idleness. To everyone except the peasants, who had to work, work, work, life could have an easy atmosphere of tolerance for human frailties. There was little sense of pressure. Even in the shops and offices, much time could be passed in casual public discussions, whenever a distraction arose; the personal relations between those working were thought important along with the work.

Perhaps this interest in the play of personalities had something to do with the Chinese tough-mindedness which many Westerners have interpreted as a low value on human life. Much of the cruelty which could be seen in modern China was caused by the superstitions and helpless fears which were part of the national decay, but other examples did sometimes show an almost inexplicable callousness. People injured in traffic accidents, for example, might lie beside the road for hours before they were helped. But I think this came less from a contempt for human life than a great value placed on it as a group undertaking, carried on by families and communities. One man's life was important as it contributed to the harmony of the larger life and when a man was hurt or dying, he had disqualified himself. It was rather like bee life, in which the hive was the important thing and dead drones were husks to be pushed aside. This devotion to human harmony instead of humans as such had probably helped prevent the Kuomintang from setting up a government that was more than a tangle of personal "deals." It may or may not aid the growth of Communist-style communal life.

In a town like Loyang, of course, an unfailing pleasure was the famous Chinese good humor, particularly among peasants and coolies. The Shuangshihpu mountain farmers might be too ill and overworked to share this, but the Loyang people, living in the edge of the more fertile coastal plains, had it in full measure. They joked under the heaviest burdens, and even when they were marching through the streets in shackles, on their way to the armies or forced labor, they often could still laugh.

Another pleasure was the sense of human equality which marked most public business and leavened dealings between the classes. Just as China was the one Asiatic country in which absolute, demanding religions had never taken root, so it was the one which had rejected caste and class customs that demanded cringing servility from most of its people. Perhaps it was their sense of humor which had saved the Chinese from this, but whatever the cause — and no matter how tyrannical class relations really were — in lesser affairs men commonly behaved toward others as if they were men too. A burdened coolie could shout at an official to get out of his way, and felt free to swear at him if he did not step quickly. A waiter could refuse to serve a customer if he felt his manner insulting, and unless business were unusually slow, the restaurant keeper would back him up. Even in the richer households, servants were treated more as members of the family than was common in Western countries.

An American's contacts with the Kuomintang minority could be pleasant too. The non-political charm of upper-class Chinese was certainly one reason for the great esteem the Kuomintang then enjoyed in America and the other countries where its agents had gone. I think it was compounded partly of the courtliness of an ancient race, partly of an innate showman's — or shopkeeper's — sense of display, partly of the fact that these Chinese from a society so unlike ours assembled all elements of life into patterns just different enough to be fascinating. I met their famous charm among strangers in public places, even among officials who I knew wanted me to go away. In 1941, most Kuomintang people were as anxious as Communists to make a good personal impression on Americans, in hope of bringing American aid a little closer. Open anti-Americanism did not break out in either faction until after our aid to the Kuomintang was assured.

A final reason why I found life under the Kuomintang so interesting was the very fact that this country was decaying to the point of collapse. The results might be harrowing but the process was always engrossing. Coming here had been like traveling into another period of history; near the middle of the twentieth century there was less in common with the contemporary West than with those historic periods of disorder and change which had produced the tragic-comic classics of our art and literature. It seemed closer to the fifteenth-century Flanders of Breughel or the sixteenth-century Spain of Cervantes than it was to the America of picture magazines and movie romances.

Since I was not very familiar with the Chinese language and not really welcome in official circles, my life in Loyang was naturally quite limited. It was a river-sitter's existence, calling for considerable sloth and a willingness to be amused by trifles. I just sat beside the

stream of hot summer days, facing away from the future, waiting for whatever might float into view.

Many days the stream would be empty. I would wake in my cave, eat, write for a while, eat, nap, then perhaps wander out to look for more details of the recent invasion and evacuation, eat again, and go to bed. Other days, the flowing hours constantly brought the small antics and crises and fragments of gossip which could make life in China such absorbing theatre.

I might be wakened by the noise of quarreling and laughter in the gulch outside my cave. I would find that the hospital on the rim of it had discovered a man was buried under the new clay stove in its kitchen. The peasant family who lived there originally had buried their father before they moved away. Now his wife had died and as they wanted to put the couple in one grave, they had come back for the old man. When both sides had stated their cases, they sat in well-shaded positions about fifty yards apart and negotiated through third parties from the neighborhood audience. The family must be allowed their corpse, but with skill and humor the question of how much stove they were to break could be drawn out through the morning. The debate did go on long enough for two or three wandering vendors of noodles and bean-milk to set up their portable stands and begin selling refreshments to the spectators.

Before noon I might have a call from the middle-school teacher who had asked me to correct the grammar in the *Outline of English Grammar* he was writing. His visits were always melancholy, because he was racked by poverty and tuberculosis, the occupational diseases of teachers here, and was so sure the book would bring him enough money to rest until his health came back. With its painful revisions and counterrevisions, his manuscript still had so many grammatical errors that if published, it would be a pamphlet like those which pre-war foreigners used to buy to laugh at: *Correctly English in Hundred Days, Familiar Rules and Intimate Mistakes in English*, and so forth. But this one was more sad than funny, not only because of the man who was writing it. In the sentences he had invented as models, there were some flashes of the old "correctly English" fantasy — "The parrot were killed in its cage, perhaps by a mouse" — but more of them reflected the ills overtaking China — "We heard the air raid alarm while we was discussing the price of food." "It is said that the officer himself is a hoarder of grains."

When I had corrected several pages, my visitor repaid me with the story of a recent ruckus in his middle school. The president of the School Association, the student council, was an arrogant and unpopular senior whose election had been railroaded through by the San Min Chu Yi Youth Corps, of which he was a leader. Not long ago, he had tried to seduce a much younger girl student in one of the classrooms after school hours. He had been caught by the girl's friends, who asked that he be tried for rape by a student jury.

A "moderate" faction among the students wanted him tried by the School Association, all members of which belonged to the Youth Corps and would undoubtedly pardon their colleague. A "radical" faction wanted him tried by the chairmen of the classes, who were elected in a fairer way and happened not to be members of the Youth Corps. At last the school principal, a good Kuomintang man, intervened. The charges against the student president were false, he declared, though a number of witnesses besides the damaged girl knew their truth. He denounced the leaders of both factions as agitators. He "nominally expelled" the leader of the "moderate" faction, which meant this boy was still allowed to attend school in fact although not in name. He really expelled the leader of the "radical" faction.

When I went into town for lunch, I found the newsman at the central corner had some English-language papers smuggled from Shanghai. I bought out his stock and spent two hours in a quiet restaurant reading down through every last tiny news item and classified ad. Never could the incongruity of the great metropolis of

Shanghai, really industrialized and Westernized, seem stranger than when one sat reading about it in a dusty little provincial capital of the blockaded interior. Even more than the news, the advertisements — for ice cream, chocolates, whiskey, brand-new movies, air-conditioned dance halls, race-meetings — pictured a world almost inconceivable in Loyang. One classified ad read: "Young American businessman with roof-garden apartment would like to meet attractive Chinese girl, not over twenty. Purpose: language exchange and outings."

That summer, though, the papers carried hints that international Shanghai, the carefree island of neutrality, was drifting into the troubles which beset the rest of the country. The society columns, which ignored Chinese Shanghai, made polite mention of the Japanese Consul General; still, every issue carried news of more Americans and other foreigners who were closing down their businesses and sailing for home. Even the bounteous material life seemed to be waning. The power company and the streetcar lines warned of further cuts in their service. A brewery advertised that beer would be sold only to customers who returned empty bottles. The auction notices spoke of the frantic buying and selling and hoarding and reselling of objects which later, as production dwindled, was to become Shanghai's main business. In primitive Loyang, these read like surrealist poetry: "Wanted to sell: an electric icebox and five electric fans, two spring beds and a case of champagne, a gallon of olives, an opera hat, a cuckoo clock, a gold shawl suitable for throwing on a piano, two angel-shaped mural chandeliers."

When I left the restaurant I gave the papers to the waiter, who looked at the photographs in them and said seriously: "How do you foreigners tell each other apart? You all look alike to me."

After a siesta in my cave, I might go call at the Protestant mission. Like so many others, the Loyang missionaries had reduced their work in recent years, for lack of money and volunteers. When the inflation began, all the Protestants had moved into the same walled compound, but these six or seven men and women rattled around lost and lonely in the big brick buildings which had been put up in the successful evangelist years. They had so little to do with the community outside their walls that they scheduled themselves on Shanghai time, which they thought closer to sun time. This was an hour earlier than the Chungking time the rest of the city used. With their great obsolete compound and their isolation, they were as typical of those last failing years of the semi-Western century in China as the worried Shanghai businessmen in their skyscraper offices.

At the gate of the mission I might be lucky enough to avoid the English-speaking Chinese pastor who liked to ejaculate, "I *love* that man!" whenever the name of Jesus Christ or Chiang Kai-shek came up. I could visit the two jolly Canadian ladies and ask why, when I passed their American co-worker on the street, the pale young woman had covered her face with her hands.

"You must have been wearing shorts," they giggled.

They told me they had once tried to borrow some American women's magazines from the unhappy girl. She reluctantly unlocked a cupboard and brought out the shiny journals with their lush pictures of lovers and bloodcurdling ads for deodorants, depilatories, and sanitary napkins. She handed them over as if she had bought them from under the counter of a disreputable cigar store. "Be sure you don't let any of the Chinese see them," she whispered.

Later in the afternoon I went to a bathhouse and found a string of fine army horses, towering ex-Japanese ones from Australia, tethered before its door. Inside, a party of young officers were sporting like porpoises in the big tank. After my bath, when they were lolling under the wistaria arbor in the courtyard, being massaged and pedicured, they were eager to talk to the foreigner. They seemed to be of that young Kuomintang army type — rather rare — who could be called fascist, but were relatively progressive in their own setting, anxious to get on with the war and free their country from the old feudal rottenness. Instead of chanting that China needed tanks, planes, and big guns from America, as the older and more conservative Kuomintang people did, they thought light automatic weapons would be useful. They asked endless questions about America but politely did not inquire why America had been helping Japan more than China. On the contrary, they implied they were in debt to America for what little aid they had received, obligated even to Americans like myself.

"We are sorry you must find it so uncomfortable in our country," one apologized. "China is too poor. There are too few automobiles, too few telephones, the buildings are too small, the food is too thin, and the girls — umm — the girls aren't red enough."

He apparently meant their faces but this stretched the talk along lines common to bathhouses, and I learned a new ditty for my collection of folk songs. Its first verse could be translated:

Say old madame, please sit down,
And listen to my song.
There's a girl in your house,
Who's really not so bad.
        She's fair . . .
        And she's fat . . .
And something about her reminds me of dumplings . . .

When the officers learned I was a writer, one smiled, bowed, shook hands with himself, and said, "Loyang chih kwei" — In Loyang paper is expensive. Finding what this meant, I had another idiom. It was an old one from Peking and implied: "You are such a fine writer and so many of your books have been printed that even in a distant provincial town like Loyang, the price of paper has gone up."

When the officers left, as I was dressing to go, the bath attendant who had been itching my feet said that Soviet military advisors, four or five of whom were still with this War Area Headquarters, sometimes came here to bathe.

"What kind of men are these Russians anyway?" he asked. "They seem to have plenty of money because they come in an automobile and have good clothes, even their underwear. But each man always pays for his own bath and tea. They never treat each other." When I asked for my own bill, I was told the officers with whom I had been chatting had secretly paid it before they left.

I had dinner with friends from the CIC who knew me well enough to be rude about my use of their language and amused themselves with some of the classic jokes about foreigners' mistakes in Chinese. One told of an American walking in the country, who was attacked by a farmer's dog but could not remember the word for "bite," only the formal expression for "dine." "Hey! Old neighbor!" he cried to the farmer. "Your dog wishes to take rice on my leg!"

After dinner there was the usual abstract wrangle between the guests and the host, to decide who would pay the bill. When it reached its predetermined end and the host paid, there was a slighter controversy, equally stylized, as each guest gave thanks and said, "The food was too fine," and the host murmured deprecatingly, "There was no food."

Later my friends took me to an opera, a new version of a centuries-old classic about a fishermen's revolt; many modern theatre people liked to present classic works, edited to make them sharper commentary on present conditions than the censors would allow in new plays. This piece was acted in a blend of old Chinese and new Western styles. The more arbitrary customs of the sceneryless Chinese opera — in which a man standing on a chair was a man in a fort, a man with a whip was a man on a horse, and so on — had been dropped, but all the dancelike pantomime with clear meaning had been kept.

The chief characters, a fisherman and his daughter, went about in a boat. To get in, they would go to the back of the empty stage, and leap lightly forward as if jumping from the shore to a sampan. Facing each other, their arms held before them, they would alternately dip at the knees, see-saw, as if balancing against a rocking boat. By the time the daughter, the bow-paddle, turned around and the pair glided rapidly across the stage on tiptoe, while their arms sketched paddling motions, the boat was there more convincingly than any prop sampan that could have been dragged in.

While the last act was on the air-raid sirens sounded, and though the alarm proved false and the opera went on in less than twenty minutes, the scurry brought one moment which would have made the perfect end for the whole stylish, sweet-sour, performance on the stage. After the audience had poured out into the dugouts lining a nearby parade ground, the actors came streaming out, still in their flowing Ming Dynasty costumes, their feathered headdresses, and their bold anti-naturalistic stage make-up. All their vivid colors — scarlet, silver, jade, mustard, plum — were ghostly in the blue moonlight as they hastened across the open space and vanished one after another into the earth, like spirits back into a tomb.

After the opera, I could find only two rickshaws on the nearly deserted streets. The pullers were taking turns hauling one another, each temporary passenger dangling an arm to tow his cart as he sleepily gossiped to entertain his engine. Both refused to pull me home. "We're tired and we have enough money for today," they said. "We're sorry, but we're only helping ourselves."

Back at the cave, the neighborhood was dark and quiet but I was hardly in bed when a commotion of yelling, cracking wood, and running feet broke out. From the eager audience in nightclothes which surged from the caves came news that a schoolteacher who lived a little farther up the gulch had taught the illegal mah-jong to some of his pupils and had been cleaning them out in a midnight game. The father of one boy had found them and chased the teacher off into the fields. Sure enough, a stocky man soon came trudging back down the gully, puffing and calling heaven to witness that Mr. Chou, the escaped teacher, was a turtle and the defiler of his turtle aunts. Another stocky man burst out from the crowd and cried with suspiciously calculated affront: "Who is shouting the name Chou all over the world? Whoever is, should be more careful. That's my name too!" In no time, a formal debate on the name and face of all Chous was in full swing, with the two parties squatting apart in the darkness, third parties going back and forth, and the neighbors who thought it too hot to sleep softly sending laughter and sarcasms from their shadowy thresholds.

Since this was such a slight kind of life, with boredom always close, I did not expect to look back on it with fondness. Nevertheless a certain nostalgia now colors my memory of Loyang and the other little cities of the Kuomintang interior where I later lived for weeks or months.

They were all a bit alike. Set in a circle of blue hills or mountains, beside a little river or lake, each was an oblong of one story courtyard buildings, keeping the shape set by the medieval city walls even if they had been torn down. Each had its crumbling temples and pagodas on sites selected centuries ago, and its street or two of semi-Western buildings. Over it night and morning echoed the songs and bugling of soldiers. Sometimes from a distance sounded the klaxons of the buses on the few country roads or the faint tootling of trains on the vestigial railway lines. For the rest, the air over the town would hum only with the easy noises of handicraft industry and family life, and the stylized cries of the street peddlers.

These semi-modern provincial cities were the end-product of a sordid phase of China's history, and the only possible reason for nostalgia is that the phase has now ended and the cities are bound to change. Despite the cruelty and misery, their people were wonderfully capable of wit and endearing foolishness, and everything they did that was pleasant now seems of special value, for only at that time and place were things done in that special style. Moreover, they were being done for the last few times. The easygoing life of Chinese city-people seems as certain to alter or disappear as were the aristocratic salons of Paris in the seventeen-eighties or the bounteous habits of the Russian landed gentry in the early nineteen hundreds. With hindsight, the people I met and enjoyed when I was river-sitting in Loyang and those other provincial towns do not seem to have been cups of mild rice wine, eddying by on their little wooden floats, sometimes drifting into backwaters for the pleasure of a spectator by the river. Instead, they were eggs, floating swiftly down towards the place where they would be bashed up for the omelet which Lenin once said a revolution was.

Indeed their whole way of life and the cities which held it now appear to have been a sort of floating structure, a big one like the rafts of lumber on the upper Yangtse, so large that the lumberman would build villages of matting on them and live there during the weeks it took to reach the lumber markets downstream. But to represent Chinese city-life most exactly, you would have to imagine this raft as being afloat on a wide and increasingly stormy ocean, the vast expanse of peasant life. The floating replica of the city, with its shrines and bus stations, its toy shops for adults and murals of Generalissimo Chiang, would be gradually sinking.

During that summer in Loyang, I began to see that the two forces which most affected the life of the urban raft were Chiang Kai-shek and the peasants, the one man and the countless masses. I made up a parable about Chiang, based on Hans Christian Andersen's story of the Emperor's new clothes. The Kuomintang mythology I have already described fitted it perfectly:

In a wretchedly governed country where the Emperor's person was supposed to symbolize all the national greatness, taxes were ruinous but it was officially claimed that as the Emperor himself was frugal and moral, this could not be a greedy or corrupt government. At last,

after the taxes demanded by his courtiers became intolerably heavier, it was announced from the palace that a new plan for exalting the Emperor, hence the country and all its people, had been learned from abroad. New clothes were to be made for the Emperor, appropriate to his nature as a moral man and a symbol. The clothes would be so moral that only those of his subjects who were moral too would be able to see them. Traitors and other immoral elements would expose themselves by claiming there were no clothes. The heavy new taxes were necessary because such fine clothes could only be manufactured of pure gold.

Nearly all the remaining wealth of the country disappeared into the palace. Famine and riots spread, but in the palace the talk was all of the Emperor's new clothes. Those who claimed to have seen them said they included knee breeches and a three-cornered hat sewn all over with gold cherries. There was also a golden hatchet for the Emperor to carry.

At last the clothes were ready. Orders were issued from the palace for every family in the capital to buy national flags from a Flag Supply Monopoly set up by one of the courtiers. Every ten families were ordered to send a quota of celebrants into the streets. At the head of his court, the Emperor sallied out for all to admire. The route of his parade was lined by secret police, so the people knelt and murmured "Oh!" and "Ah!" for the clothes, until the Emperor reached that corner where a little child cried, "But the Emperor has no clothes!"

Unless he had foreign support, I imagine his people quickly disposed of the Emperor.

I could not go out of Loyang and live in a peasant village because my CIC hosts feared it would puzzle the local officials and complicate the Co-ops' shaky position. Even in the city, though, it was impossible not to be aware of the surrounding peasant masses. This provincial capital was only a larger Shuangshihpu, compact and clearly set apart from the countryside that fed it. Less than a mile from the central corner, with its fancy shops and cement mushroom for the traffic police, lay the edge of the farmland, dotted with dusty villages which — except for decay — had changed little in centuries. Because of the drought, mild banditry was beginning that summer, and it was not thought safe to go out on the country roads after dark.

Inside the city one could also hear of the troubles which were making the humble peasants as potent an influence on modern China

as the Generalissimo in his palace of austerity. From a village about fifteen miles away came a typical account of one of their increasing attempts to protest against the government demands which were aggravating the effects of drought, pushing the farmers to the brink of starvation.

When the peasants in this village learned it would take almost their entire spring crop to fill the new army levies of wheat, they decided to appeal directly to the highest local power, General Wei Li-huang in Loyang. Since the members of protest delegations had sometimes been hauled off to forced labor, they sent only their old bound-footed women, useless to everyone except their own families.

With their canes and holiday dress, about fifty old ladies began the walk to Loyang, a two-day trip at their hobbling pace. The magistrate of their county wired to Loyang about them, so a provincial official — the "Minister of Reconstruction" as I heard it — met them before they had come halfway. Promising to describe their miserable life to General Wei, he persuaded them to go back home. The only result of their effort was that the magistrate of their county was dismissed, for making General Wei lose face by letting them start out.

From Shenchow, near the Yellow River, came another tale of peasant trouble. The farmers here suspected the Bureau Head in charge of grain requisition was demanding more than he had been ordered to, keeping the balance as squeeze. His profit was believed as high as two hundred bushels a day, but the strong peasant tradition of social obedience prevented any protest. Finally one old farmer who had been ordered to the grain requisition office for the past three days and on each was told to bring more grain for extra taxes, went home and hanged himself.

This put all the Shenchow farmers in a mutinous frame of mind. When the threat of riot was reported to Loyang, an Inspector from the provincial Grain Requisition Bureau was sent to Shenchow. He appeared to be that rare type, a conscientious Kuomintang official. Unlike the Bureau Head whom he had been sent to investigate, he happened to have been born in Shenchow and sympathized with the farmers. He soon found the gentleman had been squeezing and had him arrested by the county magistrate.

Now it developed that the jailed Bureau Head was the "man" of the Director of the provincial Grain Requisition Bureau in Loyang. Through this tie he regained his freedom, then had the Inspector who had caused his arrest jailed, for "exceeding his authority." But the Inspector was the "man" of the Assistant Director of the Grain Requisition Bureau. The Assistant Director called on the Director, and pointed out that he might get into an embarrassment for allowing the arrest of the innocent Inspector. The Director agreed and had the Inspector released.

Obviously the Director did not have a strong mind. When others of his "men," friends of the Shenchow Bureau Head, came to him and said the released Inspector might make trouble because of the unjustified arrest, he ordered his rearrest. By that time the Inspector had wisely fled to Sian, out of the province. The squeezing Bureau Head was reinstalled at Shenchow and the peasants' misery, the cause of this serio-comic game among officials, continued as before.

Towards the end of the summer, stories reaching Loyang told that a state of crisis already existed in many parts of the province. In northern Honan there had been a little rain and the situation was not yet too desperate, nevertheless, some farmers who had eaten all their wheat were actually buying it for the tax collectors, pawning their winter clothes or cutting down and selling their farmyard trees to raise the money. From southern Honan, where the drought was more serious, leaf-eating was reported. Some farmers were giving up their land and wandering away. Bloody banditry was increasing.

In August I began cycling out to the farm villages near Loyang, spending a day or two in each. While the peasants might not always tell the truth to a foreign stranger, their answers were enough alike to suggest the general picture. Taxes and requisitions had become so heavy, the average farmer knew that if the weather should get a little worse, or if this plow would break, this ox should die, he would be in serious trouble. So many of the able-bodied young men had been taken away as conscripts — nearly three quarters of them in some

villages — that most families could get along only if the old people, children, and pregnant women worked regularly in the fields.

Taxes varied from village to village, for the opportunist government collected more in the places which were easier to reach. By American standards most of them were tiny. A farmer with a little more than ten mou, or two acres of land — the minimum needed for a small family — would have to pay a basic tax of about forty Kuomintang

dollars, two American dollars, a year. Grain demanded from him for extra taxes and by military requisition might be worth four to ten American dollars a year.

This was a staggering burden, however, since everything earned or paid, bought or sold, by such a family in a year would be worth far less than a hundred American dollars, more likely less than fifty. The taxes usually took at least ten percent of their total crop, sometimes much more. Tenant farmers had to pay another twenty to sixty percent of their crop to their landlords. Before the Japanese invasion, taxes had been only about a third what they were in 1941, and those had been as great as the peasants could meet without suffering.

Furthermore, the taxes were unequal. In Loyang that summer, I met an official in charge of collecting the income, business and inheritance taxes from the non-peasant minority — the city dwellers and other well-to-do — of whom there must have been two or three million in unoccupied Honan. He admitted that in the past year he had collected taxes worth only sixty thousand American dollars. Averaged out among all the non-peasants of Honan, this would amount to only a few cents per person. Its sum was no more than the taxes collected from about ten thousand peasant families, in perhaps a hundred of Honan's tens of thousands of villages.

Most of his revenue, the official said, had been income tax from salaried workers, the white-collar class which was already in such grave straits because of the inflation. He had collected the business tax only in Loyang and a few other larger cities, because in most places the businessmen, allied with the local officials, "did not cooperate." The inheritance tax, which would strike the richest, had not been collected at all.

"It is so troublesome, and we have more important things to do," he laughed. "Now we are just letting the people know about the procedure, so in a few years, when we are ready to collect, they will be willing to pay."

I was sorry I could not live in a Honan farm village because my talks with Lao Hsiung in Shuangshihpu had shown me how likable the peasants could be as individuals. These Honanese were a more tantalizing mystery because they seemed more typical of their national class. They had none of the special handicaps — goiter, cretinism, recently deforestated and dry mountain land — which made many Shuangshihpu farmers grotesque. The low hilly country around Loyang seemed to be more open by its original nature and the trees among the fields on the sloping plains apparently guarded enough moisture in normal years. The Honan villages also were more typical: little clusters of adobe buildings housing one or two hundred families, set about half a mile apart in the fields, most of them untouched by the influence of roads, refugees, and other features of the modern world.

On my trips into the villages I could collect only random details about the peasants as people. They often staggered their schedule of crop-planting, so they could help one another harvest. They sometimes called their boys by girls' names, to fool the spirits who might want to take the valuable sons off to death. Few knew anything of the Kuomintang except Chiang Kai-shek's name, but most thought their life was more miserable than ever before, worse than under the Manchu Dynasty. They remembered their provincial warlord, Wu Pei-fu, with affection.

After a certain stage of harvest, their cotton fields were public property and anyone with the patience and need could gather the remaining shreds of the crop. They thought it lucky to share, and on a certain spring night would steal green vegetables out of one another's gardens. Some believed the war against Japan could not be won because it had been going on so long. Some were sure it would be won because so many conscripts had been taken away. They had a proverb: "The barefoot man does not fear the one with shoes," which meant the barefoot one could always take refuge in a dirty place. Most Honan villagers were allowed to elect their own Chia-Changs and Pao-Changs, and they would pick tough, sly ones who could bargain with the higher officials. Following a centuries-old tradition, many villages supported their own self-defense corps, called "Hung Ying Chang," or "Red Spears."

Few peasants had latrines in their houses because they thought it an unlucky, gravelike, omen of death to dig holes in their courtyards. They did not plant grapevines in their courts because grape leaves hung downwards, a sign of death. They had a proverb: "For the first twenty years of her life, a woman follows her mother; for the next twenty, her husband; for the last twenty, God." In the late summer of 1941, the bamboo telegraph in the Honan villages reported that "government" was going to confiscate many big trees for barges to replace those lost on the Yellow River during the Chungtiao battle; the

peasants began chopping down their own biggest trees and cutting them into lengths too short for barge-building, storing the logs for their own firewood.

The trend toward land-monopoly was present but the majority of Honan peasants still seemed to own most of the fields they farmed; usurers were a greater problem than landlords here. Deforestation of the hills had taken place so long ago, a certain balance of fertility had been restored — largely, I believe, through the use of human manure from the very dense population — but the land always had to feed just a few more people than it really could. Most peasant families had too many mouths, since the wives produced as many children as possible; sons were the only old-age insurance in a society based on human relations. The farmers had to overwork their land, planting double crops, never letting it lie fallow, never allowing its fertility to increase.

I remember the Honan peasants a little as one would a breed of animals, shy and puzzling, with strange ways and secret motives. They scattered before a questioner as half-wild creatures would before an annoying person who wanted to pet them. Their brown villages covered the plains so evenly and thickly, and there were always so many of them working in the green fields, that they seemed a species of ground-loving beastie — like prairie dogs — busy, self-contained, and mysterious. Thinking of their part in Chinese life, I remember something told me during the Pacific war, by an American mining engineer whom the State Department sent out as an advisor on mineral resources.

He said Kuomintang China had a fair number of "theoretical geologists," with Western training, expert at making maps and charts "with beautiful wavy lines." As far as he knew, not one "practical geologist" or working mining engineer had yet appeared. By upper-class standards, the handling of dirt and rocks, the messing about in the country, would have made an educated man lose face. Not a single mineral deposit in China, said this State Department man, had been discovered by a modern, Western-trained, geologist. All the mines and oil and salt wells he visited had for centuries been known to, and crudely worked by, the local peasants. The Kuomintang had "discovered" them by driving the peasants away and exploiting the deposits through its own monopolies.

This stray bit of information summed up a feeling toward which I had been moving ever since I came to China. This land really belonged to the peasants, as far as the use and care and responsibility for it could give anyone title to property. As they had under the imperial dynasties — the national mandarin hats — the peasants of Kuomintang China kept the country, its cities and wars, running. They had tragically little share in the benefits of Chinese culture but their cheerful endurance and industry had allowed this rather whimsical and impractical structure to stand longer than any other civilization in the world.

Whenever I spent a few days in peasant country, I used to toy with ideas for a monument which should be built to the peasants' generations of misery, when and if their trouble ended. It should not be heroic because they were anti-heroic, belittling themselves with painful laughter. I finally decided that the best memorial would be just a stretch of the fine kind of farmland they now could not afford to have.

It would be a gently sloping range of hills, say, with wide fertile valleys. The summits would be covered with dark forests full of game birds and animals. The streams would run brimful of clean water from the springs in the woods. In the farmland some fields

would always lie fallow and each year the crops would be a little
higher and thicker and greener. To make this range of hills into a
monument, I would add only one thing, a stone on the highest summit. Engraved on it would be a farmers' joke I heard in a village near
Loyang, a perfect example of the cruel self-mockery the peasants had
developed to ease their years of numbness and stupidity:

"One night two silly men were sleeping in the same bed. One was
bit on the leg by a bedbug, but when he tried to scratch it he got the
other's leg. He scratched so hard he tore the other's flesh and started
it bleeding.

"The other woke up and said: 'Shame on you, you've wet the bed.
We'll both go out for a leak.'

"Out they went, the two sillies, and stood side by side in the yard.
The next-door neighbor had a bag of bean-curd hanging up to drain
and as this made a dripping noise, each silly thought the other had
not finished. Each was too polite to go back in the house by himself.
They stood there for hours.

"At last there was an outcry in the neighboring house. Burglars
had been found. The two sillies thought they might be suspected, so
they ran and hid by putting their heads in a haystack. Soon the
neighbors discovered their bottoms sticking out of the hay and began
to beat them and cut them with knives. Inside the hay, one silly
whispered to the other:

" 'Don't make a sound. I think they've caught the burglars!' "

It may be a mistake, though, to get sentimental about the strange
ways and sufferings of the Chinese peasants when you know so little
of them that they can appear more mysterious than matter-of-fact.
As an antidote, I remember an old farmer I met on the highway near
Loyang, one morning while an air alarm was on.

The city-to-city traffic had stopped for the raid, and the travelers
gossiped or dozed under the trees. All vehicles had been camouflaged
with leaves, and in the city manner of charade or joke, the shields were
stylized and semi-imaginary as the scenery of traditional opera. A
motorcycle was supposed not to be there when a stalk of corn was
leaned against its handlebars. A truck was protected with small bouquets of wheat, one on each mudguard. Then the old peasant came
trotting down the center of the empty road, in the full glare of the
dangerous day. He was balancing two buckets of water on a carrying

pole. A large leaf sloshed about in each bucket. I asked him con-descendingly if he thought the leaves would make him invisible to the planes.

"Hell no!" he said, spitting into the dust. "I just put the leaves in to keep the water from splashing my pants!"

13 · Ebb-Tide

SEPTEMBER passed with no more than rumors of invasion, but in the first week of October, just as the Moon Festival started, word reached Loyang that the Japanese had crossed the Yellow River and occupied the semi-deserted town of Chengchow, sixty miles to the east. The Loyang citizens carried to their friends' houses pyramidal packages of holiday food, wrapped in scarlet paper, and with their gifts left word of Radio Tokyo's warning that this city, too, would be taken. Then for three days most families stayed home behind closed shutters to feast, the rich on fried sweet moon-cakes, the poor on persimmons. Everyone exchanged the rumor that ten thousand Japanese with seventy tanks had crossed at Chengchow and would soon push on to Loyang. Everyone also burned incense and drank toasts to the Gentlemen Rabbits who lived in the moon.

The second week of October brought official confirmation when Central News announced: "Our troops are re-attacking Chengchow from three sides." Loyang already knew it was in danger for again the government was abandoning it, fleeing west in conscripted peasant carts. But this time few private people even started to evacuate; they had spent all they could afford in May.

The Japanese crossing of the Yellow River was the event they had most feared for three years, and perhaps that was one reason why they showed no more panic. With the Japanese on the south side, the game was probably up. Their last natural defense was down. Like people in a trance, they passively waited to see whether they would be conquered. There was acid laughter among non-officials when the lesser Kuomintang bureaus accused the War Area Command of rushing its own families, furniture, and files all the way to Paochi by special train, before warning the rest of officialdom. Cynical rumors became popular:

320

"Chengchow was taken without fighting by less than a hundred Japanese. Their tanks were paper and bamboo fakes rigged on motor-cycles."

"The first Japanese got across the river as smugglers, with their guns hidden in cases of Shanghai cigarettes. Our troops didn't stop them because they were waiting to collect the squeeze."

"The richest Chengchow merchants stayed when the Japanese came, and are now on the puppet 'Peace Committee.' Some Loyang gentlemen are already forming a 'Peace Committee' here."

The price of vegetables began to rise because the farmers feared to be conscripted as carriers if they came to market, but the price of wheat, which would drop only when hoarders dumped their supplies, was fairly stable. The cost of real estate and other non-portables did not drop far, and the cost of gold and small valuables rose only slightly. Unless the air raids began again, it seemed most city-people would not even move into the villages. When a propaganda team freshly plastered the main streets with political clichés — "BUILD AND RESIST," "REMEMBER THE THREE PEOPLE'S PRIN-CIPLES," "FOLLOW THE LEADER" — it was watched with secret smiles.

By the last week of October, many refugees and smugglers from the east had reported that the few thousand Japanese in Chengchow were systematically looting the place instead of preparing for further con-quests. Some had already been moved back across the river. It was now, however, that the Loyang Kuomintang — with its own heavy evacuation almost complete — tried to alarm and empty the city. Cen-tral News reported Japanese sorties twenty and thirty miles out of Chengchow. The Loyang banks and schools were told to leave within ten days, and a few public buildings were mined for "scorching." There was much cannon practice nearby, and in a practice air alarm one dawn, more ack-ack was used, and the police were more murder-ously threatening, than during the real raids in May. Finally the Pao-Changs and Chia-Changs were ordered to tell the people to leave as soon as possible.

Since they did not say where to go or how to pay for it, few went. The whole temper of Loyang was against evacuation. It was even rumored that the War Area Command knew the Japanese would withdraw from Chengchow and was promoting a false invasion-scare as a commercial venture. If Loyang could be needlessly stampeded, those in the know would profit by cornering wheat, real estate, and nonportable goods at low panic prices.

As after the Chungtiao battle, this period of little face for the Kuomintang was also a time for hunting out scapegoats. In mid-October eleven shabby men, accused traitors, were hauled through the streets in placarded rickshaws, escorted by police officials on bicycles, then taken out behind the railway station and shot. There was a series of single executions later. The persecution of liberals and alleged Communists was also more intense; month by month and year by year this always seemed to increase.

Early in October, the Loyang CIC Director, Meng Yung-chen, had received a telegram from the Co-op Headquarters in Chungking, warning him to "see General Wei Li-huang if work is to continue." He called on the General, who advised him to leave the province for a while. He did so for a couple of weeks. A day after his return to Loyang, three secret police with pistols under their coats came to the CIC Headquarters as it was getting dark. The Director was not in, but they refused to tell their business or to come inside to wait for him. When he arrived, after dark, one of them drew his pistol, snatched him by the arm, and said: "Our chief wants to see you."

The CIC Director found this man was a friend of his father's. He shouted: "*You* wouldn't do this!" broke away, and ran into the CIC compound. The police did not follow; they rarely kidnaped their prey before witnesses, for they liked to be able to deny that a man had even been arrested — he had just disappeared, perhaps because he wanted to.

The Director told his assistant what had happened and the assistant sent a servant out to ask the police in for tea. This fifteen-year-old country boy, cheerful and vigorous, went to the gate as he always did, running confidently with a great thumping of feet. The secret police, seeing a dim uniformed figure hurrying towards them unafraid, must have thought someone of public authority was visiting the CIC. The three dread men scattered like small children caught playing dirty under a porch.

Meanwhile the CIC Director had run out to the latrine at the back of the compound, climbed the wall, and gone off to a government bureau where he had friends. They arranged for an automobile and took him to call on General Wei, who was civil Governor of Honan as well as Commander of the War Area. If the CIC Director had to be arrested, he wanted it done publicly and legally, with the charges stated. But this time General Wei refused to see him. Leaving word where he was staying, the Director went to his friends' office for the night. Next morning General Wei still refused to see him, so he realized there was no legal way for him to avoid secret, illicit arrest. He purchased false papers and fled the province disguised as a merchant — or smuggler, you might say, since traveling merchants could openly handle Japanese goods. Later he went to Chungking and this may have been the purpose of the whole spooky little game. Many others in the provinces had already been forced to flee to the capital, where — though in reasonable safety — they were under the Kuomingtang thumb.

In late October a U.S. Army colonel, an observer from the Magruder Military Mission which had recently arrived in Chungking, visited Loyang. As far as I know, he was the first official American observer to come near this front from the Kuomintang side since 1938, the year the war became static. That autumn he was the only one of his kind within several hundred miles of the Japanese experiment at Chengchow. He went no closer than Loyang. He was entertained by General Wei Li-huang, and given the official story of the Chungtiao and other recent battles. In the first week of November, on the day after the Japanese did withdraw from Chengchow and he had a unique chance to look into the current state of the war, he let himself be shipped back to Sian in General Wei's own railway car.

Two less august Americans also visited Loyang: Miss Cram and Mr. Fisk. The lady was a spry, nut-brown maiden of forty-five or fifty summers, a social worker who had spent years as a missionary in coastal China and was collecting lecture material on wartime conditions. Fisk was a correspondent, tall, pale, and diffident; he was new to China, and carefully explained he was with Miss Cram only because she spoke Chinese. As some knowledge of the Co-ops seemed obligatory for anyone describing China in those days, and the CIC was eager to be mentioned, the pair came to stay at the Loyang Headquarters where I was still living. By then the Headquarters had moved back into the city. Only a few days before, the Director had left the province under his cloud.

Miss Cram and Mr. Fisk were soon displeased, for they had heard Loyang must soon fall, and had hastened up the railway towards urgency, a front, a story. This city demoralized rather than galvanized by crisis, its shirttail out instead of its forearm bared, was an affront. It did not fit either's plans to describe a sick community awaiting the final stroke. Miss Cram told me it was not fair to criticize the Kuomintang when the Generalissimo was so plucky. Fisk said there was no market for that kind of stuff in America now.

Loyang did not even suit their clothes. Expecting air raids, rescue work, night marches, they had left their city dress behind. Fisk wore a hiking outfit, zipped and buckled and leather-cornered by a gentlemanly New York store, but nevertheless brown country clothes. Miss Cram wore many floppy sweaters and a baggy pair of men's canvas pants. Both carried Chungking letters of introduction to Loyang officials and it was a shock when these got them nowhere except waiting rooms where they sat unattended for days. They resented any suggestion that they were not dressed for official calls and had better borrow Sunday clothes from the missionaries, at least a skirt for Miss Cram. In a few days we heard their CIC address and unconventional garb had been noticed and "peach-blossom colored" questions were being asked about them.

Fisk — working alone in his clothes of expensive American material — at last presented his letter of introduction from the Kuomintang Minister of Information, and there was some consternation at Hsi Kung when this ignored visitor proved to be an official one. He was told he must move out of the CIC immediately. It was full of bad Chinese. He was invited to stay in the guest house of a Kuomintang bank, where he would meet good Chinese. He did move, just in time to be persuaded out of visiting Chengchow and the front he had traveled hundreds of miles to see. He was cordially and officially placed in the same railway car with the American colonel and hauled away.

The day he left the CIC, a minor English-speaking general was sent to escort him to the bank, and Miss Cram and I were trapped into entertaining him while Fisk finished packing. He was a "General in general" as his type was sometimes called, one of those cousins or uncles or nephews of a real general who, without military training or experience, filled out the payrolls of the Kuomintang armies. He did know the party line about the war for he described the glorious victory General Wei Li-huang had won in the Chungtiao Mountains in May. Fourteen Japanese had been killed, he said, for every Chinese lost. Then the conversation lagged until Miss Cram took over, and made this the most enjoyable encounter I ever watched between an idealistic American propagandist for the Kuomintang and a product of that government.

Miss Cram was brimming with chuckles and enthusiasm as she told of the grand things she had seen on her journey: the Red Cross, the "warphanages," the Co-ops. "Grand" was her favorite adjective and she had a way of stringing it out into "gra-a-a-ahnd," with a very English "a," then chuckling. From her teaching days she kept a habit of talking to Chinese slowly with gestures, no matter how well they spoke English. The general — a great sullen lump of a man — was a suspicious, resentful pupil; I was told later that his main interest was the trade with the Japanese which he managed for the real general to whom he was related. His English was not very good.

"I had a thrilling evening yesterday, General!" Miss Cram said. "With the boys — the organizers — from the Loyang Co-ops. Ah, they're a gra-a-a-ahnd people," she reminisced. "Fine, strong, keen, sensitive — but with gra-a-a-ahnd senses of humor!" She chuckled richly. The General looked puzzled but crafty.

"And you know, the thing that impressed me most about those boys," she went on in her distinct pedagogic manner, "was the answer they gave when I asked what they would choose first if America would send help to China. What do you think they said?"

"China needs tanks, planes, and cannon," said the General.

"No, no, no!" she wagged a finger indulgently. "That's just the point. That's what I thought they would say, but they didn't. They said: 'We want America to send us tools. We want to build what we need ourselves!' " She did not notice what the General was saying until he had almost finished reciting it again.

" . . . tanks, planes, big guns."

"No, no, no! You don't understand. TOOLS!"

"China needs . . . "

"Tools, *tools*, TOOLS!"

The nervousness which always underlay Miss Cram's professionally hail-fellow manner was coming to the surface. She leapt to her feet.

"HAMMERS!" she cried, hurrying to an imaginary table and beating it. "Tap-tap-tap," she said.

"SAWS!" she threatened, hitching a hugely trousered knee over an invisible saw-horse and getting to work with an invisible tool. 'Dz-z-z-z, dz-z-z-z," she grinned.

"BITS AND BRACES!" she roared, bending over and spiraling

her fists, her shoulders moving clockwise, her hips going counter-clockwise.

"China only needs tanks, planes, and cannon," mumbled the General feebly.

"Who swiped my dental floss?" shouted Fisk, coming in with his knapsacks all strapped, buckled, and zipped. When he found the floss, the General ushered him away with relief, away from this nest of dangerous-thinkers and belly-dancers.

On the second day of November, the Central News announced: "After several hours of heavy fighting, the Japanese have withdrawn from Chengchow. The enemy has suffered two thousand five hundred casualties." Next day the police came through the Loyang streets ordering all shopkeepers to hang out the standard-sized national flags which were part of their compulsory equipment. The Pao-Changs and Chia-Changs conscripted paraders from every neighborhood and that evening there was a victory celebration. Except for some school children who headed the procession singing their war songs with open-throated enthusiasm, the conscript marchers slogged by in shabby, bored silence.

On the following morning, I arranged for a bicycle and set off to the east. It was one of those travesties of a beautiful day which sometimes mar the spring and fall in northern China. The sky was a watery blue overhead and the sun thinly painted the country with silver gilt, but the horizons were choked with a dirty gray-white haze threatening snow or cold rain, and the sunlight was hollow, filled with biting, fretful winds. The trees standing in the naked fields had faded from yellow to sand color and were steadily dropping their leaves. The long hills north of the road to Chengchow, shielding it from the Yellow River, looked like ledges of dusty ice.

The farmers had already begun their winter of idleness and the fields were abandoned to the flocking crows, but for about thirty miles east of Loyang the highway was crowded with market-goers, traveling salesmen, country buses and public carts. Then it crossed the tributary Lo River, curving north toward the Yellow River, and entered a country which even in its dun barrenness, sharply exposed by the pale northern sunlight, reminded me of the jungly swamps of the West River delta through which I came into China the year before. Here really was the country of war again, the wide belt of wrecked and partly abandoned land which surrounded all Kuomintang territory like a protective layer of dead tissue. The road had crossed the Lo River on a makeshift pontoon span anchored below the sagging ruins of a great steel bridge, bombed or "scorched." In the country on the opposite side, it skirted the wreckage of a modern arsenal, a vast pink ruin of brick and rusting girders. Higher in the hills, it disappeared as a highway for carts or automobiles, in a welter of deep traps and earth barricades. Along the footpaths winding through the trenches moved only the travelers of war — soldiers and smugglers, a few refugees.

I stayed that night at an inn outside Kunghsien, a county town at the foot of the small spur of mountains separating Loyang and the Lo valley from the Chengchow plain. The place was jammed with soldiers; under the willows on its outskirts they were busily digging oblong and round pits: graves and foxholes. The noise of artillery was faintly audible around the flank of the mountains and the Kunghsien talk was all of the war.

Though the Japanese had left Chengchow city, they were still on this side of the river, holding the approaches to the old Peking-Hankow railway bridge north of Chengchow, which they had repaired, and to the causeways and bridges they had built across the wartime Yellow River farther east. There was talk that they had withdrawn only temporarily, and would soon reoccupy the city. Meanwhile, General Sung Tung-shuen, garrison commander of Chengchow, who allowed the Japanese to cross the river and thus made himself eligible for execution, had a chance to redeem himself by clearing them off the

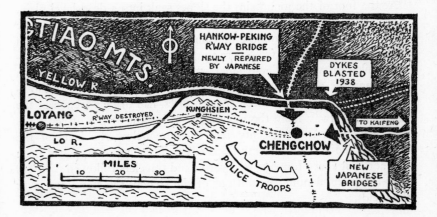

bridges; that was what the firing was about. General Tang En-po, a
central Kuomintang man and one of the Generalissimo's favorites, had
brought police troops up from southern Honan and was waiting to
put pressure on Sung from the rear and arrest him if he failed.

Next morning the Kunghsien innkeeper waked and warned away
his guests while the moon was still up; because of the soldiers,
the town was usually bombed at dawn. The early mists were so thick
when I reached the top of the mountain spur that the country below
was hidden behind a milky haze, but as the sun began to streak the
upper sky with blue and copper, explosions sounded from the abyss:
the soft thump of bombing from Kunghsien, the sharper crack of
artillery from the shores of the Yellow River ahead and to the north.

On the summits it was almost as cold as winter. The wind wailed
through the army telephone wires, and the dust blew up white as
snow. In the caves of the clay bluffs, blackened refugees squatted by
their smoky straw fires quarreling over their future plans or, if sick,
staring at one another as enigmatically as witches. Straggling com-
panies of soldiers, almost all with rifles, marched over the mountains
in both directions, herding peasants captured to carry their heavy
equipment and confiscated food and firewood. Gangs of farmers,
guarded by soldiers, worked on new trenches and forts. The explosions made the captives nervous and often they tried to run and hide;
with fierce laughter and blows the soldiers drove them back. Moving
with the assurance of hereditary nobles through the violence and
misery, the merchant smugglers with their black felt hats, good clothes,
and leather suitcases calmly rode their mules and bicycles back toward
Chengchow.

At the foot of the mountains the slopes sank into a dead-level plain,
as sharply as a rocky coast would plunge into the ocean. This was the
edge of the truly flat country of China, the great sea of earth which
stretches without break from here to the Pacific, more than three hundred miles eastward. These inner stretches of China's alluvial plain
are among the oldest inhabited regions on earth, and the wind, blow-
ing dust away from cartwheels for centuries, had made a trench of the
road leading away from the mountains. For most of the fifteen miles
to Chengchow, it lay twenty feet or more below the level of the
fields. In the last month tank-traps ten to fifteen feet deep had been
dug across it every few hundred yards, and travelers followed tortuous
new footpaths winding in and out of the trench, the traps, and over
the fields.

The air raids were finished by the time I got down the mountains, and the villages on the plain had a holiday air, with all the shops closed and the people out gossiping in the streets. Since most Kuomintang forts and soldiers were in the mountains behind, it was thought this part of the plain would be given up without resistance, if the Japanese attacked. Hoping they might be conquered peacefully, the villagers here seemed less nervous than those around Kunghsien. On their own initiative some had begun to fill in the tank-traps which cut local traffic. I saw no soldiers here, except for one group who had gone into business at a wide bridgeless stream, carrying smugglers and other travelers across piggy-back, at fifty cents a head. Over by the Yellow River the Japanese artillery banged cheerfully away in the hazy sunlight.

At the gates of most villages were bands of blue-clad farmers armed with bird guns and spears with shaggy scarlet tassels: the traditional village guards or guerrillas, the Red Spears. As I learned later, their chief work during the occupation of Chengchow had been to protect village property from the city refugees, sometimes to "tax" or rob the refugees. That morning, though, one group took an interest in me. They stopped me and asked me for my papers. I had nothing but an ordinary civil passport and they were quite properly demanding a military pass, with some heat, when an old man came hurrying out of the village. He was unusually neat and well dressed.

"You should never ask foreigners for their papers!" he scolded them.

"They are only ignorant country boys and do not know any better," he apologized to me. After more argument I was allowed to go on.

"I understand the proper courtesy to foreigners," the old man murmured, bowing as I got on my bicycle. "I am a Christian," he shouted as I cycled away. Over by the Yellow River, the guns of the other foreigners were still crackling.

In the afternoon, close to Chengchow, the road began to fill with returning refugees carrying their dusty quilts and cooking pots: pallid, sniffling, shivering in clothes too light for the season. On the last stretch, where the dead smokestacks of the city were in sight, the sunken road was nearly blocked by a column of soldiers marching east with fine style and equipment. As I had seen a Japanese plane just before I caught up with them, I began to pedal past them as quickly as I could on a bicycle twisted by a spill in a tank-trap a few miles back. At the head of the column the road trended sharply up to the level of the fields and turned so sandy, another spill was almost unavoidable. When I picked myself up and was brushing the dirt off my shirt and trousers of faded blue village homespun, I found a resplendently plump officer frowning down on me from the top of a tall white horse. General Wei Li-huang.

"Who is this foreigner?" he remarked to the wind.

"I am a journalist."

"From what paper?"

"*The New York Times*" — since I had no job at all.

"What are you doing here?" This question was directly at me.

"I have come to see your victory."

He smiled queerly but said nothing so I cycled ahead. The road crossed a railway without tracks, and an earth barricade which soldiers were hastily tearing down for the triumphal entry. Near the edge of the city a row of buglers and élite officers with red-tasseled sashes awaited General Wei, and their guards were angrily driving away some refugees who were trying to beg from the reception committee.

The dark clouds of sunset were covering the sky as I cycled on into Chengchow and I have never seen a city look so strange. After two days of travel in the brown fading countryside, covered with peasant villages so humble and worn that they seemed an organic part of the earth, this wilderness of tall, rectangular, ruined buildings for a moment made the very fact of a city, any city, seem fantastic. Though there was a small walled town of ancient gray houses at one side, most of Chengchow had been modern, clustered around the remains of the railway station. These deserted and blasted factories, warehouses, and blocks of flats, clumsily porticoed and corniced in the styles common to any European or American railway town, had the same sinister, mocking appearance as the derelict gas stations I had seen a year and a half before, in the front-line rice paddies behind Macao.

In the pitted fields between the Chengchow ruins, swarms of tattered people seemed also to be mocking urban life, for they were building hovels out of massive carved tables, cupboards and other big-city furniture. Beside the rutted streets, more scarecrows crouched, offering for sale heaps of objects which looked like the props for a practical joke when they were piled together in the mud: broken plumbing fixtures, telephones, vases, victrola records, artificial flowers, plaster statuary. This loot had been collected by the poor when the city had been abandoned to them.

Inside the zone of the pauper half-world, a few of Chengchow's more solid citizens were already back. Street-corner stalls sold noodles, peanuts, hot water and cigarettes, and the more modest shops and houses showed the faltering light of vegetable-oil lamps through their semi-barricaded doors. Many ex-Japanese pillboxes stood in this zone and, in the gathering dark, the neighborhood families were busily dismantling them, quarreling over which timber and which bricks the Japanese had torn out of whose house.

By now the smuggling trade was so well established that an isolated frontier city like Chengchow, far from being a backwater, was an important part of the Kuomintang economy. Even directly after an invasion, while it was still threatened with reinvasion, its recovery must be as swift as the repair of the most essential factory or arsenal in Chungking. As I later learned, smuggling was such a big business here that even the remains of the petty middle class — artisans and small shopkeepers — were in it on a retail scale, trundling their wheelbarrows off to the front to see what they could buy. The peasant refugees who camped on the outer fringes of Chengchow stayed because they could make some kind of living by hauling smuggled goods on into the interior.

In the center of Chengchow, however, where the banks and the offices of the bigger merchant firms stood, the streets were emptier and many buildings were sealed up. I later learned that most of Chengchow's substantial businessmen had evacuated in 1938, and while some had returned to smuggle, this did not show in the former business district because so much of the trade was handled inside the government compounds, under the auspices of official partners. All wholesale smugglers liked to keep their Chengchow operations as slight and demountable as possible, because of the risky frontline position; their homes, home offices, and important warehouses were farther from the front, on either side of it.

In the heart of Chengchow was the first proper paved avenue with concrete sidewalks I had seen since Hong Kong. The tall department stores and hotels lining it were bricked up as tightly as sepulchres but had been abandoned too early in the war to have been blackened for camouflage. In the last cold glow of the dark sunset, their elaborate decaying walls were streaked with the light, ice-cream colors of a big modern city — pistachio, mint, lemon, strawberry. With its pavement washed white by the rains of three dead years, this street was deserted except for a few dark figures hastening through before the night, and looked like a shore resort closed for the winter. At one end, it opened on a flat sea of bricks, spotted with a fuzz of brush, and empty except for a few stray goats and half a dozen ragged, non-élite soldiers squatting around a fire in the angle of two broken walls. This had been the railway station.

I went to the fire to warm my hands and ask directions, and while

I was answering the usual questions — "Which way do you go to get to America?" "Are Chinese called foreigners in America?" — an old beggar crept around the corner of a ruined platform with a burden of grass and twigs. He made the mistake of passing too close to the fire.

"That's a terribly big load you have there, dad. Are you sure you need it all?"

"Oh, your wife is sick, is she? Does she have a fever?"

"Fine! Then you don't need any fire at all. She can keep you both warm."

"Easy there, old neighbor, you can have the ashes back in the morning."

"We're just doing you a favor, old uncle. Now you don't have to carry this heavy rubbish all the way home."

"No, you're not going to get any money, old ox. But you can have this . . ."

"And this . . ."

"And this . . ."

"Funny old piece of furniture, wasn't he? The way he howled, you'd think we were trying to kill him."

As I watched the shivering soldiers pile their stolen straw on their fire, the wreckage of the Chengchow station seemed to sum up all that the Kuomingtang war had become.

This junction of the Lunghai and Peking-Hankow Railways had been one of the most vital spots in China during the first two years of fierce resistance, for the two lines had connected the great battlefields with the interior. Through the station had passed a huge number of the men sacrificed in those disastrous but hopeful years. Southern troops moving north, western troops moving east, they had waved and cheered as they were hauled through on their way to the earth. Many had perished right in the station; the Japanese knew its importance and bombed it mercilessly. When the bloodstained trains began coming back with wounded, more had been unloaded to die here slowly.

Chengchow itself was a symbol of those earlier years, for it had been saved from capture through the greatest sacrifice of peasant families, the kind who supplied soldiers. In 1938, when the rapidly advancing Japanese first approached it along the south shore of the Yellow River, the retreating Kuomintang commanders, apparently on orders from the Generalissimo, had blasted the dikes ahead of them. Since the ancient river had built its bed up above the level of the surrounding country, it changed its course and began flowing south-east, across the path of the invaders, who promptly retreated. The river sought out a new course across the plains and began emptying into the Pacific some four hundred miles south of its old mouth. For an American parallel, you might imagine that the Mississippi had somehow been diverted at St. Louis and begun flowing into the At-lantic in Georgia. But the holocaust was greater in China, where the population was thicker. As the muddy waters began spreading over thousands of square miles of flat farmland, an uncounted multitude were drowned or doomed to starvation. Their number was certainly near a million, perhaps two million. Since China went on fighting despite the disaster, the first defense of Chengchow could be called the climax of that whole heroic phase of the war.

Two of the men by the paltry fire in the ruins began fighting like wolves, snarling and biting over a piece of meat, and I was reminded of all the soldiers who had been wasted in the more recent years of stalemate and Kuomintang rot. There were the ones killed in battles ordered against their own countrymen, or by strategies planned to re-duce the power of non-central commanders. There were those who died on the terrible long marches ordered for the same reason, and the ones who perished because the nature of their government made it sure that the food and medicine due them should not reach them.

Among the wasted living were all the men damaged, by wounds or disease, for any of these reasons. There were the soldiers and con-scripts who had managed to escape from their armies but could never return to their former lives and must live as bandits in the mountains. There were those who had been so brutalized by their own misfor-tunes that they must savage each other and could rob, rape, torture, or murder their own countrymen. Three million men were believed to have been killed by the Japanese, but the number of these wasted ones was probably above ten million.

I began to wish the ruined Chengchow station could be preserved just as I saw it, in the squalor that summed up all the bitterness of such mishandled lives. The angle of ruined walls near the fire must have been used as a soldiers' camping place ever since the tracks were "scorched." Its floor was littered with abandoned hearths, little curved walls of broken, blackened brick, as carefully fitted to-gether as if each builder had been making a doll's house. In the corner of the walls lay fragments of army clothing and straw sandals, so worn that not even beggars would take them away. At the end of the walls, hardly as far from the fire as an animal would go from its cave, were the piles of excrement. By the sleeping places along the base of the walls were small bloodstains where vermin had been crushed. Higher up, countless names and a few weak attempts at pornography were scribbled.

To make the station a perfect shrine to human waste, one might add a statue of the Generalissimo, but China already had enough of those. I would add only one thing, on the east wall: an inscription I saw years later in South China, in another wrecked building used by passing soldiers.

> Last night I dreamed a troubled dream . . .
> I write this on the eastern wall,
> And hope the first sun to warm the wall,
> Will melt the trouble from my dream.

More than a dozen missionaries had stayed in Chengchow while the Japanese were there, and as neutrals — in the very last days of their neutrality — had witnessed quite fully this most recent incident in the history of the Kuomintang armies. It was an abominably sordid sequel to the great sacrifices of 1938.

They had first become uneasy, the missionaries said, in mid-September when smugglers coming across the lines reported the Japanese were improving the road from their base at Kaifeng to the banks of

the wartime Yellow River opposite Chengchow. One missionary asked the garrison commander, General Sung, if an invasion were expected. "Certainly not!" said the General affably. "The Japanese are just fixing the road so they can take their big guns back from the river when they retreat." At the end of the month a Christian puppet who came across the lines from Kaifeng to attend a revival meeting at one of the Protestant missions, said the Japanese in Kaifeng were preparing for a drive, and his puppet friends expected it to be on Chengchow.

On Tuesday, September 30, the Civil Governor of Chengchow, a young and healthy man, drank his accustomed morning cup of tea and died as suddenly as if he had been poisoned. His colleagues brought his body around to one mission and demanded its hall for his lying-in-state. As was later learned, the first Japanese crossed the river that Tuesday night. On Wednesday night the Kuomintang civil and military officials secretly fled. The missionaries learned of it when they received a curt note advising them to bury the Civil Governor's corpse themselves.

At dawn on Thursday, the ordinary people of Chengchow had their first warning when eighteen Japanese planes bombed the town. Casualties were heavy as usual, since the place was too near the front for an alarm system, and the wet, sandy soil made safe shelters expensive. Smaller waves of planes came all day and nearly everyone fled to the country.

Sounds of fighting could be heard before evening, and among those waiting in the fields the rumor spread that the Japanese had already occupied Chengchow. Some were afraid to go back, while others were driven in by the knowledge that cold and hunger could kill them more surely than the Japanese. That night the price of millet — which could be eaten without milling — skyrocketed, while the price of wheat — which had to be milled and was useless to people in flight — dropped to a record low. There was frantic packing and shuttering, and from midnight until dawn the rickshaws and wheelbarrows and carts creaked off to the west.

On Friday, retreating troops began streaming through the city, the first under strict enough discipline to blast the power plant and the barracks. The last, who came at night, were in complete disorder, frantically discarding their guns and uniforms, stealing civilian clothes, bicycles, food, and valuables. By Saturday morning Chengchow seemed empty except for the police, whose chief had gone off too hurriedly to dismiss them, and a scattering of the very poor, the old, and the sick. A few Japanese appeared on the east wall of the old town and began sniping at the police, who sensibly ran away too.

About three thousand Japanese, mostly cavalry, entered the city. They selected quarters, fortified them, and before sunset shut themselves in. That night was the wildest of the occupation. Hidden away in their hovels, far more of the poor had stayed than showed during the day. Much of this smuggling capital's large underworld had stayed; their connections made them safe, whoever was in control. Paupers and gangsters roamed the dark city, exultantly breaking into empty buildings and setting fires, at first to light their looting, later in drunken haste and abandon. The few rich shops and houses which had not already been emptied and bricked up were gutted shells by morning.

For several days Chinese looters had complete freedom, though candy, cigarettes, and liquor were often relooted from them by enemy soldiers. The Japanese as an army were busy building forts. They destroyed the old pillboxes in the center of street corners and dug their own into the sides of houses, with supply lines hacked through neighboring buildings. They chopped down the telephone lines and used the poles and wire to string a barricade south and west of the city, where most Kuomintang troops had fled. Many of the poor who stayed to loot were veteran flood refugees living in straw shacks on the edge of town, and now they found that even they had something to lose. The Japanese burned their slums without warning, wherever they wanted to clear the ground around their outer string of forts.

Within two hours of entering the city the Japanese had posted warnings not to molest the missions, and next afternoon their commander invited the missionaries to tea. He was most polite, in a satiric way.

"How much do Hatamen cigarettes cost here? . . . What? A dollar and a half a pack? Why back in our part of China they still cost only fifteen cents."

"How is the electricity here? . . . What! You don't have any now? Oh-ho. Back a hundred years, eh?"

"How long since you have visited Shanghai? . . . What! You can't get there? A pity. It's a lovely place."

He was equally merry about the war.

"We are just resting here for a while, because the Chinese run away so fast," he laughed. "Soon we will take the rest of the Peking-Hankow Railway and the Lunghai line as far as Loyang."

Then he asked the missionaries to sign a notice assuring Chinese it was safe to come back to Chengchow. Some thought they should, to avoid reprisals against mission property, but they refused as a group. The Commander's jollity returned in double force. It had grown dark and they asked for a guard to protect them from looters on the way home.

"I'm afraid not," he laughed very hard. "As a matter of fact we are no safer out there than you are," he hooted as he opened the door, and bowing, waved them into the night.

When their forts were finished, the Japanese began their systematic looting. Depots were set up for scrap iron, wheat, cotton, hemp, smuggled Japanese goods. All stocks were inventoried and sealed until they could be collected. Chinese looters were now shot on sight. The Japanese were said to have made a huge haul of smuggled goods in the official warehouses, and made an even greater haul of wheat, since most of the grain taken in summer taxes from the peasants around Chengchow had been abandoned in the Kuomintang compounds. Japanese military trucks of American make were driven over causeways improvised across the wartime Yellow River, and daily convoys hauled the plunder back to Kaifeng.

With the Japanese so busy, a shadowy sort of Chinese life revived. More people began to come out of hiding, now that they no longer feared great and constant violence. The Japanese kept the East Gate open, and some of the refugees began to come back, driven by scarcity and disorder in the country. Some street peddlers resumed business. Many whores had stayed and were able to deal with the Japanese on a commercial basis, though the casual rape of other women was not uncommon. But robbery remained the city's chief occupation. The citizens still looted empty houses at night, whenever they could find a way around the Japanese guards; by day they stole from each other.

For a while farmers from unoccupied territory brought their produce to a market at the East Gate, then Japanese soldiers stole so much they stopped coming. Meat and vegetables became unobtainable, but wheat was plentiful and cost only a fraction of its pre-invasion price. The Japanese had brought a few puppets with them from Kaifeng, apparently to share in the loot as a reward for good behavior; they were given a stock of confiscated wheat which they sold to all comers for fifteen Kuomintang dollars a tou, a high price to anyone from Japanese territory, but wonderfully low to people accustomed to paying at least seventy-five.

It was clear from the first that this was a raid, not an occupation. Except for a few spies and plainclothesmen, the invaders were all military. As with the telephone lines, they destroyed the city's material fabric whenever that suited their purpose of collecting loot and protecting its removal. Politically, they were just as contemptuous of their conquest. Beyond painting out the old Kuomintang wall slogans and painting in stereotyped mottoes for their "New Order in East Asia," they made no effort at persuasion.

In a few villages south of Chengchow, the Red Spears had offered guerrilla resistance and there the Japanese used terror as a weapon; there had been mass executions, some by immolation in wells, and anyone who ran from the Japanese for any reason was shot. Nothing like this occurred in the city, which was so empty and unresistant when the Japanese came, but all through the occupation there were scattered cases of whimsical cruelty which seemed more shocking than the great atrocities in Nanking and other earlier conquests. Those had been blows inflicted in anger on an enemy who struck back. The Chengchow brutalities were tortures capriciously inflicted on a helpless invalid.

To build their forts or carry their loot, the Japanese conscripted whatever men they could find, able-bodied or not. They kept them working for days without food; one group reported that when they complained of hunger they were given salt to eat, as a joke. They were flogged and sometimes bayoneted if they misunderstood orders; some were maltreated as a joke, because they could not speak Japanese. Men who tried to escape were buried alive, some of them head down, as a joke. I heard of two girls who tried to save themselves from rape by covering their bodies with filth; they were bayoneted to death instead, a good joke on them. In several cases when Japanese on their free days went looking for women and found a whole family hiding, they amused themselves first by forcing the fathers and brothers to violate their mothers, daughters, and sisters, another good joke.

At first the Chinese in the city cheerfully rumored a counteroffensive, though the noise of shooting in the country usually sounded more like rabbit-hunting. The missionaries were hopeful too, until mid-October when one of their female co-workers cycled in from Kunghsien, on the other side of the front. She calmly explained that her winter clothes were stored in Chengchow and she had come to get them. Fronts? Fighting? She had seen no large numbers of Chinese troops nearer than the mountains above Kunghsien, and they were building defenses. The last Chinese soldiers she saw, a small patrol, were five miles from Chengchow. She saw no Japanese until she reached the two astonished sentries who admitted her through the barricade at the edge of the city.

On October 29, the puppets sold off the last of their wheat at the bargain price of twelve dollars a tou and disappeared to Kaifeng with the prettiest Chengchow whores. Next day most of the Japanese left, toward their new bridges in the north and east. Columns of smoke were seen in those directions and it was said they were burning all the smuggled Japanese goods they had captured, thus creating a new demand. On the morning of November 1, the city was so quiet that some of the missionaries ventured downtown and saw the rear guard leave. They were hardly more than a dozen. Confident and unhurried, they loaded their trucks with personal loot and drove off.

In less than an hour the refugees were swarming back. No police appeared, and for several hours there was more looting and fighting over loot. A tide of people with axes and cleavers swarmed over the telephone-wire barricade the Japanese had built, and before any authority returned, all the wire and poles were chopped up and disappeared into hundreds of poor homes, for use or sale. In the afternoon some Kuomintang troops marched in and the victory was complete.

All that I heard from other sources confirmed the impression I got from the missionaries; this had been modern war at its lowest ebb, very much like one of the oldest and most primitive forms of war — the community raids of pre-history, before there were large governments, when local wars were part of the routine commercial life of every settlement and tribe. On the Japanese side, the Chengchow episode had apparently been nothing but a quest for loot, and they won as in a game; they took the city by default, when they upset their opponents' strategy by crossing the Yellow River at a time and place where they weren't expected. (And the Loyang rumor that their first wave had crossed disguised as cigarette smugglers appeared to be true.)

For all its bloody confusion, the Chungtiao invasion had been a battle, and in the higher mountains it had resulted in small guerrilla groups which continued to fight. But this occupation of Chengchow had been mainly an economic event. Since the Kuomintang armies had withdrawn into the mountains far from the Japanese lines, it had also been almost entirely a civilian event. With the leaders of civil resistance whisking themselves away, the whole tragedy was reduced to a juggling-about of objects of use or value. It had been a period of dog-eat-dog confusion, but because of the shocking, quiet way the Japanese came, and because the enemy soon established a kind of order inside the city, it had been a period of very niggling anarchy, expressed mainly in pilfering, chicanery, and petty cruelties. In a way, the political and military bankruptcy which thus reduced one of the most tragic situations in human experience — a city in the hands of its enemies — to a tired scrabbling among its citizens, haggling and quarreling over objects, created a more dismal and degraded picture of war than the cruel, violent one of the Chungtiao defeat. Perhaps it was the kind of thing that had to happen eventually in a country whose rulers thought objects more important than the uses to which they were put.

There had been a few skirmishes near the Yellow River when the Japanese first crossed, plus the scattered attempts at resistance by the Red Spears in the villages. For the rest, the city and its surrounding plain had presented nothing more than a panorama of people manipulating objects. They packed them and unpacked them, they pawned them, they stole them; they hid, abandoned, or sold them; they hung them in wells or trees, they cut them into shares, they tied them under their clothes. Almost everything which befell anyone happened because of something he or she had done, was doing, or intended to do, to some object.

From a petty merchant-smuggler, for example:

"After the big air-raid on October 2, I buried some of my stock under the floor of my shop and hired two coolies with wheelbarrows to take the rest to Loyang. We got out of the city safely, but in the country we were stopped in every village for inspection by Red Spears who said these were Japanese goods and took some, as a 'tax.' By evening more than half my stock was gone. That night the village where we stayed was attacked by bandits, but they must really have been Red Spears, because they robbed only the city refugees who were camping there. They stole all the rest of my stock. I stayed in the country until I heard the Japanese were not killing many people. Then I came back. I found my shop had been burned by looters, but there was an unburned shed behind it where I could hide. The looters had not found the stock I had buried, and by bartering it I could get food. What will I do if the Japanese come back? I won't be here. As soon as I can dispose of my property, I am leaving for occupied territory where business conditions are more stable."

From a middle-class woman, widow of a railway engineer: "After the big air raid I took my children and ran out into the country. When we heard the guns on this side of the river we were too frightened to come back into the city, though we had only three quilts and very little money. We spent the whole month in a little farm village with many other refugees from the city. The refugees helped each other a little, loaning cooking utensils, but the farmers were very cruel. They kept telling us they would never feed us and that we had better go to Loyang before the winter. I think they were really frightened of us, because we outnumbered them. They would not even let us pick leaves to eat from their trees. One day my twelve-year-old daughter was terribly beaten by the farmwomen when she was caught trying to steal a potato from the fields. Luckily, this daughter can draw and we found the farmers would barter food for her pictures. With her drawings and my money we were usually able to get one meal of millet porridge a day. When we came back to Chengchow, we found everything in our rooms had been stolen. I don't know what we will do if the Japanese come back. I think we will stay in the city."

From a coolie who cleaned city latrines and sold the contents to farmers: "The Japanese gave me no trouble; I am too poor. I don't have a lock on my hut — can't afford one — so when I heard they were coming, I just leaned my crap-bin across the door and took my family to the country. We stayed all month with a farmer who is one of my oldest customers and he gave us plenty to eat. When we came back we found not a thing in our hut had been touched. I'll do the same if the Japanese come back. That bin doesn't smell bad to me."

During my week at Chengchow, the objects in the city were slowly placed in a more normal pattern. On the first day there was little for sale except loot, vegetables, hot water, and cigarettes. Many shuttered or gutted stores bore chalked signs: "Sorry" or "Robbed Empty." Next day three portable businesses — rickshaws, street barbers, and fortunetellers — reappeared. The barbers were said to be making much money because so many men had sworn they would not be shaved again until the Japanese left Chengchow.

On the following day the peasants from the nearest villages brought in baskets and reed matting, which they sold for profiteers' prices since both were useful for retidying. A few "guerrilla merchants" opened shop on the sidewalks, where they sold such light smuggled goods as shoelaces, soap, and fountain pens out of suitcases. By the fourth day, the crowds in the streets had quadrupled and rickshaws were common. The sidewalk merchants seemed sure now that the Japanese were not coming back; they brought bulkier goods in from their caches in the country: thermos bottles, mirrors, felt hats. Shops with goods which neither looters nor Japanese had wanted — coffins, ladders, bedpans — opened with their stocks intact. Along the main street one could buy ink, garters, toothpaste, neckties, a red-tasseled hat for a bride, a souvenir picture of Chiang Kai-shek. The police had outlawed the sale of loot so it was displayed only on the traditional second-hand street, one block over.

By the end of the week, the stubborn resilience of its people made Chengchow well on its way back toward the half-life it had enjoyed before the Japanese came. The streets were swept clean of their dirty drifts of charred cloth and paper, shattered glass, straw and horse manure, and other débris of war. Patiently built walls of broken brick began to hide the flat wreckage of bombing. A few potted plants and caged birds appeared at the thresholds of semi-ruined houses. Several teashops opened and posters promised that a theatre would reopen soon.

Even then, however, it was a city in appearance only, an arrangement of urban objects, and would probably remain so for some time. Most officials, who had fled the first and farthest, had not come back; the rumor was that they not only feared the Japanese, but were

afraid that "the people were restless" after all their troubles. As far as I could find, no official relief agency had yet been set up although thousands were destitute and beginning to starve and many more would starve soon. The only Kuomintang organizations to return in force in the first few days were the police, and their work seemed to concern the city as a pile of objects. Secret police were said to have infiltrated Chengchow before the Japanese left, to spy out looters, and in the first week of reoccupation the jails were filled with paupers like those I had seen building hovels of furniture, taking for themselves property which had been abandoned to the Japanese. It was cynical Chengchow gossip that many men with pre-invasion debts were now trying to get rid of their creditors by denouncing them as looters.

The Political Department of the reoccupying forces had painted over most of the Japanese wall slogans by the time I arrived, but I saw no evidence of an organized Kuomintang approach to the people of this miserable city. Except for police notices ordering that looted property be returned, the wallboards for public notices were usually filled with pathetic personal ones, asking for news of lost family members. The only two new wall slogans I noticed might better not have been painted: HELP THE CHINESE SOLDIERS DRIVE OUT THE JAPANESE!   THE CENTRAL GOVERNMENT LOVES AND HELPS THE REFUGEES!

Just before I left, Kuomintang tax collectors arrived and announced that since the Japanese had stolen all the grain already collected in summer taxes, an emergency autumn tax would have to be collected from the farmers around Chengchow, to feed their government and armies. Shortly afterwards, the first of the caravans of wheat-loaded wheelbarrows — pushed by peasants from many of whom this levy took the last of their own grain reserves — began arriving in the city under armed guard.

In itself, the Chengchow invasion was a small event: the major campaigns that autumn were in Central China, around Ichang and Changsha. But the Japanese capture of the Yellow River railway bridge near Chengchow was most important. As long as they held it, the river which had stopped them for three years could offer no problems. The wretchedness of Kuomintang resistance around Chengchow, only two months before Pearl Harbor, gave further proof that the Japanese could withdraw more men and equipment for use elsewhere.

After I came back to America, I went through files of the New York *Herald Tribune* to see how it had reported on Chengchow. Although most news in October and November of 1941 showed that America's entry into war was accepted as likely and our position in the Orient was thought most precarious, I found the existing war in China just as badly reported as by the *Times* during the Chungtiao battle. The unusually thorough *Tribune* reader could glean most of the basic facts about the capture of Chengchow, but how and why it had happened, and what could be expected because of it, was not explained. Not even the significance of the Yellow River bridge was made clear.

Perhaps the most interesting thing about the Chengchow coverage was its suggestion that the Japanese had realized how useful it was to have America overestimate the Kuomintang. They seemed to be trying to help build up our complacence. Early in October, for example, a report from Japanese sources in Shanghai claimed that five thousand Chinese troops had been captured and two thousand — including a general — killed in a battle outside Chengchow. There had been skirmishing then, but if a battle of such size had occurred, I think I would have heard about it when I visited the city. Later in October, a report from occupied Peking, apparently from Japanese sources, said that two hundred thousand Chinese reinforcements were converging on Chengchow in a "desperate effort" to recapture the city. The report would have surprised the missionary lady who, at about that time, cycled across the front to fetch her winter clothes.

The *Tribune's* one editorial about the fighting in China during this period was called "China Creates a Diversion," and was based on Kuomintang claims of victory in the Ichang campaign. It advised Americans to notice how strong China was, and said Chinese strength was helping divert Japan from war with America. The other comments on China that I could find in the *Tribune* came from Kuomintang sources and followed the standard line. In his speech on the Double Tenth holiday, October 10, the Generalissimo appeared to be ignoring his own problems, emphasizing instead that America and Britain were friendly nations which had thrown a cordon around Japan, preventing further aggression. General Hsueh-yueh, commander at Changsha, was quoted as saying China's war against Japan was entering a "new, momentous phase of counteroffensive." He called on Britain, America, and Russia to "come in for the knock-out blow." H. H. Kung was quoted in a claim that the Japanese armies were so hopelessly bogged down in China, they were unable to take advantage of the world situation to seek conquest elsewhere.

Next to our press and State Department, Americans who have lived in China seem to be the strongest influence on our attitude and policy toward that country. Missionaries are probably the most important of these, since mission comment on China is circulated through our churches, and the churches can sometimes influence decisions in Washington. My trip to Chengchow gave me my first chance to see how missionaries could react to a Chinese crisis.

At first the mission compounds, the only arrangements of objects which had not been tumbled about in the past month, seemed as remarkable as their occupants. In this half-ruined city within sound of the front it was almost incredible to find little oases of the most solid Western-style comfort I had seen since leaving the coast. As Chengchow had been connected by rail with Shanghai before the war, the big mission houses had furnishings brought from there or even from abroad. No doubt they would have seemed meager and shabby if I had come direct to Chengchow from America — then the few bomb scars would have impressed me more — but they represented luxury after so many months in inns and caves farther west. The Italian Catholic mission had a herd of imported cows and the mission tables bore fresh milk, cream, butter, cheese: rarities which foreigners elsewhere in unoccupied China, except for the greatest nabobs in Chungking, only dreamed about.

All the missionaries — American, Canadian, and Italian — had stayed in Chengchow when the Japanese came. Most of their pastors and other Christian workers stayed with them. They opened their compounds to refugees and many of their parishioners remained. Among the Protestants, at least — the ones I saw the most since the Catholic compound was outside the city — there seemed to have been no screening of refugees; all were admitted until the compounds were full. Several thousand Chinese stayed under church protection while they became conquered people.

When asked why they stayed, why they had offered shelter to Chinese who wanted to stay, the missionaries were so surprised it was plain no other course had been considered. Most answered frankly that they themselves stayed to protect mission property; they had been part of that panorama of people doing things to objects. Furthermore, as men and women of courage and good will they had obviously stayed because they felt a moral duty not to desert their posts; they were still sure of their neutrality. As for sheltering Chinese, they said it was their duty to offer sanctuary to whomever came asking for it.

I began to think it was a pity that missionaries could not live as Elijah in the wilderness had — separated from mundane environment, fed as though by the birds, devoted solely to works of evangelism or benevolence. In modern China they naturally could not. As foreigners in a country constantly interfered with by foreign powers, everything they did, their very existence, had political meaning. This could lead them into situations which were awkward by political or social, if not religious, standards.

In Chengchow at least one traitor passed the insecure first days of the occupation safe in a mission compound. He was the puppet from Kaifeng who came over to attend a revival meeting; later he went out and joined the other puppets who had come with the Japanese. From a Chinese Christian pastor, I heard this man was not bad "because he warned the Christians when the Japanese were coming and when they were going." The pastor also said: "No Christian can really be a traitor." When I discussed this with one of the foreign missionaries, I was bluntly told: "Any Christian Chinese is better than a non-Christian Chinese."

Concerning the other Chinese who stayed in the missions, the only thing I know for certain was that if the occupation had been permanent — and when it began, nobody could guess it wouldn't be — every one would have been a loss to China, a gain to Japan. In view of the disagreeable things I had seen happening to refugees farther west, it could have been defensible for the missionaries to help their wards into life under the Japanese. But none of them knew of the deplorable conditions further west. Their idea of the Kuomintang hinterland had been built by American magazines, smuggled from Shanghai. They believed the discouraging things they saw in Chengchow were not typical because this was too close to the front. They thought that deep in the interior the Christian Generalissimo and his wife were building a new China.

These missionaries were fortunate in one thing at least. The whole Chengchow occupation was such a low-pressure affair, even on the Japanese side, that they were able to protect all whom they had sheltered. In some other captured cities, notably Nanking, the crowded mission compounds and other foreign-protected zones for refugees had proved merely convenient reservoirs of humanity for the Japanese to work, rape, or kill. I have heard that one Nanking missionary was a pacifist who, before the fighting stopped, persuaded Chinese soldiers to lay down their arms and seek safety in his zone. The Japanese later dragged soldiers out of this zone, doused them with gasoline, and burned them alive.

In Chengchow the adventures of the missionaries and their flocks were mainly grotesque and bloodless frictions with an un-Christian situation.

There had been the case of the Chinese Christian preacher who cycled out into the country to look after his property there. Fearing he might meet Japanese, he tied two flags to his handlebars: one with a Christian cross, one with "Welcome to the Japanese" written on it. He blundered into free territory and was caught by Red Spear guerrillas who threw him into a dark room full of other suspected traitors.

"Preach to them," they said.

Preach he did, for dear life and for nearly two hours. At length some of his audience became restive and noticed it was very quiet outside. Cautiously they opened the door and found the guerrillas

must have got bored with the whole business, for they had all gone away.

"I found the occupation a wonderful time for the Lord's work," one missionary said to me, a woman evangelist with the great convex face of a fanatic.

"What do you mean?"

"People who wouldn't listen in ordinary times would listen while the Japanese were here."

"What people were these?"

"The — ah — merchants. I let them bring their — ah — wares into my compound. Then they would listen."

I went around to her compound and found it piled with Japanese goods. She had been sheltering some of the more successful smugglers of Chengchow. A few were still there, hard-bitten old rascals who did not feel the open city was safe for their wares yet. Tucking their hands into their silk robes, they spoke to me solemnly of the peace and security brought by true belief.

One had become uneasy in the middle of the occupation and tried to escape through the East Gate with his wares. Red Spears confiscated all his Japanese goods, so he came back.

"What will you do if the Japanese return?" I asked him.

He looked upward like a wolf making sheep's eyes at heaven as he replied: "Next time I will trust in Jesus and stay in the compound."

The woman evangelist running this compound further confused me by the tale of her meeting with a drunken Japanese soldier. He asked her if she had any money and she said no, forgetting she did have a little in her purse. He searched the purse anyway, found it and took it. She was delighted to lose the money, she said, as it was a punishment which cancelled out her unwitting lie. It was she, too, who told me about the whores operating during the occupation; she lived across the street from the red-light district. She thought this prostitution was good.

"It must have saved so many of our Christian women."

In another compound, a fundamentalist one where nicotine was thought an instrument of the devil, cigarettes had always been kept on hand for Japanese who chose to visit. "They might have taken something away if we didn't entertain them the way they expected."

While I was in Chengchow the occupants of the same compound were planning to repair, at their own expense, a bridge on the public road opposite their gate. This had been in disrepair as long as they could remember but they hadn't bothered about it until the occupation, when Japanese trucks frequently drove over it and they feared that if one fell through, the Japanese would get even angrier than at a lack of cigarettes. Under the Chinese reoccupation they were repairing the bridge because they were afraid the Japanese might return.

Though the Japanese had heard a rumor that General Sung Tung-shuen's fortune was hidden in the Catholic mission and searched that compound carefully, none of the missionaries lost anything of great value. None was harmed. Most Japanese officers were excruciatingly polite to them, and the soldiers usually ignored them except when they were at liberty, drunk, and bent on looking at foreigners in foreign houses. As alien neutrals dealing with an unpredictable race of invaders, the missionaries often found themselves in non-political and non-ethical situations which smacked of Alice's Wonderland, or would have if the whimsy had not always held the threat of brutality.

A favorite afternoon pastime for drunken soldiers was to climb on the mission compound walls, with bottles, and sit for hours like a row of stubble-bearded Cheshire Cats, watching everything that went on inside. This was specially trying for two ladies from the southern United States who ran a girls' boarding school, and had a houseful of Chinese virgins. They made the girls lie on the upstairs floor, where they could not be seen from the compound walls, and with their servants kept a constant watch in the yard. The Japanese seemed to suspect, because there were always more Cheshire Cats here.

Whenever a soldier did slide into the compound, he was invited into the house, offered tea and cookies, Southern-style, and generally shown such politeness he could not muster the face to search upstairs. One soldier was so alarmed by all these Alabama manners that he ran right out of the house, forgetting his harmonica.

An officer, admitted at the gate as officers always were, gave the ladies a worse jolt. During tea they were aware, if he wasn't, that the girls upstairs were making quite a lot of noise. They must not have known a visitor was below, for they were giggling, crawling, and thumping around, apparently playing tag. The officer was courtly and spoke English well. He said he had been an English teacher in

Japan and loved American literature. He asked what the ladies' favorite book was. After they told him, they asked what his favorite book was.

He hissed with politeness and softly said: "*Little Women.*"

Toward the end of the occupation, a male missionary was accosted on the street by another English-speaking Japanese, one of the rare civilians, who asked so many questions that the missionary lost his temper.

"I've answered all your questions, now you answer one of mine," he snapped. "What right have you to question me?"

The Japanese puffed out furiously.

"I," he shouted, "Am a registered spy."

I boarded at a mission compound in Chengchow and on the day before I returned to Loyang, it was visited by some dapper Kuomintang officers who demanded the missionaries' best table linen, silver, and china. Indignantly the missionaries asked why.

"General Wei Li-huang is giving a dinner for you foreigners tonight and wants to borrow your things. You will get your invitations later."

When these came, there was none for me but the weather was rainy and the mission women did not want to go out. It was felt that the foreigners should make a numerous showing, so one husband wrote and asked if an extra guest could be brought along, and later I got a formal red card too. I had no clothes except the dilapidated cotton outfit in which I had fallen at the General's feet at the entrance of the city, but was able to borrow a fine ecclesiastical serge suit, white shirt, and dark tie.

We walked out to Wei's headquarters in the dark and the rain, past a long line of farmers cursing and spitting beside a caravan of oxcarts loaded with wheat, another installment in the repayment of the looted summer taxes. At the headquarters in the former residence of a railway official we were ushered by trim sentries into another world of the war: bright lights, uniforms of the finest imported materials, a long white-covered table with chrysanthemums in cut-glass vases without water.

The festal impression did not last, for after nearly an hour it appeared that only a fraction of the guests, foreign or Chinese, were going to come out in such weather. We finally sat down in a huddled knot, perhaps twelve people, at the end of a long table set for more than thirty. The food was sumptuous — Western-style with fresh Catholic dairy products, and apples brought by military courier all the way from Linpao, nearly two hundred miles west. But the talk never mounted to enough of a clatter to drown out the drenching rain on the outer walls, or the artillery at the river, bumping away as monotonously as a shutter in the night.

General Wei was assisted as host by a few aides, stylish young "generals in general." Some spoke English, some French, but there was really nothing to say in either language. The missionaries later declared they could imagine no reason for the party except that Wei heard the Japanese commander had given them tea and was determined to do them one better. Halfway through the meal an older missionary, embarrassed by the silence, blurted out a congratulation to General Wei, saying he had read in a Loyang paper that when the Japanese came, the General had got all his troops out of Chengchow without losing a single man. General Wei remained silent, and the remark sounded so gross said aloud that there was silence and all the foreigners began searching for small talk. One aide eulogized General Wei by listing his victories, but when he ended with the Chungtiao battle and the reconquest of Chengchow, the table again relapsed into silence. Another missionary thought it might be safe to get the General himself to talk:

"Why did the Japanese leave Chengchow?"

"They were outnumbered," said General Wei with his small smile and the silence returned.

The General ignored me until dessert, then he stared full at me.

"Where did you get the clothes?" he asked.

"I borrowed them."

"Ni shih hen yung-an," he said. "You are very 'yung-an.'" This word could mean brave, it could mean clever, or in this case it could mean just what his icy tone implied. He smiled faintly and ignored me the rest of the evening.

While I was in Chengchow, the Japanese occupation and withdrawal had seemed rather mystifying. It was nearly a month after I left before I could fit the events into any larger pattern. By then I was back in Shuangshihpu, living in Rewi Alley's caves. I had more than enough material for a book and was on my way back to Chungking. On December 10 I saw a group of village Kuomintang officials making their way up the long slope from the river, their black-clad figures bristling with the canes, medals, and scarves which were the tokens of their rank and prosperity. They had ignored me during my previous stay, but now they beamed as they hastened to shake my hand. They told me five hundred American planes had bombed Tokyo on December 7 and we were allies. A day or two later, I heard what really happened.

SENTRY EDITIONS

    (continued on next page)